Without Wheels

Alternatives to the Private Car

Terence Bendixson

WITHOUT WHEELS

Alternatives to the Private Car

INDIANA UNIVERSITY PRESS
Bloomington & London

First published in the United States in 1975
by Indiana University Press

Copyright © 1974 by Terence Bendixson

Library of Congress Cataloging in Publication Data

Bendixson, Terence.
  Without wheels.

  Includes index.
    1. Transportation, Automotive. 2. Transportation,
Automotive—Great Britain. 3. Urban transportation
policy. 4. Urban transportation policy—Great Britain.
I. Title.
HE5611.B43 1975   338.4   74-21680

ISBN 0-253-36560-0

Printed in the United States

Contents

To Frances, my collaborator,
and to Maurice for his patience

Preface

The self-defeating consequences of trying to adapt cities to cars have become more and more widely recognised in the past decade. I became aware of the contradictions as a journalist writing about towns and transport for the *Guardian* in the 1960s and subsequently saw the problem through international spectacles while working on urban transport policy at the Organisation for Economic Co-operation and Development in Paris from 1971 to 1973.

The case for change was strong enough then. The events of the winter of 1973/4—the steep rise in oil prices, the realisation that petrol would never again be plentiful and cheap, and the dawning of an era of energy conservation—make it imperative.

This book describes a set of responses to these new conditions that would enable us to reduce our dependence on private cars without jettisoning mobility. These responses are not just theories. In virtually every case they are ideas that are in use experimentally or on a day-to-day basis in one or other of the cities of Europe and North America. The result is a kind of cupboard full of possibilities that can be drawn upon in various ways to suit cities as different as Brussels and Baltimore, London and Los Angeles, Montreal and Melbourne.

In these days of storm-lashed floating currencies, the relationship between the pound and the dollar changes continually. I have therefore quoted costs in the currencies of their country of origin and have omitted equivalents. A convenient rule of thumb is to treat one pound sterling as worth two United States dollars.

London   T.B.
April 1974

1 Can we kill the Car?

Cars and trucks are part of our way of life. We use them so much that even though they pinch like countless pairs of ill-fitting shoes we just shrug our shoulders. There seems to be no choice. A businessman peers anxiously at his watch as he sits trapped in a jam on the way to an important meeting. An old woman grimaces as she waits to cross the road, her ears pierced by the noise of a heavy truck. Children tumbling out of school crinkle their noses as they register the smell of exhausts in the street. A mother tries to pacify her fractious family as they crawl back into the city on a Sunday evening after a day in the country. A householder glares at his increased car insurance premium and thinks of other bills to be paid. Passengers speeding along a motorway experience flickers of fear as they catch a first sight of fog ahead : memories cross their minds of fifty-vehicle pile-ups and people burnt alive in their seats. Commuters stand dejectedly in a queue at the end of a day's work, waiting for buses that never seem to come and are full when they do. Shoppers, as tense as infantrymen crossing a minefield, zig-zag between moving and parked cars. Drivers competing for a rare parking slot glare coldly at one another.

Anxieties and discomforts of this kind are typical symptoms of our times. They are warnings that something central to daily living is out of order.

Nearly ten years ago the citizens of San Francisco realised that the first step in countering this seemingly remorseless process is to stop feeding it, to stop building urban motorways. Since then residents in other cities from Chicago to Munich have followed their lead.

The problems are everywhere the same : the incompatibility

of giant highways with decent living conditions, and the liquidation of public transport by an advancing army of cars. The upshot is almost invariably identical, too. Protest groups form, petitions are organised, public meetings held, counter plans are advanced and the whole issue brought to a conclusion at a referendum or an election. Such episodes are like storms, they start gently, rise to a crescendo and then die away. The only memorial is generally the stub end of some vast viaduct intended by the highway engineers to channel inter-city and regional traffic into places totally unprepared to receive it.

In some countries, notably the United States, Holland and Great Britain, opinion has moved on from this position to question the sense of continuing to construct national motorway systems now that their tentacles are being blocked again and again at the portals of the cities they are intended to link.

Government response to this changing opinion has in most places been slow. Many city engineers still believe there is no alternative to catering for increasing car use and the same view remains well entrenched in all ministries of transport. Yet if living with cars is not all that advertisements of the motor industry would have us believe, the sale of cars continues to mount (and is forecast to go on doing so after a set-back due to rising oil prices) and as the men of Detroit, Coventry and Turin are quick to point out, the buyers of them and the complainers about their ill-effects are the same people. Individuals who can afford cars and have nothing to do with them are rare. As far as most people in the industry and outside are concerned, all argument ends once this fact has been established. It is taken as proof of hypocrisy of the critics. 'You drive yourself, don't you?' people ask on hearing a case being made for getting rid of cars, and on being told 'yes', they smile knowingly. The paradox of use and dislike is left unexplored.

The vastness of the numbers of vehicles made every year is probably one reason why people find it hard to believe that change is possible. The flow looks suspiciously as if it were an irreversible economic tide. Forecasts make the process seem even more tidal.

How the output of vehicles has grown over the past twenty years

	United States	Europe (European Community and EFTA)	World
1950	8,006,000	1,597,000	10,577,000
1960	7,905,000	6,022,000	16,488,000
1970	8,284,000	11,348,000	29,403,000
1971	10,672,000	11,729,000	33,204,000

(Source: Motor Vehicle Manufacturers Association of the United States, *1972 Automobile Facts and Figures*)

The numbers of cars in use and trend forecasts up to 1985

	United States	Western Europe	World
1960	61,700,000	22,600,000	97,300,000
1965	75,300,000	42,300,000	137,900,000
1970	89,300,000	64,300,000	186,800,000
Trend forecasts:			
1975	100,000,000	85,400,000	238,700,000
1980	111,000,000	108,000,000	296,600,000
1985	122,000,000	126,000,000	372,500,000

(Source: Gerald Leach, *The Motor Car and Natural Resources*, Organisation for Economic Co-operation and Development, Paris, 1972)

What the forecasters are saying is that there will be nearly a third more cars in fifteen years in the United States than today, nearly twice as many in Western Europe and almost a fourfold increase throughout the rest of the world. Admittedly the statistics were prepared before the convulsion of the world oil market, but despite that event, motor industry planners still think the forecasts will be on target give or take a few tens of millions.

Many people would agree with them because they are aware of the immense sums of money and the scale of the interests that are tied up in highway building, haulage and motor manufacturing. Furthermore, their experience tells them that alternatives to cars tend to offer an inferior service. The answers given by some German motorists to questions about the relative merits of different kinds of transport are probably typical. They said they knew that buses, trams and undergrounds were cheaper and safer than cars but they also thought them to be noisier, dirtier, slower and to offer less freedom of action and less comfort. Attitude studies of this kind suggest that people will go on using cars until the last gallon of petrol is used up and that policies aimed, for instance, at making cars more expensive and public transport cheaper or even free are unlikely by themselves to bring about more than a slight or temporary change in travel habits.

A bit more light is thrown on this subject by the experience of the bus and underground company in Stockholm. In October 1971 the officials who run the undertaking were ordered by the regional council to introduce cheap monthly passes giving unlimited and unhindered travel on all services. At the time of their introduction the passes cost per week about one hour's wages for a skilled industrial worker and it was hoped that this would lure commuters from their cars. As it turned out, few if any motorists were attracted though additional buses had to be put into service at off-peak times and weekends to cope with the extra travelling of pass-holders. Since then petrol shortages in Sweden have caused the sales of weekly and monthly passes to boom in Stockholm but how long this will go on turns on future supplies of fuel and its cost. With incomes rising steadily and fuel costs being only part of the expense of keeping a car on the road, motor manufacturers argue that the oil crisis will only cause a hiccup in the sales and use of cars.

The moral of this brief excursion into transport economics is to suggest that there is no simple or speedy way of departing from current trends of motor production and use. Time and again during the past decade, in the course of debates about cars and traffic economists have argued that if only one or two important economic changes were made the whole thrust of transport development would be launched on a completely new course. Engineers have made the same assumption about their field of expertise and insisted that if only sufficient money was invested in one or other of a range of shining new technologies, the same result would be forthcoming.

In the early 1960s the technology thought to contain the magic ingredient was the monorail and a network of lines was even proposed for central London. Currently small taxi-like vehicles running on tracks under automatic control are in vogue and development work is being done by aerospace companies such as Boeing, Messerschmidt and Hawker-Siddeley. Push-button taxis seem far more promising than monorails for in-city work but, even so, it is unlikely that they will come about as quickly or in the form that their most ardent advocates would have one believe.

Another solution to the problems raised by cars in cities upon which much hope was placed in the 1960s was the dividing up of urban areas into precincts free of through traffic. Sir Alker Tripp put forward the idea in the 1940s in a book called *Town Planning and Traffic*. It was later taken up and developed by Sir Colin Buchanan who called the enclosed parcels of land 'environmental areas'. In *Traffic in Towns*, published in 1963, he and the architects and planners who worked with him showed the principle applied to London, Leeds, Norwich and Newbury. The seed of the idea lay in the peace and quiet that can be observed in the surroundings of cathedrals such as Salisbury and Norwich and within the Temple in London. Exclude through traffic, the theory went, and people could live and work in conditions as delightful as found in any one of those places. It seemed to be the secret of living comfortably with cars. The trouble is that although precincts can be shown to be doing yeoman service in certain places under certain conditions, it is not possible to find in them a general theory which can be used to prevent the intrusion of cars and traffic in all parts of towns of all sizes. There is also the problem of cost.

Bypass a small village battered from dawn to dusk by heavy through traffic on a trunk road and the result is, without doubt, a haven of peace. Traffic past the village green may be cut by as much as eighty per cent. Build a network of urban motorways in a city in order to provide bypasses by which through traffic may avoid the streets in which people live, work, shop and go to school and the effect is not quite the same. The reasons are simple. For one thing a high proportion of the traffic found in any part of a town or city will have local business. It will consist of the cars of the residents plus the to-ing and fro-ing of the butcher, the baker and the candlestick maker. This, in turn, is because most of the trips made by most vehicles are short ones. Even in the United States, with its gigantic spreading cities, the average commuter drives nine and a half miles to work and the average shopping trip is four and a half miles each way. Motorists should be able to check this sort of thing for themselves. Make up a tally of the last ten trips made by the family car and work out how many were just around the neighbourhood and how many were long distance ones. The results should show that it is not a faceless 'them', composed of out-county commuters and trucks delivering ball bearings from Bristol to Zagreb, that create most of the danger and pollution in cities but the residents themselves, their friends and the vans that are fetching and carrying the day-to-day needs of the locality. And, outside those streets clogged by commuter parking, it is again the cars of the locals that cause blockages and ugliness.

The effect of building urban motorways is therefore not so much to lift traffic out of the existing streets as to make possible a multitude of new middle- and long-distance car trips and so add to traffic. The first reaction of most motorists to this is to ask what is wrong about such longer trips. Why should they be singled out for extermination (which will undoubtedly be their fate if urban motorways are not built)? The answer is in the form of another question. Are such roads and the traffic they bear worth the destruction they cause to established neighbourhoods; are they worth the aura of noise, dust and fumes; are they the most equitable way of spending transport funds? Or to put it another way, would people travel as they do when urban motorways are provided if they had to put their hands in their pockets and pay for these costs as they were incurring them?

In the United States traffic is not such a problem in local streets. The spreading out of cities and suburbs ensures that only a few front doors are found on any one residential street and this keeps the level of movement down. The difficulties crop up along the old main roads which are fronted by shops, factories, garages, motels and offices and which still carry very heavy flows of traffic. They are also bus routes where services are still operating. What is their role in a city arranged, as Buchanan proposed, in environmental areas? On the one hand the presence of so many people doing business and of the bus stops suggest that such routes should be treated like Nicollet Mall in Minneapolis or Oxford Street in London and made over to pedestrians, buses and taxis. On the other hand they carry large numbers of cars that could only be disentangled from the pedestrians by building bypass routes that would have to go through nearby houses, or by rebuilding the places that attract so many people elsewhere, in the form of traffic-free precincts.

Neither is a real solution because one disregards the flesh-and-blood relationship of commercial activities and movement and the other implies unlimited resources. Somehow, in some way, it is necessary to enable people who are travelling to mingle with others who have arrived, and to do so without reconstructing the entire built world.

The failure of environmental areas to resolve this conflict in large, densely built-up cities can be seen nowhere more vividly than in Bremen, the first place of any size where cars were banned from crossing the city centre. Trams and buses are allowed through but a mixture of barriers, one-way loops and foot streets prevent cars and vans from doing the same. A ring road, following for the most part the line of old fortifications, provides an alternative way for the barred traffic.

When I went to Bremen several years ago I arrived by train from Hanover and immediately went on foot to explore the precinct. Coming to the inner ring road that follows the line of the old city walls I waited at the signals in a barrage of noise and a cloud of fumes as five or six columns of vehicles roared through a complex junction on which the traffic engineers had obviously spent much time and skill. The barrier to progress on foot created by this rush of cross-town traffic left an impression quite as powerful as the delight of walking unhindered a little later on in the precinct next to the cathedral. Environmental areas, pleasant as they are in theory, turn out in practice to be prisons for pedestrians, with walls of traffic. In the early 1960s when Gunter Nasemann, the then head of the Bremen transport company, was successfully persuading the city to create the precinct, none of this was apparent. Freeing the main shopping streets of cars, diverting traffic and giving trams priority over other vehicles at traffic signals appeared to offer nothing but benefits, even though the shopkeepers (wrongly as it turned out) thought it a short cut to bankruptcy. Buchanan's advocacy of such precincts was therefore entirely understandable.

With the passage of ten years and the benefit of hindsight, it is now possible to discover where the theorists went wrong. They mistakenly assumed that watersheds can be found in cities where the movement of people on foot is so insignificant that it does not matter if their way is impeded. They also failed to distinguish between the very different kinds of road network required by buses and trams on the one hand and cars on the other. To be useful, the public transport services need to go through the midst of precincts, as in fact they do in Bremen, whereas cars have to be sent round the back of them. But once this is done, the balance of advantage between the two kinds of conveyance changes radically. Frequent and comfortable buses or trams become a much more attractive proposition and begin to merit part of the finance that would hitherto have gone into highway building.

Thinking has now evolved to this point in a number of cities such as Oxford, Nottingham and Edinburgh, yet in other cities such as Bristol and York it has barely progressed in ten years. The dread disease of ring-road-itis still stalks the corridors of their town halls.

I have gone into ring roads and precincts and 'primary road networks' in some detail because, while they represent only one facet of urban transport thinking, they have a long history and have undergone considerable evolution. But is it also necessary to draw from the experience of the past decade some more general conclusions about cars and highway building. What are the main points to emerge?

There is no single action that promises to reduce the mounting costs and discomforts imposed by cars and highways on people.

No amount of ingenious juggling by engineers and architects is capable of adapting long-established cities to accommodate large flows of traffic and vast highways, except over a period and at a cost that makes it an irrelevancy.

Learning to live with cars, by routing traffic away from where people live, is out of the question, too. It would be possible if the number of people with cars remained small or if the users of cars lived in isolated villages. It is not possible when car owners are numbered in millions and when they live in extended clusters of cities, suburbs and towns. In these circumstances living with cars means the destruction of the amenity of all and the absence of mobility for many.

There is no going back to the public transport that exists today, even if it is made free. Services have in most cases declined over the last ten or fifteen years, but even if they had not, they would fall below the expectations of people who have tasted the comfort and convenience of cars.

There is no whizz bang new technology that is going to beat the car at its own game in the next five to ten years and enable all existing forms of public transport to be pensioned off as well.

Nevertheless, the way out of this apparent *impasse* involves nothing grandiose. It rests not so much on doing things that no one has heard of before but on doing more concertedly and with a greater sense of purpose things that have somewhere been tried and found to work. It involves going on from the experience of the last ten years in small, impatient steps rather than by great impulsive ones. The purpose of this book is to describe experience that has already been built up with individually modest measures and to argue that, put together in different ways to suit the needs of different communities, they could produce revolutionary changes—mobility for all irrespective of age and income and a reduction in the damage inflicted on people by traffic and highways.

It would be facile to pretend that such a change can be wrought at the drop of a hat. The action taken in the nineteenth century when it became clear that cholera was the result of foul drinking water is a measure of what is called for. Public health standards were defined, legislation enacted, public funds provided, new sanitary equipment developed, new public institutions set up and a new profession brought into existence. As a result the impossible was achieved in the short space of thirty years. People who in their youth took it for granted that drinking water came from nearby wells, rivers and streams and that privies, buckets and open drains took care of the waste, found themselves in their later years drinking water piped from miles away and relying on vast systems of municipal sewers.

Getting rid of the ill-effects of cars in our time is potentially no more difficult and will bring no less an improvement to public health. Fifteen years could see the major part of the task completed.

2 The Car's Uncounted Costs

A Scot playing the bagpipes in the street may wake someone up. A man walking down to the post office may bump into a woman coming back from the grocer's with eggs in her shopping bag. Street incidents of this sort are happening all the time but everyone accepts that there must be give and take. The Scot would no doubt be pardoned by all but the most pig-headed Sassenachs for playing on New Year's Eve but might well have the police put on to him if he played at midnight for ten days in a row. The man posting the letter would be pardoned if his sudden swerve was to save a pram from rolling into the gutter and sworn at if he was being absentminded.

The potential of cars and lorries to inflict damages on innocent parties was recognised from the first. The Highways and Locomotives Act of 1878 contained the well-known and crippling stipulation that any horseless carriage should not go faster than four miles per hour and be preceded by a man on foot. Subsequent legislation, as William Plowden has shown in *The Motor Car and Politics*, has been soft on cars. What was never foreseen was the damage inflicted by tens of millions of vehicles or the numbing effect of their insidious build up.

At present we in Britain are about halfway to a forecast fleet of thirty million plus cars and lorries. It is possible that energy shortages have put paid to that prospect but unlikely. The motor manufacturers are quietly confident that a combination of more economical engines, speed limits and thrifty driving will circumvent all problems and, after a time, get sales booming again.

If the manufacturers are correct and the number of vehicles continues to grow, even though their use may be somewhat

1960   9·4 million

1965   12·9

1970   14·9

1975   18·1

1980   21·5

1985   24·2

1990   26·8

1995   28·5

2000   30·2

2005   31·7

2010   33·0

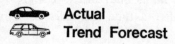

Actual
Trend Forecast

Motor Vehicles in Great Britain

curtailed, then all the external costs associated with cars will continue to grow, albeit at a somewhat slower pace. In these circumstances, congestion, once confined to the centre of cities and to rush hours (they should be called 'crawl hours') will continue to spread in space and time. Jams are already becoming more common in suburbs, at holiday resorts and in national parks and occur at weekends and late in the evening. Towns such as Brighton and Blackpool, which used to be famous for their crowded beaches, are becoming more memorable for their crowded roads. Flatford Mill, at the end of a sunken cart track overhung by trees, is nowadays virtually inaccessible in summer by car or foot. The cars of visitors to the scene of Constable's painting jam the lanes for miles around, despite a one-way system.

In the United States things have gone further. At most holiday places, cars and parking lots have become so dominant that Disneyworld, Walt Disney's 'land of magic' in Florida, is served only by Exciting! New! Public Transport. (In Britain privately-owned branch railways are evolving in a comparable direction.) The scale of American traffic congestion is hard to grasp until experienced. In New Jersey, a State as thickly peopled as north-west or south-east England, it is possible on summer weekends to crawl for a hundred miles along the Garden State Parkway, a multi-lane toll road that runs from the fringes of New York southwards along the Atlantic Coast. Until recently motorists could at least pull off and picnic on the swathes of grass that separated the two carriageways and made the road one of the most beautiful in North America. Now the once-undulating parkland accommodates a duplicate freeway.

As traffic congestion spreads, so increasing amounts of time and fuel are wasted. More fumes are poured into the air, increasing the likelihood that cities will acquire blankets of smog. At present smog is a hazard to health only in twenty-nine cities in the United States and others in Japan, but it is a serious nuisance in several in the Netherlands and Australia, and signs of it are beginning to be detected in France, Germany, Sweden and

Britain under certain climatic conditions. As the number of vehicles in use grows, as the mileage driven in urban areas increases and as congestion becomes more frequent, so these signs will become unmistakable. Sufferers from chest diseases will have their lives endangered. Others will find their eyes watering and their noses tickling. More generally, the stink of exhausts will increasingly cover up smells and scents that are part of the pleasure of life.

In the United States the seriousness of air pollution caused by cars and trucks has produced action. Modifications to vehicles have already led to improvements in air quality in the Los Angeles basin, though realisation that exhaust catalysts increase fuel consumption as well as converting pollutants into harmless emissions has been a blow. In many cities 'transportation strategies' designed to reduce use of cars are being prepared by order of the Environmental Protection Agency as a second line of defence. The possibility of controlling air pollution and reducing fuel consumption by methods of this kind to some extent offset the débâcle over catalysts.

In Europe speedy progress towards cleaner air is being made in Sweden, but within the unwieldy Commission of the European Communities it is complacently held that urgent action is unnecessary. This bodes ill for cities such as Munich and Grenoble that have hot summers and sheltered positions. Cities to watch in Britain are Leeds, which advertises itself as the 'motorway city of the North' (when will they ever learn?) and Sheffield, which is set in a bowl of hills that acts as a container for foul air. Precursors of smog have been found in both places by the Fuel Science Department at Leeds University.

Noise is a diabolical nuisance for many people, disturbing their sleep, upsetting their children, interfering with speech and interrupting their pleasure in hearing radio and television programmes. Estimates made by a Government working group on traffic noise in Britain in 1970 are that between nine and eighteen million townspeople already live on roads where noise levels are undesirably high and that between 900,000 and

2,170,000 country people suffer the same blight. (Great variations in human reactions to noise make it impossible to be precise about the numbers affected and explain the gulf between the high and low estimates.) With increases in traffic and in particular the fast growth of heavy lorry fleets, these totals will grow and the working party estimates that by 1980 up to six out of ten townspeople may have their sleep disturbed.

Traffic accidents are another drag on the morale and the economy of car-using societies. In the nine countries of the European Community sixty thousand people are killed and one and a half million injured every year. Over ten years this level of casualties promises to liquidate the equivalent of all the residents of a town the size of Nantes or Newcastle upon Tyne and to injure as many people as live in the entire south-east of England. Figures of such proportions make it clear that town-dweller and farmer alike live in the midst of a kind of no-man's-land where pedestrians and cyclists come under indiscriminate attack by passing vehicles and where knights in modernised armour engage in an interminable and lethal jousting match.

Attitudes differ about the seriousness of highway dangers. A young man showing off his prowess by creaming down the centre of a busy road on a 750 c.c. Suzuki would be unlikely to share the views of a mother shepherding three small children to school. Yet highways bring their values into conflict as no other everyday experience does. The careless kill the cautious without the cautious being able to do anything about it except stay at home.

Pedestrians and cyclists are particularly at peril and the Swedes emphasise this by calling them 'unprotected' road users. It would be an exaggeration to suggest that they are never the guilty parties in road accidents, but soft, slow objects inevitably have more to lose in any contest of strength with hard and fast ones. Potential cyclists are literally frightened off the roads. Numerous people in both Paris and London have told me this on hearing that I ride a bicycle. Bicycling *is* a dangerous activity under present conditions and the nervous are well advised to be wary of it. In America the great two-wheel revival of the last decade has been won at the cost of nearly doubling the annual death rate.

The danger of the roads is a special burden for children. Robert Louis Stevenson wrote that in his youth it was possible for a lad to wander out from the middle of Edinburgh to explore the Pentland Hills. Today few parents living in similar circumstances let their sons roam as freely. Worse still, cities have spread and the streets in their inner neighbourhoods are now lined with the cars of commuters. It may still be possible to play hopscotch on the pavements but tag in the street is desperately dangerous. Children being children, they play just the same and steadily rising accident tolls are the result. In Britain the number of youngsters from five to fourteen who were either killed or seriously injured on the roads increased by fifty-seven per cent between 1960 and 1970. Casualties amongst no other single class of road user increased as fast. The 'Green Cross Code', a new street crossing code for children introduced with an intensive advertising campaign, produced a drop in these figures but since the publicity ended they have started creeping up ominously again.

'Spaceship earth' is one of the new ideas of the last few years. It signals a realisation that the physical resources of the world are limited and capable of being exhausted by the tremendous appetite of consumer societies.

The full implications of this new insight have not yet been grasped. Increasing numbers of people are now peering at the dials and gauges in the spaceship's cockpit but their interpretations of what they see vary. At one extreme are those who read the quivering needles as saying Emergency! Emergency! Prepare to abandon ship! For them the only practical future world is one in which everyone grows his own vegetables and uses bicycles and wind generators.

At the other extreme are optimistic materialists like Herman Kahn of the Hudson Institute and co-author of *Thinking the*

Unthinkable. Kahn believes that industrial growth will not be arrested until the entire world's population has succeeded in patterning itself after suburban Americans. Conservationists are appalled by such unthinkability but Kahn calmly assures them that he has run it all through a computer and found that there will be sufficient resources for every family in a future world to have a house, a country cottage, two cars, a deep freeze, a personal submarine and a private helicopter. (I may have overdone it a bit with those helicopters but I am remembering the list from a BBC television programme in 1973.)

It is all good, clean ivory-tower fun. The conclusions the competing parties come to depend not on the facts but on which facts they choose as foundations for their prognostications. The pessimists calculate world food production in the year 2050 on the basis of outputs in India. The optimists base their forecasts on outputs in Iowa. The one group foresees disaster, the other a promised land. It is the same with energy supplies : you pays your money and you takes your choice.

But I am being too flippant. The two views not only help to get into focus the kinds of change that are necessary for survival but also hint at the ways in which the future will differ from the present. Values will change. Increased production, greater energy consumption and higher speeds, the traditional objectives of industrial societies, will have to change. A further stage in man's evolution will be necessary, not a genetic mutation but a moral one. Ways in which to use and reuse and to avoid misusing the immense but still fragile resources of spaceship earth will have to be discovered. Yet the outcome seems very unlikely to be a race of ascetic recluses. Material possessions, if not the ones Kahn suggests, seem likely to remain a dominant concern of human beings for many years.

Such a change in values will take time to affect all aspects of life but that is all the more reason for starting now. Adaptations in behaviour over the consumption of irreplaceable resources like petroleum are a case in point. To go on pouring such a uniquely valuable fuel into cars that are used to crawl wastefully to work or to nip out for a packet of cigarettes is like feeding peaches to pigs.

The energy crisis which broke upon startled motorists and other oil users in the winter of 1973/4 was a harbinger of a new era, even though it was not the result of world demand outstripping world supply. The immediate cause was political, but underlying the decision of the oil-producing countries to raise their prices was an awareness that they are selling a dwindling resource.

There is every reason to expect this pattern of price rises to repeat itself in other commodities as world demand for them rises. Economists argue that this phenomenon will in itself be sufficient to ensure that scarce resources are not depleted and that alternatives are devised. This is a comfortingly Olympian viewpoint and while no doubt true in the long run, it glosses over the immediate problems caused by sudden rises in the cost of essentials. In the case of oil, there is the plight of developing countries suddenly faced by a doubling in cost of one of their primary sources of energy. In Western countries a similar predicament faces poorer households as the prices of transport and heating rise remorselessly.

Running a car is already an expensive proposition. When fuel was 36 pence a gallon a ten-thousand-miles-a-year man could expect to pay £578 to run a one-litre car and £688 to run a two-litre one. Fuel represents about a fifth of these costs so a doubling in the price of petrol would increase annual costs by between £100 and £150. For the well-paid executive such increases may be manageable, but for those with average incomes who can only just manage to afford cars, even a fifty per cent rise in fuel prices is bound to impose strains. Public transport might be an alternative but if services continue to decline and fares to increase as in recent years, cars will remain indispensable even for getting to work and people will be obliged to skimp on other things.

The situation is even more serious in the United States, where road vehicles consume about half of all crude oil compared with seventeen per cent in Europe. (Throughout the world road vehicles accounted for twelve per cent of all oil production in 1970.) The reason for this tremendous consumption is partly the huge number of vehicles in use and the longer distances travelled, both within towns and between them, but largely the sheer weight of the typical Detroit-built land cruiser. Each one weighs nearly four thousand pounds, or twice its European equivalent, and burns its own weight in fuel every year.

But changes are on the way. In the United States sales of small cars have soared and an act imposing a fifty-five mile an hour maximum speed limit has been passed by Congress. In Britain Lord Stokes of British Leyland has announced that the next generation of cars will be designed on a 'fifty-fifty' principle —fifty miles per gallon of petrol at fifty miles an hour. Things are clearly not going to be left to go on as they are but the motor industry is hoping that, with a few adroit adjustments, the changes will over ten years turn out to be slight. The fallacy in this argument lies in failure to consider the implications of a doubling in the number of vehicles over the next twenty to thirty years in the developed countries alone. Even on the wildly optimistic assumption that petrol consumption per mile can be halved, total demand for motor fuel in Europe, North America and Japan would remain at present levels. Beside this it is necessary to put the efforts of American and European motor manufacturers to introduce the car habit into Africa, South-East Asia, India and South America, and the probability that the communists will obediently follow the example of the capitalists they so much detest.

Three main aspects of the interaction of cars and energy supplies can now be identified : the difficulties of poorer countries and poorer people faced by higher fuel prices; the prospect that world demand for motor fuel will go on increasing despite the introduction of more economical vehicles; and, hanging like a cloud above all, the steady exhaustion of an irreplaceable resource.

Building mathematical models to analyse situations of this

complexity is difficult enough Making reasonable assumptions on which to base them requires wisdom of a high order. Nothing illustrates this better than the debate between the classical economists and the environmentalists over the modelling exercise financed by the Club of Rome and published in *Limits to Growth*. The one saw it as rubbish and the other as divine inspiration.

Pending the results of further efforts to plot a way through the maze of unfolding energy inputs and outputs, it is necessary to be cautious. It is not a time to push on at high speed with building inter-city motorways. This has been recognised in the United States where the Highway Trust Fund, the notorious cornucopia of petrol taxes used to finance 42,000 miles of inter-state freeways, will be wound up—many would say ten years too late—in 1977.

In Europe the extension of motorway networks is still amongst the sacred cows of transport policy and new routes can be seen munching their way through the landscape of all countries. The resource implications of their continuance, and the inducement to travel by car they give, has hardly been looked at. In Britain about eighteen per cent of all the mileage done by road vehicles occurs on inter-city motorways and trunk roads and because high speeds are the rule, fuel consumption is heavy too. The Department of Transportation in Washington has looked at the opportunities for cutting down on the fuel used for inter-city travel and estimates that, under American highway conditions, a maximum speed limit of fifty miles an hour and a change to coaches and trains by half of the number of car passengers would reduce total petrol consumption by about six per cent. This is not by itself a big amount, but then, no single measure will achieve huge economies.

Countries like Britain and France, that have not completed motorway networks conceived in the petrol-swilling 'fifties and 'sixties, have an opening not available to the Americans—the diversion of motorway funds to railway improvements and coach services. Railway modernisation would include new interchanges between urban and inter-urban systems. Coaches which tend to use established trunk roads serving towns and villages along the way would be better off with local bypasses than motorways. Fuel savings beyond those available from throttling back on existing motorways would result from cutting down on motorway construction. Motorists would go not just less fast but less far, particularly in the growing area of pleasure driving. Instead of racing two hundred miles on a weekend excursion they might meander for fifty. The differences in the annual mileages done by cars in countries with extensive motorway systems, such as Germany and the United States, and those without, such as France and Britain, bears this out. The high cost of petrol in France and the huge number of second cars in the United States pull down the figures for those countries but the absence of comparable distortions in the Anglo-German comparison makes it sounder.

*Average annual mileage driven
by cars in four countries in 1970*

Britain	8,125
France	6,625
Germany	10,312
United States	9,812

A nice illustration of the effect of reducing weight on fuel consumption is the bicycle. Cut it down to the unbelievable eighteen pounds of an alloy racer and a fit man can pedal along for hours at twenty-five miles an hour just using metabolic energy, better known as sweat. Such a way of getting about may not be everybody's cup of tea but it is a winner in the conservation of fuel.

Alex Moulton, the father of the shock-absorber plus small-wheel bicycle, is, as might be expected, an authority on this and on the energy characteristics of mechanically powered transport as well. In a paper delivered at the Royal Institution in London in

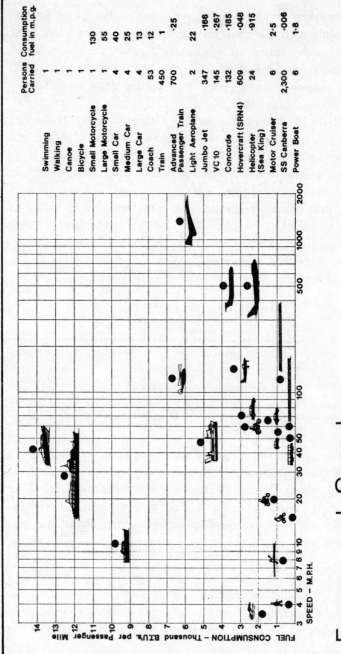

	Persons Carried	Consumption fuel in m.p.g.
Swimming	1	
Walking	1	
Canoe	1	
Bicycle	1	
Small Motorcycle	1	130
Large Motorcycle	1	55
Small Car	4	40
Medium Car	4	25
Large Car	4	13
Coach	53	12
Train	450	1
Advanced Passenger Train	700	·25
Light Aeroplane	2	22
Jumbo Jet	347	·166
VC 10	145	·267
Concorde	132	·185
Hovercraft (SRN4)	609	·048
Helicopter (Sea King)	24	·915
Motor Cruiser	6	2·5
SS Canberra	2,300	·006
Power Boat	6	1·8

FUEL CONSUMPTION – Thousand B.T.U.'s per Passenger Mile

SPEED – M.P.H.

Energy and Speed

February 1973 he showed that, with certain provisos, buses are more economical than trains and both of them more so than cars. The most important proviso is how many seats are filled. An illustration of this, calculated from Moulton's figures, is that a Morris Mini doing forty miles to the gallon and carrying four people will be more economical than a twelve-miles-to-the-gallon coach carrying twelve. Less fuel would be burned if the coach party was sent off in three minis.

This is one reason for looking carefully at proposals to build undergrounds or to open disused railways. If the trains using them are not going to be full, they are likely to be uneconomical in fuel terms. There are other reasons for looking quizzically at them that I will come to later.

Doing more with less fuel is such a new idea in passenger transport (though the truck makers have been doing it for years) that the implications are still unclear. The more one thinks about it the more promising minibus-sized vehicles appear to be. Their advantages on grounds of passenger miles per gallon were brought out by Gerald Leach in a report for the Organisation for Economic Co-operation and Development called 'The Motor Car and Natural Resources'. Leach did an exercise similar to Moulton's, but on slightly different assumptions, and showed that a vehicle with a one-and-a-half litre engine and seats for six or eight people—a Volkswagen Microbus for example—was the most economical motor vehicle going. Add to this its capacity to give door-to-door service on every kind of road from motorways to country lanes and it begins to look like an important element in a transport policy designed to conserve energy.

As the energy inputs and outputs of different modes of transport become better understood it will become possible to take into account the fuel needed to *make* vehicles as well as to operate them. This is likely to push engineers in the direction of long-life, light-weight vehicles, noticeable already in designs for push-button taxis, but pending this level of sophistication, it is clear that great economies can be achieved by moving towards

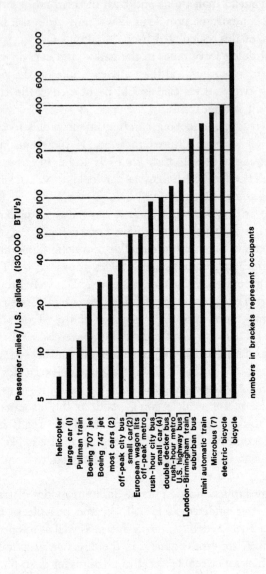

Passenger-miles/U.S. gallons (130,000 BTU's)

helicopter
large car (1)
Pullman train
Boeing 707 jet
Boeing 747 jet
most cars (2)
off-peak city bus
small car (2)
European wagon lits
off-peak metro
rush-hour city bus
small car (4)
double decker bus
rush-hour metro
U.S. highway bus
London-Birmingham train
suburban bus
mini automatic train
Microbus (7)
electric bicycle
bicycle

numbers in brackets represent occupants

Another View of Transport and Energy

vehicles that are built to last like London taxis (they generally do 250,000 miles) and that have the passenger capacity of a minibus.

Land is another natural resource on which cars and highways lay heavy claim. Slightly less than a quarter of the surface of a typical American city is needed to provide 'tracks' for cars and trucks. 'Stations' or parking places demand additional square miles of paving, though transport planners are not accustomed to taking this into their calculations. Between a quarter and a third of a drive-in city will thus be dangerous concrete wasteland where people are regularly killed and injured. The pre-car-age city was different. In 1966, before any motorways were built, only about fourteen per cent of the surface of London (not a place that strikes one as being empty of roads) was covered by highways and railways.

Many pressures are at work in creating the spreading, loose-knit modern city and it would be an error to attribute the process solely to cars and trucks. Suburbs have a long history and are not just a form of development that provides *lebensraum* for cars. They are a response to aspirations for gardens, peace and psychological space too. Advocates of high-density living need to bear this in mind. However, densities are such an inadequate index of liveability because so much turns on layout and on extent. Thus, while not departing from the densities found in suburbs, it is possible to arrange the buildings in many different ways, some of which compel people to use cars all the time and some much less so. The almost military uniformity of houses set in their own quarter acre as in Houston in Texas, a sprawling oil port of about one and a quarter million people, is a car sales-man's paradise. It seems miles to anywhere and walking is out of the question. Cluster the same houses together into a series of 'villages' set in parkland and playing fields, on the other hand, and the outcome is places with the same overall density but better suited to being served by buses or trams because walking distances are cut down. Assume the village model is followed further and that town planning controls are used to ensure that shops, schools, offices and small-scale factories are gathered together in its middle, and still greater use can be expected of walking and public transport and less of cars. The extent of roads and parking lots will diminish proportionately.

Adopt the Houston or Detroit model and it becomes obligatory to design everything on drive-in principles. The city centre becomes progressively a car centre. Constantinos Doxiadis, the Greek urbanist, shows this process at work in downtown Detroit in a report called *Urban America and the Role of Industry*, done for the United States National Association of Manufacturers. In a series of maps covering a period of fifty years he shows *dementia automobilis*, a black disease of expressways, streets, alleys and parking lots, gradually blotting out the central square mile of the city. Between 1929 and 1968 this car space expanded from less than half to more than two-thirds of the centre. And in a list of eight other United States cities Doxiadis shows car space nowhere falling below thirty-five per cent in their central business districts.

City	Year	Acres	Streets	Parking	Streets and Parking
			Percentage of Land in Central District devoted to:		
Los Angeles	1960	401	35	24	59
Dallas (core)	1961	344	35	18	53
Detroit	1953	690	38	11	49
Minneapolis	1958	580	34	14	48
Dallas (central district)	1961	1362	28	13	41
Chicago	1956	677	31	10	41
Winston-Salem	1961	334	25	15	40
Cincinnati	1955	330	—*	—*	40
Charlotte	1958	473	29	9	38
Chattanooga	1960	246	22	13	35

* *Not known*
Source: Doxiadis, *Urban America and the Role of Industry*

Few people expect cities in Europe to spread out as much as those in America or their central areas to become as dominated by car space but the differences are of degree, not of kind. The canal banks of Amsterdam are linear car parks. The former *quais* along the Seine in Paris are expressways. Just as in the United States so in Europe, all public and private institutions that play a part in financing and development of buildings act on an assumption that the future lies with private cars and trucks. So long as they do the proportion of urban land devoted to roads and parking will increase remorselessly.

'Everyone has a car.' The statement is uttered again and again until the majority of people believe it. The belief is crucial to understanding our predicament because it helps to create acceptance for concentrating public money on catering for the greatest possible use of cars. But does everyone have a car? Not in the United States. One in five households there is without one and amongst the fast-growing ranks of the elderly, nearly every other household is without one. There are regional differences too. In the group of heavily urbanised states stretching from New York State to Virginia one household in four is carless.

In European countries two to three out of five households are without cars but transport planners in most places are following faithfully in the thoughtways laid out by their opposite numbers across the Atlantic. A typical example is the transport plan for Greater Manchester produced under the chairmanship of the Manchester City Engineer in 1971. At that date half the households studied had no cars and forecasts indicated that a quarter would still be without them in 1984. Nevertheless a recommendation was made to invest more than four-fifths of the capital available for transport in highways. On Tyneside, where car ownership is forecast to grow more slowly, a comparable plan recommended spending sixty-two per cent of all transport funds up to 1984 on highways. The influence of these land-use transportation plans on policy is a theme I shall return to (pp. 98 and 234). The plans and the philosophy of the professionals who prepare them pervade everything that has happened in urban transport for the past decade. In this context it is necessary only to say that the plans invariably concentrate on the numbers of households *with* cars and never examine those *without*. They also neglect to look within households that have cars to see who drives and who does not.

If the planners took a breakfast-table look at an average three-person British household they would find, more often than not, that the man takes the family car to work, leaving his wife and child to walk or go by bus. The number of people in this partially car-less situation is, of course, far larger than the number of households without cars. The exact total depends on the age at which it is assumed young people would benefit from being independently mobile. If the age frontier is set at fifteen, then between six and seven out of ten Britons are more often than not dependent on walking or public transport to get about. Set the qualifying age lower and the number increases. Until very recently the American answer to this problem was to assume that households would buy second cars and to let public transport run down still further, thereby worsening the predicament of the young, the elderly and the poor. Two out of five Americans over the age of fifteen were members of this 'transportation poor' in 1970.

Mayer Hillman, a research worker at Political and Economic Planning in London, has waged an almost single-handed fight against the inequity of conventional assumptions about car ownership. Using detailed figures of how children, grannies, 'teenagers, housewives and other real people get about, or fail to do so, he has exposed the baselessness of plans that talk about universal car ownership and the blindness of planners who become lyrical about cars freeing the family. The following figures give the meat of Hillman's report, *Personal Mobility and Transport Policy*, and show that everywhere but in small towns the majority of adults are likely to be without access to cars except by begging, borrowing or stealing a ride from someone else.

The access of individuals to cars in Britain

	Households with Cars		Households without Cars	
	Percentage of Adults with Driving Licences	Percentage of Adults without Driving Licences	Percentage of Adults with Driving Licences	Percentage of Adults without Driving Licences
Country Village	48	20	5	28
Small Town	55	16	5	24
New Town	37	25	7	31
Provincial City Suburb	31	15	6	48
Inner London	26	16	5	53

The figures in this table have been rounded.

Looking ahead, Hillman forecast that even in the year 2001 only fifty-seven per cent of individuals in Britain are likely to have driving licences.

Little study has been made of the effects of pouring public finance into transport systems that improve the mobility of some and reduce it for others. The resentment of teenagers left to hang around in a dull suburb with no way of escaping is described by Herbert Gans in *The Levittowners*. Researchers in Chicago have shown that there is a higher than average probability that people who are unemployed will not have cars. Much more tentative suggestions have been made in the United States about links between lack of mobility and crime. It is a world of shadows. It is as if those with cars have made a secret agreement to pretend that those without do not exist. Ignore them and they will go away.

The privations of the car-less are not yet as bad in Europe as they are in the United States but a literature is beginning to accumulate on them just the same. Sociologists in Sweden have exposed a syndrome that is given additional relevance by the rising cost of petrol. Those caught up in it are householders who have moved out to the fringes of cities to obtain houses at prices they can afford or because flats to rent are not available closer in. Public transport to carry them to their jobs does not exist or takes so long that it is impractical, and so they have to buy cars. The combined cost of house and car then forces them to skimp on other necessities.

Ray Pahl, an English sociologist, reported similar problems amongst idyllic-looking commuter estates on the fringes of Greater London in *Urbs in Ruris*. Seeing beyond the semblance of gentility, he found that life was not all 'rum and Rovers'. It was a grim struggle to make ends meet.

Providing public transport to link people scattered out on the fringes of cities to all their possible destinations is no easy task. Sumner Myers, head of urban transport at the Institute of Public Administration in Washington, has argued, with characteristic dash, that the most promising solution is to give free cars to those without. The proposal does help to clear the air. It is a reminder that as the structure of cities evolves from being based on trains, buses, trams and walking to being based on cars, old forms of transport are less and less satisfactory. Services to carry people between many points just do not exist, or if they do, they take half a day to make the trip, which amounts to the same thing.

Giant forces are at work shaping these trends. The motor industry is the biggest engineering complex in the world and it is supported by powerful highway building industries in every country. In Britain two or three million pounds are poured into building new or improved highways every day. The Government's object is to complete a 'primary network of three thousand five hundred miles of high standard strategic trunk routes of which about two thousand will be motorway' during the 1980s. It is the same all over the Continent. In the Netherlands the Ministry of Transport, Water Control and Public Works is intent on building one thousand six hundred and eighty-seven miles of motorways between 1968 and 1985 and plans to construct a further one thousand one hundred and eighty-seven miles after that. In Germany three thousand five hundred and eight miles of *autobahnen* were in use in 1973 and seven hundred and fifty miles more were under construction. In France a six- and eight-lane highway round Paris, which has already established itself as the most dangerous road in the city, was no sooner completed in 1973 than the Minister of Transport gave his blessing to a super *périphérique* to relieve it of super congestion. In Britain, too, the proud new motorways of only seven or ten years ago are already groaning with traffic. The M6 is one of them and plans for a duplicate M6 to run parallel to it between Birmingham and central Lancashire are under consideration.

The process of which all these incidents are a part has not just given a new shape to human settlements but it has played a synergetic role (the two plus two equals five effect) in changing life itself. Cars have been part of a social revolution in which millions of 'have-nots' have succeeded in achieving the status of 'haves'. People who own and use cars therefore live and probably think differently from those who do not. They have arrived; they have succeeded. All this tends to give the process a sacrosanctity. It has become a religion. It has articles of faith—the motorist's right to the freedom of the road; it has a priesthood—the highway and traffic engineers; it has an array of costly tabernacles that have already been described in terms previously reserved for cathedrals (Reyner Banham says in *Los Angeles* that the city's freeway system is 'one of the greater works of Man' and that 'the Santa Monica/San Diego intersection is a work of art') and it has a vast, unthinking following. Motorisation is indeed a religion with an impressive record but like others before it, it has grown greedy, corrupt and careless. A Reformation is due.

3 There Will Always be a Neighbourhood

The nineteenth-century city (its husks still dominate much of our thinking of what a city is) was a creature of the railway and the tram. Canals may have been in at the confinement but the midwife came on flanged steel wheels. Before that time life for all but a few aristocrats was circumscribed by what could be accomplished on foot. For ordinary people the world consisted either of farm and fields or mill and cottages.

The railways first made possible cities of a size and a hellishness hitherto unknown (Mestre, the unknown twin city of Venice over on the mainland, is a time machine for anyone wishing to visit Sheffield or Pittsburg as they were in 1890) and then enabled the better off to escape them. The destination of the escapers was the suburbs, often thought of as another nineteenth-century phenomenon but in fact a much older one. Little dormitories for yesteryear's tired executives were built in the eighteenth century outside the walls of York where they now happen to be in the path of a misconceived proposal for an inner ring road. The French with their sharply defined conception of a city called this parasitical kind of development a *faubourg* or false city. By their standards the spanking new houses put up in the eighteenth century outside London at Islington would have been just such a place.

Railways and trams gave this process a tremendous push and permitted the growth of suburbs on an unprecedented scale. The Cheap Trains Act of 1883 changed the railway clientèle a little and enabled better-paid industrial workers to escape to the suburbs but even by the end of the century most of the people riding on the services fanning out from the great Victorian termini were middle class. The same applied to underground railways in their early decades. A print of Baker Street Station on the London Metropolitan Railway shortly after it was opened in 1862 shows the men wearing top hats and the women billowing taffeta skirts. Those were not the clothes of working people.

All this began to change in the present century as wages increased and bus services enabled the gaps in the starfish pattern of development that had grown up along the railways to be filled in with continuous blankets of houses. The top hat and taffeta brigade were by then beginning to buy cars, though they owned fewer than one-and-a-half million of them in Britain in 1939. So for most people life was still a matter of local activity and local relationships centring round neighbours and workmates and nearby shops and pubs. Nine times out of ten, transport will have meant walking. Even in 1966 more people travelled to work in Britain on foot and bicycle than by car.

The 1930s did, however, witness a loosening of certain constraints on the location of industry. In the nineteenth century virtually all factory production had taken place next to a river, a canal or a railway. Suburban factory estates such as Team Valley on Tyneside and Slough in Buckinghamshire ('Come friendly bombs and fall on Slough . . .' Sir John Betjeman was subsequently to ask) established a new pattern. They were located next to railways but also beside main roads leading to and from nearby cities and many of those who worked at them arrived by bus.

The consumer society was being born. First 2LO and then the BBC began broadcasting from Alexandra Palace. People began to buy radios in plywood cases with grilles cut to resemble a rising, or was it a setting, sun? Goods of this kind, made in the bungalow factories of the trading estates, had to be distributed to ten thousand shops up and down the country and they had to be handled with care. It was not a kind of work the railways were accustomed to or well equipped to handle. Trucks were ideally suited to it and the number in use multiplied five-fold between 1920 and 1939.

During the last thirty years all these trends have tended to intensify. Consumers have become more numerous and richer. Refrigerators and TV sets, power drills and central heating have followed the radio and the mantelpiece clock with its Big Ben chimes and become the possessions of the many. Millions of suburban houses have been built. More new factories have been commissioned next to the bypasses and main roads fringing the cities. The number of cars in use has multiplied eight or nine times and six or seven out of ten of them are used to go to work. The phrase 'urban sprawl' has entered the language and a reaction against it has set in. In Britain it has led to a programme of new towns without parallel in the world and in the United States to a number of prototype planned communities. Behind all such endeavours lies the evangelical writing of Ebenezer Howard, who argued, as long ago as 1898, that the channelling of urban growth into new towns, clustering round mother cities, would lead to 'social cities'. Letchworth Garden City, which got under way in Hertfordshire in 1903, was a first tentative step in this new direction. Columbia, a planned community being built near Washington, is a more recent one and James Rouse, its initiator, is, like Howard, a visionary businessman.

As far as transport is concerned, few changes are more important than the growing tendency for people to live away from where they work and to follow leisure pursuits that require lots of space. People working in shops and offices in city centres have been less affected than others. They may now live further out in the suburbs than they did thirty years ago but difficulties over parking—made greater by the introduction of meters in the 1950s—mean that many of them still travel by bus or train. They can also take new jobs without setting off chain reactions of change in other aspects of their lives. Thus a girl who works as a sales assistant in British Home Stores one year may only have to cross the street if she gets a chance of a better job at Littlewoods. The same bus will still serve to take her to and from home every day.

But as each year goes by, people who work pushing pens rather than ingots of iron or at any rate in some kind of service employment, find there are more and more opportunities for them in the suburbs. For one thing factory work becomes less a matter of dark satanic mills and more a question of design, research and marketing. Furthermore, classic city-centre employers such as insurance companies, newspapers and universities have begun to move to the suburbs and to locate themselves near airports and golf courses. Hotels have followed them. Bus services between the new suburban houses and these new suburban jobs are frequently non-existent or so time-consuming as to be out of the question. Or even if there is a service that enables a chemist or a machinist to get to his job one year, when he gets a chance of a promotion by moving to another firm elsewhere, it is ten to one that there will not be.

This process of growing and spreading and loosening up that is currently characteristic of all cities has not escaped the attention of urban geographers. In describing it they have even found it necessary to stop using the word city because of its associations with conditions that Plato knew and which he might still have recognised in Bristol or Boston in 1840. Patrick Geddes, an imaginative Scots planner, was one of the first to see that the twentieth-century city required redefinition and put forward the term 'city region' to convey the idea of an expanded sphere of influence. Americans use the term 'metropolitan area' to do the same job and the United States Bureau of the Census has devised an elaborate set of rules for defining the boundaries of what they call SSMAs (Standard Statistical Metropolitan Areas). The object of these rules is to make comparisons less specious than when they are based on areas contained within administrative boundaries.

Doxiadis has coined yet another term in the course of trying to show that city regions are not just geographers' abstractions but are to do with living. His label for the theatre of activity of the mobile modern townsman is 'daily urban system'. Within the compass of such a system may be found a range of jobs, shops and places of recreation capable of satisfying all ambitions apart from those pursued on holidays and long weekends.

Has this process of expansion and integration run its course? Jean Gottmann, the French geographer, argues that it has not and has identified in that 400-mile belt of cities stretching along the United States' eastern seaboard from Boston to Washington what he terms a megalopolis. He does not mean by this to infer that it is commonplace for Bostonians to commute to Washington, though no doubt a few Congressmen do, or that families in Philadelphia go to dentists in New York. The primary sinews of megalopolis are not airways or highways, though it has both, but flows of information and goods and money and networks of contacts. Megalopolis is happening in Europe too : between Rotterdam and the Ruhr, Paris and Le Havre, and London and Lancashire.

Doxiadis, never one to lie down before a challenge, has gone one further than Gottmann and identified a subsequent stage in the evolution of human settlements which he calls 'oecumenopolis' —the world city. He is focusing on Marshall McLuhan's global village but from a different perspective. Oecumenopolis is a thin trickle of hippies crossing the Khyber Pass on their way to Katmandu. It is the flick of a switch that projects into the parlour, albeit second-hand, sights and sounds that it took Marco Polo years of hardship to witness.

But I digress. Back in the city region institutional adaptations are going on that are playing an important part in the way we live. Regional shopping centres replace corner shops. Regional general hospitals replace cottage hospitals. Town halls that have been important centres of government for ninety years are transformed into mere outposts of new metropolitan and county authorities.

Some see in this process economies of scale, others a greedy concentration of power, but either way it is clear that the changes depend heavily on certain assumptions about the availability of transport. In the case of health services, for instance, it is exclusively the existence of cars and ambulances that makes it possible for a hospital board to close down a maternity unit in a small country town and oblige expectant mothers and their husbands and visitors to go to a regional general hospital eight or ten miles away. The official explanation for such a change is that it is too costly to maintain skilled staff in small towns.

The battleship mentality of those who manage public institutions (like their brothers, the take-over barons in private business) is nowhere better illustrated than in schooling. Forty years ago it was taken for granted that schools needed to be within walking distance of their pupils. Since then the control of schooling has been regionalised and the new education authorities, far from experimenting with ways to keep schools local, humane and intimate, have plumped for 2,000-place comprehensives exuding the atmosphere of pea-packing factories. The transport implications of this emerge from a plan published in 1972 for Coventry. It forecasts that the thrust to large comprehensives with wider catchment areas will result in the thirty-seven per cent of children who took the bus to school in 1967 rising to forty-four per cent by 1976.

Commentators seeking to describe the difference between life in the walk-in and the drive-in city argue that mill and cottage communities are giving way to non-spatial ones based on common interests. Twentieth-century man, instead of walking to the pub to chat with his neighbours, telephones to a friend sixty miles away or drives for, say, twenty minutes to be with like-minded enthusiasts for stock-car racing or players of medieval musical instruments. Professor Melvin Webber of the University of California argues that perceptions of cities as places are withering away altogether and being replaced by a sense of what he calls a 'non-place realm'. Webber's argument rests on the observation that human beings perceive their surroundings first of all in terms of the people they know and the social groups they are part of, and only then as assemblies of buildings. The human environment dominates the physical one. Individuals trained as architects, engineers, surveyors, and a few other kinds of highly specialised beings, may see things the other way round but that only serves to confirm the original proposition.

Webber has made a valuable contribution to the understanding of city living, but it seems to me he errs in assuming that membership of a far-flung community of interest *replaces* reliance on local contacts and dissolves all perception of locality. If he argued that the new dimension given to life brought about by cars and telephones is a *supplement* to neighbourhood living, I think he would be getting closer to the truth. For families with children who play with other children nearby, for housewives who chat across fences, for residents who unite to oppose some threat to their locality, neighbourhood continues to be something vivid. It is not predominantly a physical concept. You cannot draw a boundary round a particular district and say this is the neighbourhood of all the people living within it, though they try and do that in new towns. Perceptions of neighbourhood, like those of a non-place realm, stem from contacts with people and taking part in activities. Two housewives living in adjacent houses may have different views about what constitutes their neighbourhood because they belong to different clubs, because one goes often to the public library and the other to play bingo, and because they shop in different streets. Nevertheless, as Nicholas Taylor says in *The Village in the City*, both will be able to define precisely what they see as constituting *their* neighbourhood, and they will do so by referring to land-marks. I would guess that Webber's failure to recognise the continued existence of neighbourhood is explained partly by his own globe-trotting habits and partly by the peculiarly rootless circumstances of suburban Californian life. In California, if people do in fact jump into their cars every time they leave their houses, if they scatter like chaff before the wind when they go to work, if they shop only at distant drive-ins where everyone is a stranger, then perhaps, under those conditions, neighbourhood is killed and only community of interest remains.

If the same process has not proceeded so far in Britain, if the characters David Riesman found in Main Street, USA, and portrayed in *The Lonely Crowd* are not yet stereotypes in High Street, UK, part of the explanation may be that cars are not yet so ubiquitous.

Needless to say, living at the scale of neighbourhoods or of city regions are not alternatives. A total return to the introspective, small-scale life of the village is no more possible than it is practical. We don't want to be Marie Antoinettes, playing at being shepherds and shepherdesses. The real choice is a matter of emphasis. For the past twenty-five years the scales have been tipped in favour of the regional style of life. Parks within walking distance of houses have had motorways constructed across them, thereby obliging residents wanting a stroll amidst greenery to get into their cars. Houses within walking distance of city centres have had inner ring roads driven through them, thereby forcing their occupants out to places where they have to use transport to get to the shops. Regional sports centres, regional hospitals and regional parks have all been mooted and pronounced good. Regional shopping centres have swept across France and Germany and have begun to appear in Britain. Schools have been centralised. Local government has been made less local. Big business has got bigger.

New highways and the growing use of cars have been as intimately linked with this process of aggrandisement as the development of civilian aviation to the growth of multi-nationals. Until there were aeroplanes, executives in companies like Unilever and Ford could not get about to keep an eye on the shop.

The immense importance attached to building roads—in Whitehall the word motorway has taken on an almost mystical quality—stems from a confusion of process with substance. Because of it Glasgow, Belfast, the north-eastern region of England, and other areas where successive governments have attempted to stimulate economic and social development, have new roads of a capacity far in excess of likely traffic today or tomorrow. Anyone who thinks the result is progress should go and look at the Grand Canyons of concrete that now cut up the central parts of Glasgow and Newcastle upon Tyne and the great wind-swept wastelands that have been created. If that is development why is it that the far more flourishing towns of the south have so much less of it?

It is time to abandon a single-minded pursuit of regional organisations and a belief in motorways as a measure of progress. Bigger is better is an administrative ideal, not a democratic one. Effort should be switched to creating local institutions and to promoting the use of inexpensive, low-speed, low-energy modes of transport suited to getting to them. Local government should decentralise to 'little town halls', manned by staff from all departments. Local schools should be reopened and teaching ideas adapted to suit them. The cult of the regional, Olympic-sized swimming pool reachable only by bus or car should be replaced by smaller pools within walking and cycling distance. Town planning permission should be freely given to the opening of shops amongst and within houses (once upon a time anyone could turn their front parlour into a shop) and not at all to out-of-town drive-in shopping centres. Money hitherto spent on regional highways should be devoted to creating networks of safe and direct footways and cycle-ways enabling people to get to and from local destinations. Funds should be spent on putting short lengths of existing roads in cuttings or on overpasses so that slower unprotected travellers can pass unhindered over and under them. Traffic signals should invariably be equipped with 'little green men' that enable people on foot to get a guarantee of priority over motor vehicles.

Such a change of philosophy would be an immeasurable gain in equity, since opportunities that are now being progressively withdrawn from the reach of those without cars would be returned to them. Some of the strengths of a neighbourhood approach to accessibility emerge from comparing it with the idea of free transport that has become fashionable in left-wing circles during the past few years. Free transport advocates assume that mobility is an unquestionable good and that it is necessary only to correct its maldistribution. They therefore propose to add to the frenetic to-ing and fro-ing of the motorised society and to pile yet more customers into wasteful vehicles. The result, as Ivan Illich says in *Energy and Equity*, is complete sell-out to General Motors and an unnecessary squandering of resources.

One obstacle to giving emphasis to neighbourhoods is the belief that the greater the mobility the greater the choice. This is an argument often put forward by proponents of Los Angeles and its criss-cross of freeways. Given the possibility of traversing the region at a steady sixty-five miles an hour, it is said that anyone with a car can, within sixty minutes, make contact with millions of jobs and umpteen friends, shops, cinemas and so on. Forgetting for the moment the plight of those without cars and other hidden costs of drive-in cities, the factor that this statement omits is time. Any individual can pack into his life only a limited number of jobs, friends and shopping expeditions. But as high-speed regional travel seldom means devoting smaller total amounts of time to travelling (it usually means spending more), regional man will find he has less time to spend at his destinations. Angelinos try to compensate for this loss by using their cars as destinations. They eat in them, talk business in them, lacquer their nails in them and make love in them. There is even an apocryphal tale of a family that bought a caravan and made the freeways, and their attendant parking lots, their home. Nothing could better demonstrate the ability of human beings to make the best of a bad job.

Developing the potential of neighbourhoods by decentralisation and creating information systems that would increase access to local opportunities holds out the promise of an urban society that is more equitable and less energy hungry than is possible in drive-in cities. A neighbourhood approach would not condemn people to living in hermetic compartments where they would be forced to suffocate in their own parochiality. Contact and inter-action would continue through improved public transport and telecommunications. Travel between neighbourhoods would go on but activity within them would be enhanced.

4 Leg Power

Shoe shops are said to outnumber all others in a typical high street. Dolcis, Bata, Manfield, Bally, they are certainly ten a penny in Oxford Street in London and a figure tucked away in a corner of the Government's monthly green book of statistics shows that selling shoes is big business. In 1972 shoppers spent a walloping £547,000,000 on footwear or about a third of what they spent on cars and motor cycles.

One explanation for the size of the shoe budget in the motor age (putting aside the skyscraping price of shoes with equally skyscraping soles and heels) is the irreducibility of walking. Just as you cannot keep a good man down, apparently you cannot stop one from walking. According to Sigmund Asmervik in *Transportation of Man*, pedometer tests show that people walk three to four miles a day in all western countries come rain, hell or high water. Vehicles extend man's range but they are not substitutes for walking. If car owners take only two steps from their front doors to their driving seats and never walk from their houses, they merely transfer the start of their perambulations to those places where they park. Nowadays only people with chauffeurs get taken from door to door.

The distance that people are prepared to walk once they are on their feet seems to vary with age, income and state of mind. Surveys made on both sides of the Atlantic indicate that the elderly and the poor walk further than other sorts of people but that both are out-distanced by that indefatigable and foot-sore animal, the tourist. Despite these variations, four hundred yards does seem to be an important watershed in walking. Up to that distance most people walk, though they make considerable use of bicycles or mopeds if they are available. Between four hundred and a thousand yards walking remains important but is increasingly replaced by two-wheelers which dominate the field up to about two miles. Beyond that distance cars, buses and trams take over.

All this came out in a survey carried out in 1966 for a Netherlands Government commission to promote public transport. Not many countries can show such heavy use of bicycles or of those two-wheeled hornets Dutchmen call *bromfietsen* or *'brommers'*, but one reason for using the Dutch figures is that rising petrol prices are likely to push other countries in the same direction. Even before the fuel crisis, congestion and disillusionment with public transport seemed to be leading people to buy mopeds. Sales of motorbikes with engines of up to 50 c.c. increased in Britain from 4,000 in December 1972 to 6,700 a year later, an increase of nearly seventy per cent. All indications are that this was only the beginning of a surge of interest in low-powered, low-speed, one-man vehicles. With attractive devices like the 'Charger' electric motorcycle coming into the market (fifty miles range at thirty miles an hour after a one penny charge) it seems almost certain to increase.

One of the most repeated criticisms of transportation plans is that they fail to consider pedestrians and cyclists. A study done in Helsinki in 1970 gives some idea of the importance of what is overlooked. It showed that more than half of all trips made by adults and children over fifteen years old, and as many as three-quarters of all trips to buy food, were made on foot. Variations were found between outer and inner suburbs but the general picture is borne out by studies elsewhere.

Cyclists had a brief heyday in the 1930s when tracks were laid for them through the daisies and dandelions of trunk-road verges, but since then they have been ignored or discounted. Sir Colin Buchanan's treatment of them in *Traffic in Towns* was typical of attitudes during the early 1960s. When he came to examine the red-brick market town of Newbury in Berkshire, he found that seventeen per cent of trips to work were made by bicycle. (Buses and walking accounted for thirty-six per cent

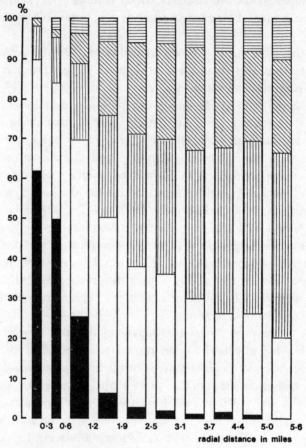

%

100
90
80
70
60
50
40
30
20
10
0

0·3 0·6 1·2 1·9 2·5 3·1 3·7 4·4 5·0 5·6

radial distance in miles

▤ Other Modes of Transport
▨ Public Transport
▥ Private Car
☐ Bicycle and Moped
■ On Foot

Mode of Transport in Holland
in 1966

more.) That is a considerable minority; nevertheless the report said 'it would be very expensive, and probably impracticable, to build a completely separate system of tracks for bicycles'. That left open the possibility of some more modest network but it was not taken up. The report merely proposed the investment of four and a half million pounds on urban motorways.

Nothing much is ever gained by using hindsight to damn those who have gone before but it is tantalising to consider what might have been the outcome had Sir Colin made a strong case for bus priorities and cycleways instead of urban motorways at Newbury. One thing is certain. The ideas he did put forward were ignored by the former Ministry of Transport and the Borough Council. The town has been systematically butchered to make way for the most objectionable kind of inner relief road and even though an opportunity has been created to turn the market places into pedestrian precincts crossed only by buses, it has not been grasped.

Subsequent surveys in other cities show 7·5 per cent of all trips to work being made on bicycles in London in 1964, 22 per cent in Cambridge in 1967 (and the same use throughout the day), 11 per cent in Stevenage in 1971 and 22 per cent in Peterborough at about the same date. The flatness of the Fens and the rarity of rain explain the popularity of bicycling in Cambridge and Peterborough, a fact confirmed by answers about travel to work in the 1966 sample census. East Anglia topped the list with about a quarter of all trips being made by bicycle. Wales and Scotland with their rain-drenched moors and mountains came at the bottom. As might be expected, the situation was somewhere in between round London and in the Midlands, where only some towns are hilly and rain is intermittent. Information of this kind may dampen the hopes of bicycle fanatics but it gives reason to believe that cycling would, if given encouragement, make a come-back in flatter and drier regions. Experience in Stevenage, where twenty-three miles of cycleways and ninety underpasses make bicycling unusually safe, bears this out.

Bicycles are to children what cars are to grown-ups. Or at least they could be if there were not so many cars. As it is, the gleaming Raleighs that arrive at tenth or twelfth birthdays all too often have to be left at home. Parents hedge their use with limitations because they are afraid of the dangerousness of the roads. In Stevenage, where the cycleways reduce parental fears, eight per cent of children cycle to school and amongst secondary school pupils, who have further to go than their younger brothers and sisters, the figure is over seventeen per cent. Peterborough is another exception, not because it has cycleways, but presumably because so many fathers ride bicycles. Given this example, two out of five secondary school children pedal to their classes and at one school the figure is almost three out of five.

Accidents loom large in the contemporary history of walking and bicycling and suggest that parental anxieties are not unjustified. In the ten years up to 1970 the number of pedestrians killed or seriously injured in Britain increased from over 22,000 to nearly 28,000 a year and the likelihood of a child between the ages of ten and fourteen being killed or maimed doubled. Deaths amongst young cyclists increased as well and if fatalities amongst adolescent and adult ones declined, it was because there was less cycling. That is hardly surprising. Traffic fumes were thickening; circuitous, one-way schemes were being introduced; roundabouts—the bicyclist's nightmare—were multiplying; and built-up areas were becoming more spread out. Among those cyclists who soldiered on through these persecuting conditions, accidents per mile pedalled did increase.

The picture in the United States was not dissimilar, despite immense investment in urban motorways designed to disentangle fast and slow traffic. The number of pedestrians killed annually increased from nearly 8,000 to over 10,000 between 1960 and 1972 while deaths amongst cyclists grew from 540 to about 1,100. Freeways failed to reduce this toll because the majority of these victims were struck down on ordinary town streets where all car trips begin or end.

Governments have not turned a blind eye on this depressing

picture but they have made errors of judgement in trying to do something about it. Road safety has been approached from a through-the-windscreen point of view. The first consideration has been to prevent pedestrians from getting in the way of vehicles. (The safety of bicyclists has been ignored.) The psychological and physical requirements of people on foot have been disregarded. Prime examples of this blinkered approach are the tunnels that have been driven under busy intersections. With the passage of time they become dark, urine-smelling, graffiti-scrawled warrens because they are not 'defensible space' in the language of Oscar Newman, the author of a book of that name. All public places in cities that cannot be policed by the eyes of people at windows, in passing vehicles or across the street acquire this character. People associate them with crime and become afraid of them. Oscar Newman has shown how such never-never lands are created by ill-designed slabs of municipal flats but the same applies to highway engineering. The hidden places in pedestrian subways become hideouts for muggers and handbag snatchers and because of this what was intended as an aid to walking becomes a barrier to it.

Physical barriers such as flights of steps down to subways or up to bridges form obstacles of a different kind. They are deterrents to movement because they demand exertion. Kerbside railings designed to stop people from crossing shopping streets and to protect them from fast-moving traffic, and pedestrian crossings that oblige walkers to wait in a barrage of noise and fumes, fall into the same category.

The procedures for deciding whether or not to install crossings giving pedestrians the right to hold up wheeled traffic show the insidious way in which the cards are stacked against unprotected road users. In Britain everything turns on a formula designed by the Department of the Environment. It has the military-sounding name of PV^2 and the rule is that for a zebra crossing to be justified, result of multiplying (P), the number of pedestrians crossing the road in one hour, by (V), the number of vehicles, and then squaring the answer, must come to more than a hundred million. This criterion is just reached where, in the course of sixty minutes, one hundred adult pedestrians struggle to cross a road being used by just over one vehicle every four seconds or one thousand an hour.

Notice the word *adult*. Children on foot are not counted on the grounds that 'lollipop men'—mostly women—are provided where they cross roads in large numbers. But lollipop men only guard school routes. The safety of children walking to see friends, going shopping or playing is dismissed as irrelevant. It remains for parents to restrict the freedom of their children, to spend time shepherding them or to let them risk their lives. In a world where more and more married women go out to work (the proportion rose from thirty-three to forty-four per cent in the ten years up to 1971) the 'risk it' option is increasingly taken. Not surprisingly, road accidents among children are rising faster than those amongst older pedestrians.

Pelican crossings, traffic lights on straight stretches of road that can be used to stop heavy flows of traffic at the push of a button, illustrate another facet of the same problem. (PV^2 has to reach an astronomical five hundred million for one of them to be justified!) The signals are set to give people on foot a minimum of ten and a maximum of twenty-two seconds to cross. How far the signals are adjusted towards the maximum depends on the width of the road and the number of people trying to cross it. British Standard Man, aged thirty-five and strong in wind and limb, has no difficulty in coping whatever the time allotted. For the young and the old and women with prams and push-chairs it is not so comfortable. These kinds of people were found in Nottingham to take *on average* eleven seconds to cross a thirty-foot-wide street and five seconds to cross each lane of a four-lane road.

The official view is that the permitted timings are fair to all parties (though modifications to them are under consideration) and the best compromise that can be arranged. Yet the whole business is a triumph of craftsmanship in a situation so patently unsound as to require a major overhaul. The reality is illustrated by the TV road safety advertisement that shows a child being smashed by a car, followed by a picture of a hammer hitting a peach. How did we ever let our peaches get mixed up with millions of swinging hammers? And what sort of pride can we take in having calculatedly to build up fear in our children so that they can survive in the mechanical jungle we have created?

Another aspect of the pedestrian's nightmare is 'things on the pavement'. Over the years traffic engineers have assiduously cultivated a forest of traffic lights, parking instruction poles, traffic signs, parking meters and traffic-signal control boxes on what used to be pedestrian territory. Parking meters were once the most effective of this array of anti-pedestrian weapons. Their head-high upper works might have been purpose built to knock out the teeth or at least bruise the faces of passers-by on dark and dirty nights. Recently, however, a weapon has been introduced aimed not just at damaging but defoliating people on foot. It is a small groin-high box, camouflaged battleship grey, that is part of the equipment for controlling sequences of traffic signals.

Government and local authorities peck away at corners of this predicament but show reluctance to study walking and bicycling in their entirety. Trends of decline are treated with equanimity. Thus the 1972 Coventry plan reports that while thirty per cent of the people who both lived and worked in the city walked or cycled to work in 1967, the percentage can be expected to fall to twenty-four in 1974 and to twenty-two in 1981. Such shifts are treated as if inevitable. No proposals are made to invest funds in footways and cycleways. The development plan for the new Tees-side Polytechnic illustrates another facet of this fatalistic obsession with catering for cars. The accommodation is for 7,000 students with lodging for 3,000 of them and parking for 4,700 cars. An assumption has clearly been made that very large numbers of students will in future have cars. Yet at Cambridge ninety-three per cent of all trips in and out of the university are by bicycle. A modern polytechnic may be a very different animal from a medieval university but there are still alternatives to designing it on the principles of a drive-in shopping centre.

Pedestrians and cyclists, like motorists, need clearly-defined networks of safe, convenient and attractive ways enabling them to go everywhere without having to plunge into morasses of traffic. This is what pavements are meant—but in today's conditions fail—to be. The simple kerbstone, brilliant invention though it may be, is no longer sufficient to guarantee safe and comfortable passage. Further innovation is necessary.

It is sensible to look at people on foot first because they are everybody. Much has already been done, particularly in Germany, to create magnificent central precincts in which people can shop and stroll in comfort. They are not only a commercial success but a human one too. People promenade in them when the shops are shut and even in the rain. Jorg Kühnemann, one of my former colleagues at OECD, insisted that this was true and he had made a detailed study of precincts in about ten cities. Once established, such sanctuaries for pedestrians need to be treated, not as self-contained, but as starting and finishing points, and staging posts, for footways leading all over a town and into the country round it. In advocating such networks, it is no more necessary to show that anyone will walk from one side of a town to another than it is to show, in advocating a road network, that anyone will drive from one end of it to another. The case for creating footway systems rests on the fact that the accumulated movements of all pedestrians call for them and that the more convenient the network the more use will be made of it. This is straight traffic engineering thinking. It just happens that with one or two exceptions, such as Kenneth Claxton at Stevenage and Nils Rosén in Sweden, most engineers apply it exclusively to vehicles and never to people or to cyclists.

What might such a network of footways consist of? Everything will depend on the importance attached to traffic. If it is considered untouchable, then expensive double-decking will follow. Venice, with its elegant footbridges oversailing the canals, exemplifies this approach. Leonardo da Vinci, a transport engineer amongst his other skills, applied the idea to a conventional town in a drawing that shows people and vehicles moving on different levels. *Traffic in Towns* helped to succour belief in an updated version of the principle because it contained a drawing of London's Oxford Street rebuilt in multi-deck fashion. This picture was widely published with reviews of the report and Sir Colin Buchanan said later that he wished it had never been included. Many people thought it summed up all he was trying to say.

The upper-level pedestrian ways at the new Barbican near St Paul's Cathedral and in the vicinity of the Festival Hall on the South Bank in London show the snags of double-decking. The footways are expensive, dull and windswept and their existence has not eliminated the need for people to walk on the ground. Furthermore, those who do are condemned to dingy gloom. At one time it seemed likely that Piccadilly Circus would be rebuilt on similar principles with Eros sitting on top of a huge concrete umbrella. Commonsense now appears to have prevailed and studies are being made of the practicality of extending the underground concourse and ticket hall into a broad ramp opening out in the direction of Leicester Square.

One of the few places where overhead ways seem to work well is in the centre of Minneapolis in the American Middle West, where the street layout is as stern and geometrical as in a Roman camp. This regularity, and the ownership of a number of entire blocks by single companies, has made it possible for footbridges to be thrown across streets between adjacent blocks. Inside buildings the footways become public corridors lined by shops and businesses normally found only at ground level. Conditions on the ground have not been neglected and one street has been turned into one of the most distinguished pedestrian malls anywhere. So successful has the whole operation been that the city aims to have sixty-four bridges in use by 1985, providing a network of indoor ways extending across the whole city centre and on into vast multi-storey car parks built on top of an encircling freeway. The highways are not something to be imitated but there may be other cities where railway stations could be connected to nearby office buildings by similar, short, enclosed bridges. The bleak, open, spaciousness of the London footways is a precedent not to be copied.

In cities with undergrounds, where people have good reasons for being below street level, extensive concourses that make it possible to walk under roads make sense. Montreal has gone further with this idea than anywhere else and visitors to Place Ville Marie can explore hundreds of shops, restaurants, hotels and offices without venturing out into the winds of winter or the slush of spring. As long ago as 1971 there were two miles of malls and the network has been steadily expanded since then. Given an underworld of this extent and the probability that large numbers of people may spend long periods down there, it becomes important to let in daylight. Sunken gardens, open to the sun and sky, do this at Montreal.

Much shorter but equally spacious malls have been built below ground at Munich to enable people to walk under an inner ring road and enter the central precinct. Most of them are lobbies for the *U-Bahn* or *S-Bahn,* which means they are always busy and all are linked to the streets above by banks of escalators. Shops, kiosks and doorways to the basements of adjacent department stores add further liveliness but only a special Olympic Games budget or some other miracle makes this kind of civic splendour possible.

Constructing pedestrian underpasses as lavish as those in the middle of Munich at all the points where a citywide footway network would intersect main highways would be out of the question. Even the most modest set of underpasses needed to serve a busy intersection were found to cost £500,000 by the Greater London Council in 1970. This sum included the price of escalators but not of any property. A set of bridges served by moving stairs would, it turned out, be less expensive—about £200,000—but would be ugly.

Problems of cost are likely to prove an even greater obstacle to the installation of moving pavements and other whizzy aids to walking. Books and conferences galore have been devoted to them in recent years but the vision of a city served by never-stop transport seems as far off as ever. The rising price of energy is likely to push it even further into the future.

Short-distance devices of this genre may involve moving belts, platforms supported by revolving screws with variable helices, or, like San Francisco's cable cars, a continuously moving cable that can be grabbed or released by a mechanical hand, but whatever the technology the generating principle is the same. It is to eliminate loss of time through waiting. The widespread publicity given to moving belts has broadcast the impression that they are the most promising kind of never-stop technology but devices with seats are as numerous. One, the VEC 'moving sofa', made by the French Cytec Company, was demonstrated on the vast concrete deck of La Défense in Paris while I was living there in 1972. The sofas of a VEC are attached to a belt and can be slowed down from a maximum of about sixteen miles an hour to about one and a half miles an hour to enable passengers to leap aboard. Once you are sitting down the sofa moves away sideways, giving you the feeling that you are being pulled by an elastic band. Children love it, particularly those over the age of twenty.

Exhibition sites, Disneylands, international airports and other places thronged by millions and under the control of one management, can often make use of new technologies of this kind. Fitting them into existing cities, where property is in a thousand different hands and where streets and buildings may still follow the lines of former cow tracks, is more difficult. A few years ago the Dunlop Company decided that London Bridge, which is crossed morning and evening by thousands of commuters, was an ideal place for some elevated travelators. They therefore put the idea to the City Corporation which was then rebuilding the bridge but nothing came of it. There were problems of cost and aesthetics. A more profound difficulty emerged from studies of the continuation of the moving pavements to Liverpool Street Station. Travelators of the kind

Dunlop's had in mind cannot be made to go round corners. Getting them into Bishopsgate would therefore have involved taking slices off the fronts of some of the most expensive commercial buildings in the world. Minneapolis with its neat grid of streets and upper-level footways is, on the other hand, more amenable to such straight-arrow technology. Travelators may therefore be installed along some of the main overhead ways there during the next ten years.

Conventional moving pavements of the kind in use at Schipol and Los Angeles airports and in underground interchanges such as Montparnasse in Paris and Bank in London go at one and a half miles an hour and users of them have to walk to gain any advantage in time. Enormous amounts of inventiveness have been devoted to trying to overcome this problem and as long ago as 1900 a successful two-speed travelator, consisting of parallel belts moving at two and a half and five miles an hour, was successfully installed above the Quai d'Orsay and several other streets in Paris. Passengers stepped on to the slow belt and from it on to the faster one. Millions used the device during the life of the exhibition held that year and those of them who had read the early editions of *When the Sleeper Wakes* must have wondered if H. G. Wells was justified in being called a writer of science fiction. It was, after all, only a year before that he had written : 'Under the balcony this extraordinary roadway ran swiftly to his right, an endless flow rushing along as fast as a 19th century express train, an endless platform of narrow transverse overlapping slats . . .'

The problem for the moving belt men now as then is to accelerate passengers to a speed faster than walking without knocking them off balance. One modern mechanism which does this has been designed by the Batelle Institute. It is called an 'integrator' and Dunlop's are the licensees for it in Britain. A prototype that accelerates a walker to a speed of seven and a half miles an hour in the space of a few yards is working at Batelle's laboratories in Geneva. The prospective traveller first steps on to some metal slats that are moving forward like the flat part of an escalator but as the slats start to slide sideways as well, he is speeded up and turned through ninety degrees. 'Integration' is uncanny but it works.

Never-stop devices can handle large numbers of people, which is one reason why they are already in use linking different railway stations or railways and metros as at Montparnasse. Another possibility is to use them to extend the area that is within, say, five minutes' walk of a suburban railway station. Let's assume someone arriving at such a station is prepared to walk for five minutes. At an ordinary walking pace he will be able to go a quarter of a mile. Install a six-mile-an-hour never-stop and it becomes possible to go half a mile in the same time. Raise the speed to nine miles an hour and a university campus or hospital three-quarters of a mile from a station may be reached in five minutes. A never-stop running overhead in a glazed tube would, moreover, cause little disturbance to places it passed through.

The first time this idea has come up in Britain is in a report on *South East London and the Fleet Line*, prepared by Lord Llewelyn-Davies for London Transport. It shows how moving belts would encourage more people to use the new Fleet Underground Line and so increase the return on the investment. There is now some doubt whether the line will be extended to south-east London but that does not invalidate the arguments for moving pavements or other never-stop devices. They could be installed at existing suburban stations.

So much for high technology. Inexpensive ways to improve the ease of walking are more important and the most promising is to win back for people on foot some of the space presently occupied by parked and moving cars. Widen pavements all over the city. It is as simple as that. For twenty-five years the reverse has been going on. Streets have been widened, pavements narrowed and pedestrians driven to the wall. The result has been increased traffic congestion and more difficult walking. Widened pavements would achieve a diametrically opposite effect. They would give pedestrians more room, making it quicker and easier to get about on foot. They would mop up parking space and reduce the scope for using cars. Last, but not least, they would change the atmosphere of streets, turn them from corridors into outdoor rooms.

Conquering space from cars can begin in city centres by turning all narrow side streets over entirely to people on foot. Norwich pioneered this in Britain. Main shopping streets, the majority of which are bus routes, are more difficult. In most German and Swiss towns (Bremen and Zurich are exceptions) public transport has been expelled, along with all other traffic, in the pursuit of pure untrammelled architectural space. An alternative is to clear out the cars and widen the pavements while keeping the buses, trams and taxis running down narrowed roadways. Nicollet Mall in Minneapolis, Oxford Street in London, and other streets in Newcastle upon Tyne, Leicester and Reading show how pavements can be widened and trees planted while still enabling people to get a bus or taxi just outside Woolworth's or Marks & Spencer's. For shoppers with parcels it is a great advantage. Nicollet Mall, with its flowers, fountains, seats and ornamental clock shows that a very attractive job can be made of this kind of semi-precinct.

Queen Street, Oxford, where paving slabs have been laid from wall to wall and buses confined to a central strip bounded by bollards, exhibits a variant of this approach. (A picture of it is on the dust cover.) The wall-to-wall paving turns a one-time corridor into a room even though there is little space for flowers and fountains. Cracks in the flagstones suggest that a mistake was made over the strength needed to carry double-decker buses, but that should not be irremediable.

Queen Street-style paving is needed in shopping streets on main roads in suburbs too. Why should conditions be improved just for visitors to city centres? Vehicles frequently race through suburban shopping streets at forty miles an hour. If, as the police insist, signed speed limits are disregarded, then it is time to modify the behaviour of drivers by redesigning the paving and the architecture of *rues corridors*. The modifications should be aimed at slowing traffic down to five or ten miles an hour. The cost would be low, the time taken to effect the changes slight. The destruction of trying to build bypasses through houses behind the shops would be avoided.

One way to warn drivers approaching semi-precincts would be to lay in the roads what one of my neighbour's children calls 'camel humps' and what others have dubbed 'sleeping policemen'. The Transport and Road Research Laboratory has since published a report backing up the infant-school intuition of my young friend. After looking at a circus full of camel and dromedary humps, the boffins concluded that platforms four inches high, stretching down a road for twelve feet, promise to alert dozy drivers without endangering them in skids (*Road Humps for the Control of Vehicle Speeds*, LR 597).

Semi-precincts in all streets fronted by rows of shops and schools would increase space for pedestrians and increase the number of safe crossing places too. Something more modest would have to suffice at other points where safer crossings are needed. Mr Hore-Belisha's flashing orange lollipops were the first attempt at this kind of thing in Britain, then came zebra markings on the road, then traffic signals which pedestrians can control and finally zig-zag markings on the approaches to zebras. They have not been without effect. In London accidents to pedestrians using crossings have been reduced one-quarter by the latest of this series of measures—the zig-zags. How can this pressure on drivers be kept up? An answer could lie in a shortened version of the semi-precinct, a widening of the pavements and a narrowing of the road, aimed at slowing down traffic to make it less menacing. Again the object would be to affect the psychology of drivers. Research is needed to identify what changes to the appearance and layout of streets would have the most sobering effect on driver behaviour.

All the measures described hitherto deal with traffic rather as a fire brigade deals with fires. Is there a trouble spot at this point or that? All right, rush and pour some water on it. But it is also possible to treat entire districts so as to exclude through traffic, increase safety and win back space for pedestrians.

The simplest technique is that used by the City of Westminster at Pimlico in London where a web of one-way streets has been devilishly put together to create a maze that brings any trespassing driver back to where he entered, or just next to it. A marked reduction in accidents has followed and additional space has been gained for pedestrians by billowing out the pavements at street junctions. This slows down vehicles entering the area and creates room for trees and benches.

A more complex approach is being slowly introduced throughout the inner parts of Stockholm. The first to be treated against traffic disease is a handsome, mixed residential and commercial quarter called Östermalm. It has been divided into three zones and an array of bollards, foot streets, one-way regulations and bus lanes used to ensure that only pedestrians, bicyclists and buses may go from one to the next. Residents with cars wishing to cross from one side of Östermalm to the other have to dodge out on to a boundary road, go along it for a bit, and then dodge back again. Alien short-cutters are kept out altogether.

Needless to say, the diversion of short-cutting traffic back on to the boundary roads, all of which are bus routes, has increased congestion on them. Bus-only lanes have therefore been introduced there too, to make sure that public transport does not suffer. Within Östermalm the conversion of a street into a pedestrian mall has given space-starved residents room to stroll and sit in the sun and provided somewhere for small children to bicycle and play pavement games. In Södermalm, the second district to be given this kind of treatment, a broad tree-lined boulevard, formerly much used by commuters, is being turned into a park. One of the City Council's aims in doing this is to entice families with children back to the inner parts of Stockholm.

As in Britain so in Sweden environmental improvements of this kind have not been without their critics. At Östermalm shopkeepers complained of loss of trade and residents said they feared to venture out at night into their newly quiet streets. Perhaps the worst problems have occurred along the fringe roads where traffic is now canalised. Householders living on these roads, looking enviously at the peace and quiet created just around the corner, feel hard done by and with justification.

The Stockholm authorities attempt to avoid confrontations between different groups of residents by putting proposals to them while these are still under preparation. And in Östermalm they have met fears of prowlers by arranging for the police to make extra patrols through the streets.

The problems of those living on the fringes remain. Noise blight can be alleviated in the short term by government grants towards the cost of sound-proofing. In Britain householders affected by aircraft noise at London Airport can claim such grants but under restricted conditions. The Land Compensation Act 1973 provides further grants for householders affected by the noise of traffic from new and improved roads. This Act now needs to be extended to include residents affected by traffic management measures on existing roads. Beyond these possibilities there is the longer-term prospect of quieter vehicles. Only this will enable townspeople in all streets to live with open windows.

The starting point for the Pimlico and Stockholm improvements just described was the exclusion of through traffic. The result is the creation of urban villages where living and walking take precedence over the rush of motor vehicles. The same philosophy can, however, be applied within single residential streets to reduce the dominance of parked cars. The Dutch are beginning to do this at Delft, using their incomparable skill with brick paving to turn streets previously lined with cars and bespattered with crankcase oil into cosy 'town yards'. Brick paving is laid down from wall to wall, householders are given 'front gardens' consisting of raised planting boxes, and bays for parking are clearly defined. Drivers turning into such sanctums are warned of the fact by the device of carrying the pavement across the road. The result is a camel hump for cars and the elimination of kerbs for people walking with prams or shopping baskets. In the more suburban circumstances of Runcorn New Town, near Liverpool, the same watch-out-you-are-entering-forbidden-territory message is conveyed to motorists by putting, or in some cases leaving, boulders at the corners of narrowed-down entrances to streets full of houses.

Large, remote and technocratic planning departments are unsuited to work of this kind. Residents are better equipped than outsiders to know what is wanted in their streets, as has been discovered by planners working on the modernisation of houses under general improvement area powers. Councillors and officials should confine themselves initially to revealing possibilities and explaining what funds are available. The most urgent need may not be traffic changes at all but better rubbish collection. Little towns halls or municipal outposts staffed by officials knowledge-able in all services are the proper scale of organisation to learn about such issues and to deal sensitively with them. Such offices could double as 'surgeries' for elected representatives. Every locality needs one.

People living in towns like Worcester, Oxford and Nottingham, towns with canals running through them, have been able to walk out into the country for as long as anyone can remember. In one or two places—Bath and Scarborough, for instance—disused railway lines are being transmuted into routes for walkers and cyclists as well. And in the West Country the Countryside Com-mission is promoting a seventy-mile-long path from Plymouth to Dartmoor. Pleasant but more modest footpaths of this kind that go out to commons, village pubs and outlooks are needed in all towns. If they are not provided people can hardly be blamed for piling into their cars to go to the country. Sweating it out in a car in a traffic jam may not be much fun but it will be a lesser evil than trying to walk or cycle along the same road.

Let's have a look, beginning at the centre of a city and moving outwards, to see what would happen if all these ideas were knitted together. To start with, many streets would be given over entirely to walking, with deliveries taking place outside busy hours, as is universally the case in Continental precincts. In many other main shopping streets the pavements would be broad and only buses and taxis allowed in. If there were a giant inner ring road with tunnels under it they might have to be renovated to make them less objectionable. Beyond the inner ring there would be semi-precincts at shopping centres strung along main roads and in front of schools; there would be a new generation of super-zebra and super-pelican crossings where the pavements would be widened out and the roadways narrowed down. Throughout the town as a whole traffic would be managed so as to create a series of urban villages closed to short-cutting drivers. Within these places living would take precedence over moving, parks would be created in former avenues and many streets modified into town yards. Further opportunities for walking would be created by opening up new short cuts for pedestrians through school playing fields, over rivers and through hospital grounds; canal tow-paths, riverside walks and other routes would lead out into the surrounding country. Walkers would have the freedom of the city.

Changes in thinking and practice as extensive as this call for new men, new organisations, new technical manuals and new powers. In Britain these are more important than new grants, since local authorities will, after April 1975, be able to spend highway funds on footways under financial provisions associated with the reform of local government. In countries where central governments issue finance for specific purposes, grants for footways and cycleways will need to be introduced at the same rate as those for highways.

Professional attention can only be focused on the needs of 'unprotected' travellers by setting up groups of engineers, planners and architects to study them and cater for them. This has already been done in Gothenburg in Sweden. Ideally there should be a chief footway engineer and a chief cycleway engineer alongside the chief highway engineer in every local authority. Decentralisation to little city halls provides another method for directing the attention of professionals away from freeways for cars and towards freeways for people.

One task facing engineers concerned with improving conditions for pedestrians will be to go back and reconsider the indefensible footways created during the past fifteen years. In some cases there may be no alternative to blowing or blocking them up. Such desperate action was taken with one new housing project in St Louis after it had become too dangerous to live in. But this is likely to be the exception. In most cases it should be possible to eliminate shadowy hiding places, improve lighting, introduce shops, cafés, pubs or activities of some kind that attract customers and increase the amount of surveillance of people by one another. The old adage about safety in numbers is nowhere truer than on footways.

Another candidate for change is the shiny, sky-blue booklet called *Roads in Urban Areas*, published by the old Ministry of Transport in 1966. It is the highway engineer's bible and enunciates with chilling clarity that the layout of roads shall accord with the type, volume and speed of traffic they will carry. Off-road factors are entirely secondary. Given this kind of start-with-the-traffic-then-design-the-world-around-it approach, splayed open corners and standardised eighteen- to twenty-four-foot-wide carriageways that encourage speeding are inevitable. Any new version of the handbook (the Department of the Environment is considering one) should put off-road considerations first and traffic second. The difference this might produce may be gauged from the conclusion of Dutch engineers working on town yards in Delft. They decided that maximum speeds of thirteen to sixteen miles per hour were appropriate in residential streets—half those recommended in the Ministry handbook.

On to bicycling and let me first try to get its role into perspective. I must confess to being a great enthusiast for bicycles. I have ridden one in London and Paris for the last ten years and after buying a tandem in 1973 went on a cycling holiday through France, Corsica and Tuscany with one of my children who was then nine. That makes it sound more exhausting than it really was. We put the tandem on a train five times and only pedalled four hundred miles. It was not a rest cure but it was fun. Nevertheless I realise that bicycles are anathema to some people and totally unsuitable for many purposes even for those who like them.

But this does not destroy the case for spending public money on catering for cyclists. Public money is spent on schools that are used only by children and swimming pools used only by swimmers. Clearways for cyclists would be a corresponding public good. They would cost their users little and be open to children, the poor, and well-buttered executives searching for good health.

There is also what might be called a fair play argument for devoting public funds to cyclists. Motor vehicles as currently used are like particularly vicious parasites. Left unchecked they eliminate all rivals not because they are intrinsically superior but because, like ivy or bindweed, they can suffocate and destroy. Anyone who has tried to bicycle through conventional city traffic will know how accurate a description this is. Cars and trucks poison the air and hog all the space. Clearing paths for cyclists through traffic is a way of redressing this imbalance and of widening choice in travel.

How many people will avail themselves of the opportunity and how much will depend on the weather, the terrain, the availability of alternatives and personal predilection. Even if only half the population were to have bicycles and to use them instead of cars for only one or two out of every five trips, there could be a major saving in resources. Vernon Goold, Mayor of Weston-super-Mare, who, with his wife the Mayoress, took to cycling in January 1974, put it this way to a reporter on the *Bristol Evening Post*: 'I'm not a cycling enthusiast and it was the first time for many, many years that we had cycled anywhere, but we felt there were many occasions when we could cycle or walk instead of using a car.' Making cycling safer and more convenient would add to the incidence of such occasions.

The first place in Britain outside a new town where pedal-power has been taken seriously is Cambridge. No one who has ever seen the flurry of gowns and spokes along King's Parade in term time will be in any doubt why, but it is worth stressing that the townspeople use bicycles as well. They go shopping on them on Saturdays and to work on them on week days. As a result of all this cycling activity, trips on foot and bicycle form more than half of all week-day movements amongst the 150,000 people who live in the city and its surrounding villages.

A firm of consultants called Travers Morgan and Partners found this out by surveying travel in Cambridge in 1967 and when they came to report four years later they proposed that several streets in the middle of the town should be reserved for pedestrians, cyclists and buses. They also noted that cyclists had several routes into the city to themselves because they crossed the River Cam by bridges that are too narrow for cars and lorries. Building on this precedent, they recommended the construction of cycleways beside two main roads leading into the city and proposed that bicycle hire depots should be established at fringe car parks so that visitors could 'park and pedal'. They even looked into the problems faced by cyclists when they reached the middle of the town and prodded the colleges to make greater efforts to provide cycle stands.

From the cyclist's point of view, the bridges over the Cam which cannot be used by cars are of inestimable importance. They work like cattle grids or stiles. They permit some to pass; they are barriers to others. They restrain travel by car; they do not hinder the movement of people. Filters of this sort can be set out across any street. They may consist of nothing more than rows of bollards four feet apart, though trees would be more elegant, and they are the secret in catering for cyclists without upheaval.

But, of course, this is exactly what has been done in Stockholm at Östermalm and Södermalm. People in buses, on bicycles and on foot may cross these areas, those in cars and trucks may not. And the same arrangement is proposed for the middle of Cambridge. Imagine cycling across a city consisting of numerous protected places of this kind. Cyclists would have an almost continuous passage along safe, direct and convenient routes but without a penny having been spent on tracks for them. Danger would, of course, remain where they had to cross the more

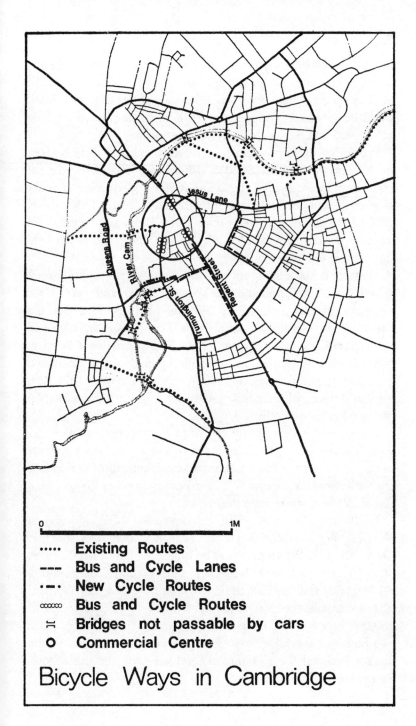

Jesus Lane

Queens Road

River Cam

Regent Street

Trumpington St.

0   1M

.....   **Existing Routes**
---   **Bus and Cycle Lanes**
-·-·   **New Cycle Routes**
∞∞∞   **Bus and Cycle Routes**
⌶   **Bridges not passable by cars**
o   **Commercial Centre**

Bicycle Ways in Cambridge

heavily used roads between the urban villages. In dense old parts of cities, crossings for pedestrians and cyclists could be installed at these points. In more open suburban places highway funds could be spent on putting main roads in cuttings or in creating broad underpasses for pedestrians and cyclists.

Proof that cycleways can be created in existing cities is given by Västerås in central Sweden, where over forty-five miles of them were in use in 1971, including routes underpassing an inner ring road and leading right into the city centre. Once there, cyclists can use several streets reserved for buses and bicycles and some pedestrian malls as well, though they are obliged to dismount in the busier ones.

Västerås is not a bankrupt provincial city where people cannot afford cars. The population is about 100,000 and two of the biggest engineering firms in Sweden—ASEA and Svenska Metallverken—have their main works there. Wages are high and car ownership is above the very high Swedish national average. Nevertheless the proportion of people cycling to work increased from twenty-five per cent in 1966 to thirty per cent in 1971 and, up to a distance of three miles, more use is made of bicycles than of any other kind of vehicle.

All this pedalling is partly explained by the existence of cycleways but also by the location of the two huge engineering plants in the middle of the town where parking is difficult. Corresponding limitations on parking will be necessary in other towns where the object is to encourage the use of cycleways.

In Britain the most vivid demonstration of confidence in bicycling yet has been given by the New Town Development Corporation at Peterborough. The building of thirty-eight miles of main cycleways and thirty-four miles of minor ones costing £1,700,000, was announced in 1973 as part of a development plan to enable the population of the city to double to about 200,000 people. The Corporation's *Cycleways Report* contains two points of special interest. One is a clear enunciation of the linkage between the planning of land uses and the use of low-energy forms of transport :

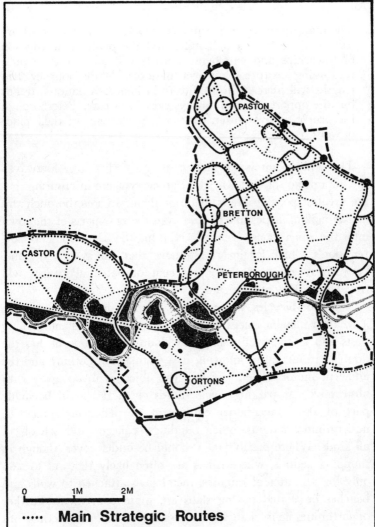

| 0 | 1M | 2M |

····· **Main Strategic Routes**

······ **Other Cycleway Routes**

🠢 **Park**

•—•— **Primary Roads**

– – **City Boundary**

○ **Commercial Centre**

Bicycle Ways in Peterborough

The majority of cycle journeys to work, shops and school are less than one and a half miles and the planned distribution of townships and employment areas will allow this to be a continuing feature of travel patterns. Work journey trip lengths will increase in the future in line with national trends but the opportunity will always exist in Greater Peterborough for people to live within easy cycling distance of their place of work.

The other point is one that came up earlier over footways : the importance of cycleways that go everywhere in ensuring that the greatest possible use is made of them. In Peterborough this means making it possible to ride from the new parts of the town into the older ones. Kenneth Hutton, the Development Corporation's Chief Engineer, estimates that unless this is done, between twenty and thirty per cent of potential cyclists will travel to work by other means.

Riders of bicycles, like motorists, need to have somewhere to leave their metallic steeds. Parking meters make excellent hitching posts and as the cyclist slings his chain around one he has the double satisfaction of knowing it is costing him nothing and the adjacent motorist plenty. But if the object is to do away with obstructive car parking, cycle stands or racks should be made part of the conventional equipment of pedestrian precincts, underground stations, office buildings, colleges and schools of all kinds. Where possible they should be under cover, though in shopping centres, where riders are often likely to want to stop only for a matter of minutes, metal jaws attached to walls and benches or slotted paving slabs are more convenient. Further opportunities lie in changing the wording of planning permissions to make clear that parking space should be designed for bicycles as well as cars. With the amount of space needed by one car able to accommodate up to ten bicycles, here as elsewhere there is a saving in resources to be had by promoting pedal power.

Special efforts need to be made at railway stations in order to encourage people to bike and ride or ride and bike. Whether any arrangements exist seems to depend on a mixture of chance and history. Cambridge, with thousands of bikes, has nowhere at the station for people to put them and they stand against some nearby railings four or five deep. Waterloo Station in London, a place only the brave cycle to, has a splendid cathedral for receiving them. More consistency is needed. Cyclists should be able to count on finding somewhere to leave their machines under cover at all stations as a matter of course.

Bicycling for pleasure has increased phenomenally in the United States in recent years. Young people, disenchanted with cars and industrial pollution in all its forms, have taken to it enthusiastically. Imports of ultra-light-weight French racing bikes with ten- (or even fifteen-speed) *dérailleur* gears have soared and the Avenue de la Grande Armée, for ninety years the centre of the French cycle industry, has become, at least for young American tourists, another rendezvous in Paris.

It may be scarcely believable, but the result of all this enthusiasm was to lift bicycle sales higher than car sales in 1972. Bicycle-only days have been introduced at university campuses and pollution-conscious states like Oregon have passed bills allocating petrol and oil taxes to the construction of footways and cycleways. Books, pamphlets and guides of all sorts have proliferated. I have one called *The Bicyclist's Guide for Manhattan* which, in addition to warning riders about the city's bath-sized potholes, contains an 'ethnic epicurean' tour through the lower East Side. This velo-gastronomy is strongly recommended for Sunday mornings.

Some impressions of bicycling for pleasure in Britain can be gleaned from the Travers Morgan report on Cambridge. It shows that about a quarter of all weekday cycle trips and rather more at weekends are done for recreation. About one in five of the city's residents are thus involved in cycling for pleasure.

Once out in the country, cyclists have thousands of miles of quiet country lanes to pedal along. With a good map and a little ingenuity they may go from Land's End to John O'Groat's or from Calais to Bordeaux without using a main road. Getting to those peaceful lanes through the suburban and semi-urban fringes of cities, where traffic is often at its thickest at weekends, is the problem. One way to leap-frog the traffic is to put your bicycle on a train. It is an unbeatable combination and one that the railways should do more to publicise. Amtrak, the semi-nationalised American passenger railway system, has seen the market potential in it and carries bicycles over long distances for a nominal two dollars. British Rail charges an expensive half fare but is being pressed by the British Cycling Bureau to follow Amtrak's example. Special hooks on which bicycles may be hung in guards' vans are just as important. Most French trains have them.

The Peterborough cycleways report observes something else that seems equally pertinent: 'Experience in Stevenage suggests that, once a comprehensive system is available, demand for pleasure cycling increases and there is pressure to extend the present cycleways system along country lanes and into the surrounding countryside.' As with footways, so with cycleways, they need to run from town into country and in many cases can probably be combined.

Finding routes of this kind should not be too difficult. In 1973 Maurice Fabre, an enterprising member of the staff of *Elle*, the fashion magazine, wrote about the opportunities for touring all over France using 'secondary roads with more trees than cars', and then described a circuit running out from the Porte de Clignancourt in Paris. Needless to say the article was decorated with photos of a macaroni-limbed blonde who took care to *'regard au miroir avant l'étape'* (not in order to avoid being crushed by an overtaking tractor but to see that her eyelashes were in place) and for whom bicycling seemed, as much as anything, part of the interminable campaign that French women wage against *la cellulite*. 'There is nothing better than bicycling to give firmness to the muscles of the bottom, to smooth the buttocks and keep fatty tissue at bay', wrote the good M. Fabre below a closeup of an elegantly saddled posterior: 'It is the best antidote to the desk chair.'

It would be a mistake to dismiss this side of cycling as frippery. Keeping fit and looking young preoccupy many people. The creation of cycleways and the promotion of cycling offers a practical and inexpensive way of catering for it and probably a far better one than health clubs and saunas. However, country lanes can be dangerous. Drivers race through them because they know all too well that trees outnumber cars and that the likelihood of meeting other vehicles is small. Country continuations of town cycleways may therefore have to be closed to vehicles or, if that is not possible, to all except those having business along them. Some research in the Peak National Park in Derbyshire should help to show what might be involved. It is aimed at sorting out conflicts between horsemen, cyclists, walkers and motorists throughout an area of fifty square miles. Theo Burrell, Director of the Park Planning Board and initiator of 'park and walk' in the Goyt Valley, is responsible. Just as the Goyt experiment showed how a small part of a national park could be closed to cars without hindering humans, so the 'routes for people' project should help to show how cyclists can be protected from traffic over a much wider area. The results could therefore be of value to engineers who are trying to disentangle incompatible kinds of movement on the fringes of cities.

Having looked at ways of speeding up walkers, it is only fair to see what can be done for bicyclists. How much can their machines be improved? An article on 'Bicycle Technology' in *Scientific American* of March 1973 argued that the answer is 'very little'. Measured by how much energy is needed to move a given weight a given distance, a man on a bicycle is about fifteen times more efficient than a man on foot (as well as being several times faster) and well ahead of his nearest competitors, the salmon and the horse. S. S. Wilson, author of the article and an Oxford don, said :

In order to make this excellent performance possible, the bicycle has evolved so that it is the optimum design ergonomically. It uses the right muscles (those of the thighs, the

82

most powerful in the body) in the right motion (a smooth rotary action of the feet) at the right speed (sixty to eighty revolutions per minute). Such a design must transmit power efficiently (by means of ball bearings and the bush-roller chain); it must minimise rolling resistance (by means of the pneumatic tyre), and it must be the minimum weight in order to reduce the effort of pedalling uphill.

Assuming that fundamental ergonomic improvements in bicycle design are unlikely, it is worth looking at other ways in which safety and convenience could be increased. Better brakes and puncture-proof tyres are at the top of my list. Greater protection from rain would be an advantage too but not if it involves shields or hoods that will increase wind resistance, that arch opponent of the cyclist. Roofing over the tops of cycleways would eliminate this problem and it might be done in towns as it already is over footways. Canvas awnings are stretched over foot streets in some cities in Japan and there are covered ways between virtually all buildings at the University of York. Other possibilities are special clothing or shields against water thrown up from the road.

Amsterdam's famous Provos gave currency to the idea of distinctive free bicycles that anyone could pick up and put down at will. The idea still tantalises many people and Eric Britton of Ecoplan International, a firm of Paris consultants, believes that the secret may lie in almost damage-proof, free-for-all machines that could be ridden without fear of punctures or chains coming off their sprockets. Another advantage of having idiosyncratic design would be that stolen ones could be quickly identified. I remain sceptical of the practicality of the idea outside small enclosed communities. Leaving the technology of the bicycle largely as it is but making machines available for hire seems more promising.

Already places as far flung as Santa Barbara in California and the Parc St Cloud outside Paris have rental depots (in Santa Barbara you can rent tricycles and at St Cloud double tandems). Historic towns where parking is particularly difficult and resorts where people may like to abandon the cares of motoring for the relaxation of cycling, are among commercially promising sites. The hiring business would probably need to be combined with running a shop or with something else. One possibility is that hire depots could be combined with bike stores at railway and bus stations. This would enable bike owners to get repairs done and improve cash flow for the entrepreneur.

My own experience of exploring Pisa and Lucca on a bicycle convinces me that no other form of transport is half as good in that kind of city. At five miles an hour one can see most things, stop instantly, and have the comfort of sitting down while doing it. Parking problems do not exist. On top of this the exercise enables one to eat with gusto and sleep soundly, though a bottle of wine at lunch can be a mistake if one hopes to get on during the afternoon. The middle of Pisa is already closed to all traffic except buses, bicycles and deliveries. Traffic could be excluded from a wider area if fringe car parks were established where one could park and ride or park and pedal. For resorts overwhelmed by tourist traffic and determined not to let it destroy what the visitors came to see, bicycles offer real hope. Just as the nineteenth-century spa flourished if it could demonstrate an ample supply of medicinal waters, so its twentieth-century successor should aim to provide a useful supply of 'medicinal' transport. S. S. Wilson's article in *Scientific American* provides a text with which an imaginative mayor or council leader could campaign for this kind of policy : 'Since the bicycle makes little demand on materials or energy resources, contributes little or no pollution, makes a positive contribution to health, and causes little death or injury, it can be regarded as the most benevolent of machines.'

There remains the ultimate technological possibility of assisting leg power with some kind of motor. Innumerable variations exist on the theme of the minimum personal vehicle and with seven out of ten car trips being made by a single person, the potential for mopeds, motor cycles, scooters and developments of them is great. Figures from Stockholm are typical of the way in which cars are used in large cities.

Car occupancy in Stockholm in 1971 (in percentages)

	Driver only	One passenger	Two passengers	Three or more passengers
Work trips	85	12	2	1
Other trips	67	25	6	2
All trips	71	22	5	2

Increasing fuel prices are already opening the eyes of many people to economical scooters. Limits on the use of cars aimed at clearing a way for public transport and reducing nuisances should give impetus to this interest. However, if the exposed users of such small and fragile machines are left mixed up with cars and lorries, accidents will soar in number. The setting aside of routes for bicyclists and riders of low-powered, personal transports promises a way to reap the advantages of machines that can do up to 170 miles on a gallon of petrol while avoiding increases in accidents. Experience in Stevenage makes it clear that bicycles and mopeds can co-exist safely.

Just as in the case of walking, institutional reforms are needed to realise the potential of two-wheeled transport. Starts have been made in several American states which have allocated petrol taxes to the construction of cycle and footways and a growing number of United States' cities have designated cycle routes. In Britain, London Transport has started looking at opportunities for storing bicycles at underground stations and the Greater London Council has instructed its officers to report on cycleways and cycle parking. Norwich, Daventry and Portsmouth are other towns to watch.

Engineers nurtured on the brute requirements of motor vehicles have much to learn if they are to cater for the light-weight and modest space requirements of bicycles. Paving for cycleways costs only about one-sixth of road paving and a twelve-foot width of it can carry five times as many people as a twenty-four-foot-wide town road carrying cars at normal passenger loadings. Harnessing gravity to aid riders is another challenge for cycleway designers. Kenneth Claxton, former Chief Engineer at Stevenage, and architect of the new town's pioneering cycleways, encapsulates his experience in the phrase 'two up, one down'. This is a recipe for underpasses. For best results they should be designed so that the roadway goes up two yards while the cycleway goes down only one. Cyclists may then wheeee down into the slight dip and whizzzz up the other side. Gravity is servant, not master. An underpass of this kind, big enough for pedestrians and cyclists, costs about £10,000 in a new town; it would be much more in an existing one if sewer pipes and telephone conduits had to be moved.

Needless to say *Roads in Urban Areas* (see p. 30) is pessimistic about the future of cycling and says nothing about the inhibiting effect on it of heavy traffic, lengthy one-way detours and traffic signals set to suit thirty-mile-an-hour cars and not cyclists quietly pedalling along at half that speed. The handbook is another, no doubt unconscious, facet of the auto conspiracy. It enforces the *status quo* and disregards the opportunity for promoting the use of economical modes of transport by catering properly for them. This disregard of promotional action is cemented into place with a recommendation to highway engineers not to consider building cycleways unless existing flows of bicycles exceed 1,500 a day. It is that dim old 1966 thinking again and it needs revision.

For the sake of clarity I have written about walking and bicycling as if they are largely unconnected but when it comes to catering for them on the ground they need to be seen as complementary. Young hellions who terrify old people by riding them down on pavements, objectionable though they are, do not necessarily contradict this observation. Conflicts do not seem to arise at Stevenage, where footways and cycleways run parallel and are separated by railings only at underpasses and where cycle racks are provided within the central precinct. The two forms of movement live happily side by side and accidents are almost unknown. Sometimes, if the precinct is fairly empty, cyclists even ride slowly through it though they generally dismount. If compatibility seems less evident in older cities, it would be wise to give cyclists a better deal before automatically assuming that they are a threat to pedestrians.

There are few higher priorities in transport planning than catering properly for people on foot and on bicycles. It would conserve petrol, reduce accidents, quell noise, fumes and dust, and give a fillip to local living. The motor manufacturers may pander to our longings to get away from it all, the airlines may offer to shrink the earth for us, and maybe such dreams are necessary. But for most of the time and for most people cars are not available and life revolves round where we live or work. All available facts support this view. It may be unfashionable, dull and parochial to lay emphasis on the continued importance of the neighbourhood but it is a vital theatre of life and walking and cycling are part of it.

5 Must We Take the Bus?

Public transport means buses to most people in Britain. Londoners may take the tube and railways are important to commuters in a handful of other large cities, but for every one trip by train eight are made by bus. On the Continent and even in the United States the same rule applies except that in some places trams replace buses.

Improvements to passenger transport in cities therefore mean, at least in the short term, better bus and tram services. There is no choice. New undergrounds take a decade to design and build and cost so much that few places can show sufficient flows of movement to justify investment in them. This is not really surprising if one remembers that up to 64,000 people an hour can travel along just one track of a modern urban railway and that such flows are reached only in New York City. Buildings need to be packed together and their occupants need to be packed in too if movement of such intensity is to occur. In fact, exactly the opposite is happening as cities spread out, jobs proliferate in the outer suburbs and the populations of old residential districts decline. Given such conditions it is likely that the trains of an underground will be heavily used only during rush hours and will be wasted for the rest of the time. Buses are a less expensive and more versatile way of coping with this situation in all but the largest cities.

I know this observation will earn me the ill-will of some people who believe that undergrounds are an alternative to motorways. There is something about railways that attracts intense loyalty. It is partly their inherent dependability. Neither congestion, nor rain, nor even fog (and snow) can bring them to a standstill though labour disputes can and do. But I suspect too that systems of transport based on tracks appeal to the tidy-minded. There is precision about them and they are so evidently under control. Highways and their vehicles are, by comparison, unpredictable, loose-fitting and some would say ill-disciplined. Despite all this, buses in one form or another are potentially able to do just about everything undergrounds can and a great many things they cannot. They have, moreover, a city's entire road network at their disposal.

So much for the heady atmosphere of theory. Down in the real world one finds wind-swept bus shelters, bronchial passengers and a decline in the use of buses in the past twenty years that has been nothing less than phenomenal. Between 1951 and 1971 the number of people carried by buses in Britain dropped by half, a black record approached by few industries, though it is true that cinema attendances were falling about as fast. To find a parallel in transport it is necessary to go back to the nineteenth century and consider the collapse of the stage coaches at the coming of the railways.

In the 1960s it was common for busmen to attribute the predicament of their industry to the change from a six- to a five-day week, which not only lost them the fares of their Saturday commuters but also made it more difficult for them to recruit drivers. The conquest of the cinema by television and the availability of a growing fleet of private cars were advanced as contributing causes of decline. All these changes did, no doubt, cause people to travel less by bus but there were other equally powerful forces at work. The miasma of congestion was destroying the regularity and dependability of services. Passengers found themselves waiting longer at stops and taking longer to get to their destinations once they were aboard. Faced with such frustrations they first cursed the conductor, lowering staff morale, and secondly vowed never to ride in a blasted bus again if they could possibly help it. It all helped to make cars, which were being greatly improved at that time, seem effortlessly superior.

As if this were not bad enough, busmen in Britain found themselves locked into a set of crippling economic conventions. These had their origins in the Road Traffic Act of 1930 when buses had few rivals and found little difficulty in making profits. Profitability was therefore expected of them even when their passengers started deserting them. Fifteen years of skimping and scraping ensued, as the companies tried to pay all or most of their running costs out of dwindling or at least slow-rising incomes. Maintenance depots got grottier, staff canteens got grimier and the buses themselves got older and creakier.

It was hardly an atmosphere to attract lively and dynamic young managers. Even though the buses were still carrying over thirty million passengers a day in 1965, bright young men went into more promising careers, managing supermarkets and running travel agencies while those who clung on in municipal transport assumed an air of increasingly demoralised pessimism. Just at a time when imagination and a flair for adaptability were most needed they were most lacking. The bus companies seemed like mastodons caught in the grip of an approaching ice age. Either they withdrew services or they went on running ones that had been in existence for twenty or thirty years and in many cases much longer.

Towards the end of the decade things began to look up. Barbara Castle's 1968 Transport Act ushered in a period of institutional reorganisation which has still to run its course. It established, too, the principle that public transport, like highways, was a proper object for government financial support. Sporadic measures to restrain the use of private cars, to introduce more comfortable buses, to organise priorities for public transport over other traffic and to experiment with taxi-like bus services have followed. In one or two cases—Leicester in 1972/3 for instance —a twenty-year decline in passengers has been turned into an increase.

Buses as we know them have a future and will increasingly be seen to have one as measures are taken to free them from congestion and restore their dependability. But by themselves they cannot possibly cater for all the different occasions on which people wish to travel. Many journeys involve routes, or luggage, or necessitate a degree of comfort or privacy that it is beyond the ability of buses to provide. Taxis and hired cars can fill these gaps and must be considered as much a part of passenger transport as their bigger brothers.

Events of recent years support this observation. Pell-mell decline in travel by big vehicles that shuttle slowly to and fro on fixed routes and expect passengers to wait patiently for them at the kerb has been accompanied by marked growth in the use of little vehicles that dart hither and thither, taking their passengers from door to door. This has happened partly because congestion affects bus services worse than taxis. Even a fire somewhere in the area holds buses up but taxis are always able to take to the back streets whatever the cause of a blockage. Despite this difference the fall of the bus and the simultaneous rise of the taxi say something about changes going on in the market for public transport that it would be a mistake to ignore.

I propose, first of all, to look more closely at the institutional underpinnings of urban transport and to go on afterwards to consider traffic management and bus operations.

The importance of institutional reform cannot be exaggerated. Progress of a real kind is very seldom made without it. The setting up of a 'transport community' or *Verkehrsverbund* in Hamburg in 1965 is the outstanding institutional innovation of our time in this field. The community markets the services of, and devises a revenue-sharing formula for, numerous bus, train and tram companies in a metropolitan region of two and a half million people. Its existence enables passengers to buy through-tickets and transfer speedily from the vehicles of one operator to another even though the control of operations remains decentralised. The fruits of this impressive organisational innovation have been marked. A twenty per cent saving in running costs was achieved following the formation of the community and a three to five per cent increase in passengers on the buses and trams has been notched up every year since 1969. Patronage of the *S-Bahn* or suburban railways has increased even more. Munich has since followed Hamburg's example and the formation of other transport communities is being considered in numerous cities, including Copenhagen and the San Francisco Bay area.

In Britain the corresponding change was the establishment of passenger transport authorities and executives in four English provincial conurbations in 1968. The passenger transport executives, which have names like the South-East Lancashire and North-East Cheshire (or SELNEC PTE) are now coming under the control of the new metropolitan counties but, like water authorities, they are given some independence by their power to levy property taxes or rates.

Barbara Castle and her Ministry of Transport officials had many reasons for creating these new bodies but some were of over-riding importance. One was to integrate the independent but overlapping operations of town and country buses. The two kinds of service can be seen running side by side in most large cities and can be distinguished by their contrasting liveries. In Leicester cream and maroon-striped buses run by the town hall share the roads with the scarlet vehicles of the Midland Red, one of the subsidiaries of the National Bus Company, which has its headquarters in London. In Reading the city's buses are plum-coloured while those of Alder Valley, the NBC's subsidiary, are pale cherry. These divisions of responsibility lead to anomalies that are absurd from the passengers' point of view. Half-empty country buses sweep majestically past long queues of townspeople whom they could quite well carry but are forbidden to do so by long-irrelevant licensing conventions. All the passenger transport executives have tried to negotiate a way through these difficulties but with a marked lack of success. So much so that it is now widely felt that a different approach is necessary. The purchase by the West Midlands Executive of a small part of the National Bus Company's Midlands Red network is an important precedent.

Other objectives of Mrs Castle's Act were the meshing of railway and bus services, the inception of planning in public transport and the exposure of the bankrupting effects on public transport of continuing to pour money single-mindedly into building highways and car parks. It was necessary, as Mrs Castle was fond of saying, to have regard for—'the totality of transport'.

During discussions about the distribution of functions in the new local government system established in April 1974, it looked as if the arrangements for public transport in the shire counties would resemble those in the great cities but in the event the Government opted for an uncomfortable split of responsibilities. Transport planning and highway building have been given to the shire counties, while the running of the buses has gone to the districts within them. This arrangement has satisfied virtually no one and contrasts sadly with the new freedom given to local authorities to subsidise the running of passenger services.

The failure of the passenger transport executives to contrive marriages between the town and country buses, and the division of responsibility for the planning and operation of public transport in the shire counties can only be put right by further legislation. The most promising solution would be to transfer the National Bus Company undertakings to the counties within which they run, leaving only the inter-city and inter-regional services of the NBC to be run as a national operation. The shire counties should, at the same time, be made responsible for running the town buses.

Such changes would produce more than administrative tidiness. They would put responsibility for the management of passenger transport and the planning of highways into a single set of hands and tie in with anticipated changes to the way in which the Treasury allocates funds to local authorities. Hitherto the Treasury has pursued a policy which might be summed up as 'Nanny Whitehall knows best'. Under this system different classes of project have been eligible for greater or lesser proportions of government finance. Trunk and certain departmental road improvements have been supported by one hundred per cent grants, other main roads have received seventy-five per cent and bus stations twenty-five per cent grants. Councils being only human, it is not surprising that road building has been the top priority, which is, of course, what Whitehall intended. (A similar distortion of local judgement has been brought about in the United States by the ninety per cent grants offered by Washington towards the construction of interstate highways.) As if this were not enough, the allocation of Treasury finance towards, say, the replacement of a bad bus service by a subsidised and more frequent one, was outlawed.

Stevenage New Town Development Corporation, the first of the new towns, was also the first public body to dynamite this convention and the explosive it used is contained in a two-volume report by Professor Nathaniel Lichfield, published in 1969. Lichfield was asked to consider whether, in view of the continued growth of the town's population and of car ownership, it would be wiser to spend four and a half million pounds on a series of flyovers or to improve the bus services. No question like this had ever been asked in the course of the conventional land-use transportation studies going on in other places, so it is not surprising that the answer was a fresh one too. Lichfield's report said :

> Taking all in all, it is a conclusion from this analysis that, on the assumptions and forecasts made for the community as a whole, a combination of an enhanced bus service and the ground level road system is better than building the elevated road works and supplying a reduced or residual bus service.

The study broke new ground by comparing the until then incomparable and by throwing doubt on the popular wisdom that a decline in the use of buses is inevitable and that it is 'cheaper' to build roads than to do anything else. I will come back later to the 'superbuses' that were introduced in Stevenage as a result of Lichfield's recommendations. I want here to draw attention to two ideas that made them possible. One was that the financing of passenger services and road building should be considered as equally valid objects of public expenditure and that Treasury funds should be interchangeable between them. The other was that the well-being of very large numbers of people who do not have cars depended on acceptance of this flexibility.

With the reform of local government the experience built up at Stevenage will be made general. The old specific grant system is being abandoned and will be replaced in 1975/6 by a 'transport supplementary grant' that local authorities will be able to spend in accord with their own priorities. Whitehall will confine itself to scrutinising annual proposals for transport policies covering the control of parking, subsidies to public transport, traffic management and capital investment in highways, bus stations and the like. In Whitehall's own estimate, contained in the 1973 Blue Book on *Public Expenditure to 1977–78*, one effect of the new freedom will be that 'Local authorities (especially in urban areas) are likely to shift resources from major road schemes to public transport'.

This, then, will be the context for bus operations for the rest of the decade. It would be preferable if the operating companies could be smaller so that they would be closer to their passengers but the scale of the industry is already large and chopping it up into little bits is impractical. A combination of energetic marketing of bus services on the one hand and open competition with taxis on the other are equally promising guarantees of good service.

A few years ago it seemed that the only way to inject new thinking into road passenger transport was to put in new men from outside. However, as money for new equipment has begun to flow in so men with ideas already in the industry have been able to get active. In Harrogate it is now possible to telephone for a little chauffeur coach to pick you up at your door. In Edinburgh all the conventional buses are linked to headquarters by radio telephone; in Leicester an inspector at a control centre can assess traffic conditions through remote TV cameras and adjust services accordingly.

New men are still needed (every undertaking should have a marketing manager at chief officer level) but it would be a mistake to assume that the industry is without talent. It is still suffering the effects of its years in the doldrums but its human resources need fertiliser rather than weed killer. One source of stimulus would be to cross-post staff between the railways and the bus companies. Tony Ridley, Director General of the Tyne-side Executive believes this would help to breed men with a total transport outlook.

Changes in the working conditions of the men who drive the buses are needed as urgently. No company is typical but some facts from Reading, which pays above normal wages because it is outside the Employers Federation, help give a picture of what is involved. To start with, the drivers, eight out of ten of whom drive without conductors, work a six-day, 48-hour week for between £50 and £55 and regularly take to the road on Sundays, bank holidays and evenings. The hours are hard too. A quarter of all duties start at six or seven in the morning and the men doing them do not finally knock off until twelve hours later. They get four hours free time in the middle of the day but it still means getting up at five or six in the morning and not getting home before seven or eight at night. Other duties (they are worked in a roster) start at six, seven or eleven in the morning, run for eight hours, and are less awkward, but wives complain about the irregularity of it all and this puts pressure on the men. On top of this there is the stress of handling a ninety-passenger double-decker in heavy traffic and taking tickets as well. It is the kind of routine that is associated in the public mind with hypertensive, rat-race executives.

Some lessening of stress can be achieved by means of bus lanes and other measures to reduce congestion. Selling tickets and giving change can be simplified too. Smaller towns may introduce flat fares and sell tickets in bulk at discount. Larger ones can follow Stockholm's example and offer monthly season tickets that give unlimited travel. Eliminating the deterrent of twelve-hour days and six-day weeks is equally important if the bus industry is to expand and improve its services.

The employment of part-time drivers to cover peak periods is one possibility, although it has so far been rejected by the trades unions. They see it as a threat to the pay of fulltime staff and in an industry where management and labour are so ponderously structured, no one has yet found a way to negotiate round the problem. This is in marked contrast to the taxi industry where, because companies are small and union strength correspondingly weak, innovations such as part-time working and even women drivers have been tried on a small scale, found to be acceptable and increasingly adopted.

An alternative way to get more value out of a given number of buses and crews is to promote the staggering of office and factory work hours. All indications are that employees are favourable to it, but with so many facets of life, from TV programmes to shop hours geared to a nine-to-five work day, it would be unwise to expect too much. Nevertheless, 'flexitime', as it is increasingly called, should be part of every bus company's marketing policy since it promises shorter queues and fewer standing passengers on the one hand and a flattening of peak demand on the other. Busmen will find that companies making the punch-card clocks needed by large companies operating on 'flexitime' (small firms usually make do with a sign-in book) will help them by providing pamphlets and sending experts to public meetings.

Another way to overcome the labour problems associated with travel peaks is to persuade employers to shoulder part of the responsibility for getting their staffs to and from work. Some firms already hire private buses to collect shift workers or employees who cannot get to their jobs by public transport. The drivers of such vehicles are either part-timers or they work other contracts throughout the day. Company-owned minibuses can be used in the same role and either devoted to other purposes during the day or driven by men whose main job is doing something else. Minibuses based on Ford Transit or Volkswagen chassis are more manœuvreable than big buses, can be driven without special licences, and taken home by their drivers. Assuming such minibus drivers collect six or eight people on the way to work and replace five or six cars, there will be a corresponding reduction in the need for highway and parking space and a flattening in the rush-hour demand for fulltime busmen as well. The pooling of cars to get to work is another way of pursuing the same objectives and I will return to it later. Success in triggering off the adoption of such practices rests on the introduction of some kind of lever. It could be an extra tax on parking space at factories and offices. It could be the withdrawal of the tax concessions that persuade companies to buy cars for their employees.

Small buses can be used to provide commuters with a very personal kind of service. One refinement, appropriate for senior members of staffs, is to give them pocket bleepers of the kind used to call surgeons to telephones in hospitals. These would be used at work during the day and taken home at night. A radio caller would then be installed in the bus and as the driver approached the houses of his riders he would press a button to buzz the appropriate bleeper. The person hearing the call would put on his coat and walk out of his front door to the bus. The low cost of bleeper systems makes this idea less science fictional than it may at first seem. It was put forward by British Leyland at an exhibition on better buses at the Transport and Road Research Laboratory in 1973.

So much for getting more buses on to the roads during the twenty hours a week when travel is at a peak. It is no less important to maintain high-frequency services during the other 148 hours. The effect of doing this can be gathered from the results of the Stevenage superbus experiments. The guinea pigs were 13,500 residents who had previously been accustomed to a twelve-minute service by day that stretched to thirty minutes in the evenings and on Sundays, and shortened to an irregular eight and a half minutes at rush hours. These frequencies were progressively improved until a bus came every five minutes by day and every ten minutes at other times. Adult fares were lowered from a stepped three to nine pence to a flat four pence, a kink was cut out of the route, reducing the time taken between suburb and town centre from thirteen to ten minutes, and single-decker buses in bright new colours were put into service in place of double deckers. When the new service was got underway time tables were pushed through the letter boxes of all potential users of it, first-day riders were issued with lapel buttons saying 'I am a superbus rider', and buses painted in different colours were put on display for the residents to choose the one they liked best.

The effect of the revolution was to increase the number of passengers carried per week from 19,700 to 41,500. The number of people using cars to get to the town centre and the industrial estate dropped by four per cent, while the number using cars to go to destinations not served by superbuses increased by ten per cent. Results outside the rush hours were even more remarkable. As the various phases of the experiment were brought into play, off-peak travellers increased from 15,850 to 26,700 a week and the biggest jump occurred when the fare was reduced from six pence to four pence. Housewives, elderly people and children were unchained from their houses.

Peter Buckles, a former research worker at University College, London, who was one of the official assessors of the project, says that construction of the flyover roads would have had very different effects. Driving to work would have been made easier for those with cars but those going to work by bus, and large numbers wanting to get about for other purposes, would have been penalised. Buckles says too that conventional transportation studies fail to reveal this because only the transfer of *existing* travellers from cars to buses is taken into account in calculating the 'benefits' of any policy. Yet at Stevenage over ninety per cent of the benefits accruing to the superbus service were the result of *generated* travel.

Maintaining a high-frequency bus service throughout the day has the added advantage of smoothing out peaks and troughs in the demand for drivers. Adding taxis and hire cars to bus fleets and moving drivers between the two kinds of vehicles, depending on demand for travel, can be used to achieve the same effect. In an undertaking with a mixed fleet some drivers might start their working day at six in the morning driving a double-decker, switch to a minibus or a taxi at mid-morning and finish at two in the afternoon. Other drivers would start later, driving a minibus, and convert to a double-decker for the evening rush hour. In both cases the men would work a varied eight-hour day.

Busmen persistently pour scorn on proposals to use smaller vehicles and say that as wages represent between seventy and eighty per cent of their operating costs, little is to be gained by using a less expensive vehicle. This may be true but it may not. If one assumes that more passengers can be attracted to a small vehicle and persuaded to pay more because they are being offered a better service, then a small vehicle may be able to make more money than a big one. One advantage of a small vehicle is that, with fewer seats to fill, it will be bound to make fewer stops than a bigger one. It may also be able to stop wherever anyone waves to it, to move away from a fixed route and pick up or put down passengers at their front doors. The country garage proprietor who keeps a coach for taking darts teams or Womens' Institutes on outings, but switches to a car to carry families to airports, accepts that it is possible to run vehicles with different economic and service characteristics in close harness. City operators have become too standardised and need to look more closely at their country cousins.

Superbus One at Stevenage has now been joined by Superbus Two, a sixpenny flat-fare service connecting another neighbourhood to the town centre and the industrial estate. Further expansion is held up by a problem that faces the entire bus industry— a shortage of vehicles and spare parts. Some busmen get almost apoplectic on this subject, which is tied to troubles with the single-decker 'National', produced by British Leyland. It is a new design built in a new factory in Cumberland and it has suffered teething troubles that have put newly delivered vehicles off the road and greatly embarrassed some operators. Noise is another problem with early model Nationals and a particularly unwelcome one in view of the growing number of pedestrian precincts to which buses are admitted. In these places, where the only other sounds are people walking and talking, a conventional bus can be about as neighbourly as a tank. Both manufacturers and operators have begun to realise this and efforts are beginning to be made to reduce engine noise both inside and outside. Most results so far flow from packing sound absorbent materials around the engine housing but engines that are designed to be quiet are on the way. Leyland have delivered a muffled double-decker to the SELNEC authority for trials in and around Manchester and Rolls Royce have delivered another one with a quiet, low-pollution, methane-burning engine to Teesside. But, as usual where environmental matters are concerned, the Swedes are in the van. Their Scania single-deckers, which are made under licence by Metro Cammell in Birmingham, are nearly as quiet as family-sized cars and the company is being pressed to improve them further by Stockholm city transport. The undertaking ordered 110 new buses from Scania and Volvo ln 1973 and specified that they should emit no more than seventy-eight decibels. The importance of reaching this standard was emphasised by a stipulation in the contract that a fine would be imposed on a manufacturer whose buses emitted eighty decibels and that vehicles exceeding this level would be rejected. At seventy-eight decibels, a bus would be less than half as noisy as most buses today and quieter than most cars.

As noise-measuring scales are not yet as familiar as those for temperature, it is perhaps worth explaining these figures. The decibel is the basic unit for measuring sound pressure, but because of the complex way in which human ears work, it is not possible to use a single scale like Centigrade to give guidance about all kinds of noise. Different scales have therefore been devised that give greater weight to certain frequencies and tones. Decibels (dB), modified according to one particular set of weightings—the (A) scale—are the common index for measuring sound pressure from surface transport. Another oddity of decibel scales stems from the immense range of sound frequencies detectable by ear. This has made it necessary to give the points on the scales of measurement a 2, 4, 8, 16, or geometrical, relationship to one another. As a result a ten dB(A) increase in sound level is a doubling and a twenty dB(A) increase a quadrupling in the apparent loudness or annoyance of a sound.

So far I have said virtually nothing about the bane of traffic jams. At Stevenage, with its miles of cycleways and modern road layout, they hardly exist despite above average levels of car ownership. The superbuses are accordingly dependable and regular. Few old cities are so fortunate and in few would it be possible today to run a five-minute service of clockwork dependability, even assuming that there were no staff shortages. In London the effect of congestion on long, cross-city bus routes is disastrous. Five red double-deckers nose to tail are not unknown round the corner from where I live and the old gag about the Number 11 being called the banana bus 'because it comes in bunches' is a fair one.

For some reason busmen are reticent about the effects of traffic on their services and even adjust their schedules to conceal the extent to which buses are slowed down by congestion. It would be much better if they published annual reports saying how much of their passengers' time, how much fuel and how many drivers' hours are wasted. The effects on fares of eliminating this waste and the improvement in services that would result from running existing fleets of vehicles on uncongested roads should be calculated as well. The marketing of bus services involves providing the general public with information that is politically important as well as with travel data.

Timings taken by the SELNEC undertaking on a nine-and-a-half mile route into Manchester on a quiet Sunday morning in 1973 show the sort of delays that are the everyday experience of bus commuters. The service is one scheduled to take forty-six minutes ordinarily and fifty-eight minutes during rush hours. Three buses taking part in the early morning test took thirty-six, thirty-three and thirty-five minutes respectively, including time taken by simulated passengers to get on and off. Thus even the off-peak schedule has ten minutes of waste built into it.

Bus lanes are widely thought of as a way to deal with congestion and increasing numbers are being painted on the roads.

They can be useful but experience makes it clear that they are not the panacea they were once thought to be. Bus lanes are regularly blocked by parked vehicles and they are not suited to being used by slow and express services that also need to pass one another. Some other set of techniques is needed that makes it possible to manipulate congestion so that it does not interfere with buses and other vehicles that make better use of roads than private cars.

When Michael Thomson (the author of *Motorways in London*) was at the London School of Economics he called this approach to traffic 'planned congestion' and as far as I know he coined the expression. The basic principle is simplicity itself. It is a matter of hunting through a town's roads to find places where motorists can be obliged to queue *where they only get in one another's way*. Special traffic signals erected at these points may then be employed to hold cars while giving buses and other priority vehicles free passage at the same or at other points : short-cutting through back streets to get round such check points can be prevented by blocking roads off or by one-way systems.

Southampton has already treated an individual main road in this fashion and Nottingham is working on a town-wide variant of the same principles, the first part of which is expected to be ready in 1975. A simplified version of this sheep-and-goats approach to traffic management, one well-suited to towns of up to about 100,000 people and circled by an outer ring road, was put forward by the Oxford Movement for Transport Planning Reform in 1971. The main points in it were parking controls in the centre of the city, barriers to cars on main roads between the suburbs and improved radial and circular bus services. Visitors from outside the town were expected to park their cars on the fringes and ride to the centre. City residents going between suburbs were expected to go by bus or bicycle or, if they wished to drive to go out to a ring road outside the town, round and in again. The overall effect was to divide Oxford into several 'rooms' or urban villages.

When these proposals were put forward they were ahead of

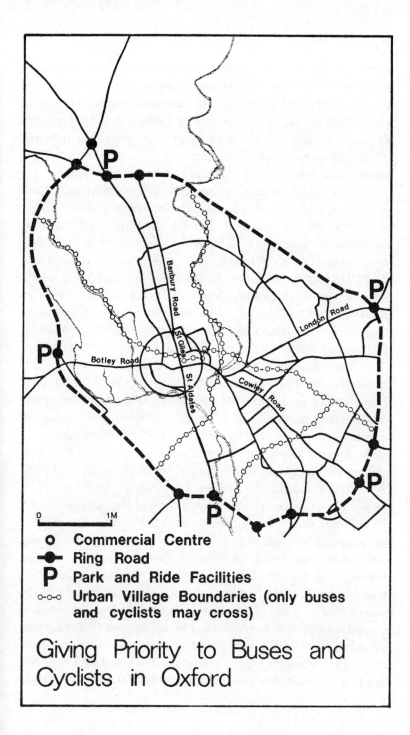

Banbury Road

St Giles

Botley Road

St Aldates

London Road

Cowley Road

0   1M

○   **Commercial Centre**
●—●   **Ring Road**
P   **Park and Ride Facilities**
○—○—○   **Urban Village Boundaries (only buses and cyclists may cross)**

Giving Priority to Buses and Cyclists in Oxford

their time but not without precedent. In essence they were merely an extension to the scale of an entire town of principles for limiting traffic and improving environmental conditions already successfully in use in the centres of Bremen and Gothenburg. Oxford has since joined the ranks of those cities that have rejected urban motorways, has introduced bus lanes on several main roads and is developing park-and-ride interchanges.

Southampton's experience in planned congestion is technologically more sophisticated and more limited in scope. It covers Bitterne Road, the main route into the city from the Portsmouth direction and a historic bottleneck because it is one of only three bridges over the River Itchen. The problem as the Council saw it in 1971 was to disentangle 66 buses carrying over 3,800 people into the city every morning from 2,916 cars and other vehicles carrying 4,400 people. The solution was designed by Barry Cooper, at that time Chief Traffic Engineer in Southampton, and now an officer of the new Oxfordshire County Council.

Bitterne Road is best thought of as a great river into which buses and cars flow by means of a large number of tributaries. Buses had for many years been routed down some of these tributaries and as the numbers of cars in use increased, became increasingly caught up in queues where the tributaries joined the main stream. These queues were caused by traffic lights controlling the junctions. Others formed up in the main road itself as too many vehicles tried to squeeze along it. Cooper therefore looked for a way by which he could channel the buses down one set of free-flowing tributaries while sending the cars down another set where they could be held back and prevented from causing jams on the main river. In the event this was done by designating some of the tributaries as one-way streets with against-the-flow bus lanes, while putting traffic signals at the mouths of the others so as to meter the flows of cars leaving them. The rate of this metering was in turn governed by sensors that measure traffic flows further down the main stream. The techniques employed are those of electronic and signal enginering and not of civil engineering and they save bus passengers from three and a half to eight minutes every morning, depending on what time they travel. So far the time taken by cars has not increased but if the number being used increases, the queues in the car tributaries will lengthen. However, even if they do, the buses will remain unaffected.

Electronic engineering is being used in Bitterne Road to make better use of existing space but it is only one of a growing bag of highway controls, some of which are for managing traffic while others speed public transport vehicles on their way. I intend to concentrate on traffic management systems because they are alternatives to highway construction, but devices such as electronic 'guns' that enable buses to shoot off the red lights as they approach crossings, monitoring equipment that makes it possible for a bus controller to see where all his vehicles are and plug gaps in disrupted schedules and other operational aids are important too.

Nottingham, where a Robin Hood transport policy for robbing greedy cars of space and giving it to economical buses was announced in 1972, is a test bed for both kinds of techniques. Their introduction follows a change of political control and the appointment of Frank Higgins, a clear-sighted headmaster, to be Chairman of the city's Transport Committee. He has since been elected to a comparable post on the new Nottinghamshire County Council. Higgins set out to give pedestrians the freedom of the city centre and bus passengers freedom to get to and from it. He also scrapped a £150,000,000 highway building programme, including thirty-four miles of urban motorways, that had been put forward in 1967.

By the spring of 1974 pavements had been widened in numerous streets in the city centre, on-street parking swept away, and two five-minute 'inner circle' bus services introduced to enable people to get to and from the country bus stations and multistorey car parks and the shops. Both these services are free of fares and cost £75,000 a year. Up to one hundred thousand people use them every week and women with children, pushchairs and parcels can be seen boarding them happily without having to fumble for change. One unexpected side effect of this innovation is the fillip it has given to other bus services. By the second half of 1973 nearly one hundred thousand additional fare-paying riders were being carried every month and revenue was up by £20,000.

On the electronic side, 'guns' have been ordered for sixteen buses to enable them to turn traffic signals green and work is going ahead with designing sheep-and-goats barriers for all the main roads leading into the city from the west. In a report called *Zones and Collars* published in February 1974 the corporation identified four objectives for this revolutionary experiment in traffic control: making travel by bus more attractive; reducing traffic on residential roads; protecting pedestrians; and reducing the need to build new highways. The report also sets out six different steps which need to be taken in order to achieve them:

Zone controls a set of techniques for limiting the rate at which vehicles leave side roads thereby permitting main road traffic, including buses, to run more freely.

Collar control a set of techniques for limiting traffic entering the inner city thereby reducing delay to bus passengers.

Bus priorities to enable buses to bypass any queues.

Additional buses to reduce passenger waiting times.

City centre parking controls to reduce commuting by car.

Park-and-ride interchanges to give out-of-town motorists an alternative way to commute into the city.

'Zone control' is initially being introduced in two outer suburban districts, one measuring about a mile and the other about two miles square. The techniques involved are very similar to those designed by Barry Cooper for Bitterne Road in Southampton. Cars will be metered out of some exits and buses allowed to pass without hindrance along bus-only lanes next to them or on other roads. The controls will be switched on only at peak periods.

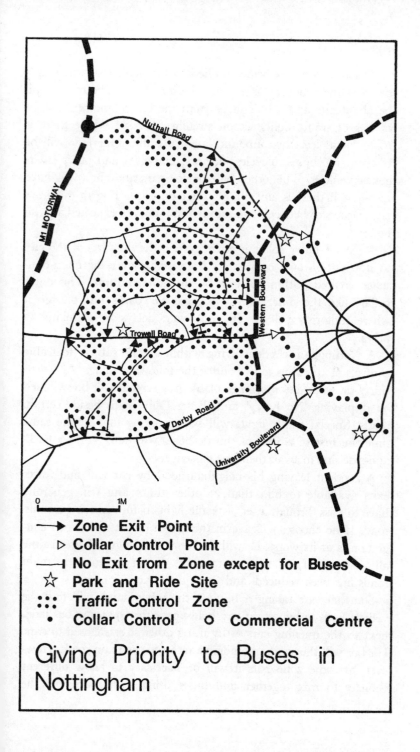

Key:

→ Zone Exit Point
▷ Collar Control Point
⊢ No Exit from Zone except for Buses
☆ Park and Ride Site
∷ Traffic Control Zone
• Collar Control   ○ Commercial Centre

Giving Priority to Buses in Nottingham

'Collar control' is being applied to six main roads at points between the suburban zones and the inner city. The collars will be about one and a half miles from the centre and will consist of sets of traffic lights set on stretches of road where there is room for at least two inbound lanes of traffic. One lane will be reserved for buses, bicycles, doctors, midwives and other emergency vehicles. The other will be for cars and they will have to queue if there is any risk of congestion occurring in the inner city. Delays of between two and ten minutes are expected at rush hours.

A second outer collar is envisaged on the outskirts of the city to stop out-of-town commuters from taking over the main-road space created within the city by the zone controls. This outer collar, like the inner one, will have car parks just outside it where motorists will be able to avoid delays by changing to buses.

A Nottingham resident living within a zone subject to traffic controls of this kind might notice the following things. At seven-thirty on week-day mornings blank grey screens will be switched on displaying 'No Entry' and 'Buses Only' signs beside certain roads. Special traffic lights will start working too. At the same time the first of a fleet of shuttle buses will enter various park-and-ride sites to await their first passengers.

A resident leaving his neighbourhood by car will find fewer exits available to him than at other times and will generally have to pass through a set of traffic lights before entering a main road. If he chooses to leave in the height of the rush when congestion is at its worst, he will find that the length of green time allowed to him and other motorists as they try to enter the main roads has been reduced, and that queues are forming.

Someone else taking a bus, on the other hand, will find the vehicle he is in bypassing any hold-ups, either by using bus lanes next to the queuing cars or by using other streets closed to cars. His bus will thus gain unhindered access to the main roads. However, at some zone-exits it will be necessary to allow different vehicles to mix together and buses using such routes will be

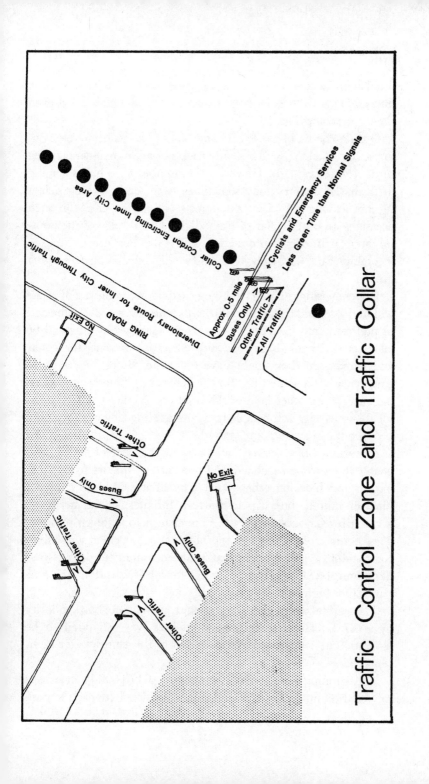

Traffic Control Zone and Traffic Collar

fitted with devices to increase the green time of signals. A little flurry of cars will therefore be released on to the main road each time a bus comes out.

Out on the main roads cars and buses alike will now be moving smoothly along with a steady trickle of additional cars joining them from side roads. However, the number of vehicles coming in from the country may sometimes swell, causing long delays to cars leaving suburban side streets within the city. On such occasions an outer collar of traffic lights on the edge of the built-up area will come into action and give less green time to incoming cars. As elsewhere buses will bypass any resulting queues.

Drivers wishing to enter the inner city along main radial roads will find a second collar of traffic lights where they will be directed to pull over into 'cars only' lanes. Here again green time will be allocated to them so as to avoid congestion beyond the collar and here again they might have to queue. Buses, bicycles and emergency vehicles destined for the inner city will, however, swish past, using the other lane of the roadway. Vehicles not destined for the inner city will be able to use an existing ring road running between the inner and outer suburbs.

Electronic links between all parts in the control system will enable flows to be regulated and prevent any queues from backing up and blocking other roads. The effect will be to reduce a nineteen-minute bus trip to thirteen minutes, while increasing a car trip over the same route from sixteen to eighteen minutes. Two hours later, when the morning rush is over, it will all be switched off. A road system that has been running under railway-like control will revert to the free-for-all we tend to think is natural for highways.

The capital cost of doing this and giving 206 buses priority over 6,700 cars and 680 other vehicles was estimated to be £325,000 at 1973 prices but over half of this sum was for additional buses.

The running costs were estimated at £170,000 a year, less any charges made for park-and-ride which is, of course, the positive side of what some may consider a restrictive system. The buses will shuttle to and fro between car parks at the tips of two boomerang-shaped routes, both of which will pass through the middle of the city.

Experience already gained with park-and-ride suggests that motorists will change if offered sufficient inducement. Railways have long gained travellers on this basis by offering them speed and freedom from congestion. Nottingham aims to achieve the same effect with the carrot of express buses and the stick of collar controls and limits on city-centre parking. Leslie Smith, General Manager of Leicester City Transport is the leading practitioner of park-and-ride in Britain. He ran his first shoppers' service in 1966 and at the end of 1973 had two permanent interchanges in operation. One called Park 'N' Ride South is about one mile from the city centre and serves shoppers only. The other, Park 'N' Ride North, is about twice as far from the centre and is served by buses timed to serve commuters as well as shoppers. In the month before Christmas 1973 nearly 440 shoppers a day used south side interchange while over 259 shoppers and commuters used the north side one. The best single day recorded was the last Saturday before Christmas when over 1,000 shoppers used each side.

Every possible medium is employed in Leicester to publicise park-and-ride. Free time-table leaflets are given away at shops, window stickers are put up at bus stops and in shops, and advertisements are placed in local newspapers. Leslie Smith misses no opportunity to appear on local radio and he got extra publicity for Park 'N' Ride North by inviting an actress who was appearing in the city to perform the opening ceremony for it.

The service has been given coherence and an air of permanence by employing design consultants to produce all the graphics—including a Park 'N' Ride symbol—and the use of colour coding, green for Park 'N' Ride South and orange for North. A popular touch has been added to the whole operation by the use of a lantern-jawed, quasi-military character called Captain Leicester. He appears in the shops in the form of life-sized plywood time-table dispensers and in cartoons, where he plays a Batmanesque role:

> Deep in the heart of the city . . . Captain Leicester waits in his specially constructed concrete bunker . . . Christmas is nigh, and the barbarian hordes are massing ready to attack and engulf the city in smoking, choking turmoil . . . Honk. Chug. Splut. Clang. . . . And yet Captain Leicester stands alone. Will his faithful troops—the park'n'riders—pitch into the battle?

And so on.

More staid transport general managers may call this gimmickry but they cannot deny that Leicester has one of the most ably run bus undertakings in Britain. The number of passengers carried per mile is very high and the undertaking has persistently made a profit even in the leanest of years. Leslie Smith's flair for publicity is part of the explanation.

It is no coincidence that park-and-ride is more fully developed in Leicester than elsewhere. The idea was succinctly set out in the *Leicester Traffic Plan* of 1964, the first in Britain to be based on mathematical modelling (London's was started earlier but completed much later). By today's standards the proposed motorways are impossibly grandiose. They would have cost £107,000,000 over twenty years (at 1963 prices) but at least they were combined with the idea of interchange car parks for visitors to the city centre. And, the plan suggested, 'In order to gain practical experience it would be advisable to build some experimental interchange car parks at established local shopping centres and to run experimental bus services (with low or even no charges)'.

The first park-and-ride experiment was tried only two years later, though not at a shopping centre. The idea of combining this sort of interchange with suburban shopping was perhaps thought too dangerous. Motorists might have parked but not bothered to ride. However, the initiative for park-and-ride in Leicester has come from the bus side. The political leadership is complacent and has yet to limit the use of cars in order to improve conditions for pedestrians and bus passengers. This is brought out in a report, *Park 'N' Ride: Further Developments*, issued by Leslie Smith in February 1974 :

> Experience has shown that Park 'N' Ride can be operated successfully, both for commuter and shopper services. Since we now have successful Park 'N' Ride services operating from the south and north of the city, the logical next step would be to provide a service for the populous area in the County to the west of the city, followed by a facility on the eastern edge of Leicester.
>
> These experiments in Park 'N' Ride have been provided on the same basis as the original pioneering enterprise of bus operators, i.e. providing facilities in advance of demand. This is a very expensive service these days in terms of buses and labour costs and I would suggest that the time has come to make a policy decision that further extensions of Park 'N' Ride facilities should only be provided as part of the parking policy within a comprehensive transportation policy. Unless there is a direct relationship between the increase of parking facilities via Park 'N' Ride car parks and the reduction in parking facilities within the city, no meaningful progress will be made in relieving the congestion on the roads in the central area.

Tremendous scope exists for improving mobility in all cities by giving buses priorities over cars, using the techniques pioneered in Southampton, Oxford and Nottingham. In Britain, where urban motorways are the exception, the use of the new techniques will be concentrated on existing main roads, but in the United States, where urban freeways are the rule, similar methods are increasingly being used to eliminate congestion and increase the flows of people on such special roads.

In Los Angeles, for instance, traffic lights are being installed on the approach ramps to all freeways. As in Southampton and Nottingham, these signals will hold cars in queues when monitoring equipment reports that mainstream traffic is falling below a certain speed, and as in Britain, buses will bypass the cars by using bus-only lanes. Some entry points are already equipped with these controls and the California Highways Department expects the entire Los Angeles freeway system to be fitted with them by 1977. Congestion will then begin to build up on the other main roads if shared transport services have not been developed to provide a substitute for one-man cars.

A different method of giving buses priorities over cars on freeways is in use in Washington, D.C., on an interstate route called the Shirley Highway. It is a two-lane busway in the middle of a six-lane freeway running from Virginia into the federal capital and it has shown a remarkable capacity to attract commuters and reduce driving, though anyone who has tried to park a car in downtown Washington may not be surprised by that. At the point where the buses leave the interstate Highway and enter the ordinary city streets their progress is further hastened by bus-only lanes and a set of computer programmes for biassing the traffic lights in favour of buses. (A similar system being used to manage ninety-five sets of traffic lights in central Glasgow increases bus speeds by eight per cent and saves travellers' time, estimated to be worth £100,000.)

The effect of the Washington busway was deployed before media men in the summer of 1971 when a car was pitted against a bus in a fourteen-mile race from Fairfax County to a point near the White House. The two vehicles started at eight in the morning and although the car initially raced off down the freeway at sixty-five miles an hour, the lumbering tortoise, in best Aesopian fashion, overtook it on the busway and arrived in about half the time. The actual finishing times were 8.35 a.m. for the bus, 9.05 for the car.

Results of this sort have helped fuel a bitter row between pro-bus and pro-subway camps in the United States, and particularly in Washington, D.C., where the Federal Government is building a subway that is likely to cost $4,000,000,000. Opponents of the project point to the potential of bus priorities to make better use of existing and improved highways and to provide service to all parts of the region within a few years and say that the funds being poured into the subway would pay for a minibus for every seven persons in the region. The financial difficulties being experienced by the BART (Bay Area Rapid Transit) subway in San Francisco, despite high fares that only the middle classes can afford, add heat to the argument.

Cities in Britain such as Birmingham, Leeds and Glasgow, that have followed United States practice and built radial motorways, would do well to look closely at freeway-flier buses to get more use out of them. By combining Los Angeles-style motorway entry controls with a bus-only lane on the motorway they could theoretically get three hundred buses or about 24,000 passengers an hour along a single twelve-foot-wide strip of roadway.

Happily by no means all cities in Europe are already cut about by urban motorways. For them the first step towards improved public transport will be to introduce zones, collars and park-and-ride though there may be places where new bus-only roads are justified. Runcorn New Town in Cheshire has a figure-of-eight-shaped busway as its cortex and Redditch, to the south of Birmingham, is building bus-only roads too. In both cases the busways go to the middle of shopping centres, groups of factories and houses and they intersect with footways that fan out amongst all the surrounding buildings. In Runcorn in particular the town is arranged round the busways, with the convenience of pedestrians and walkers being given priority over that of car users.

So far no busways have been built in any old towns in Britain but several are recommended in a 1972 plan for Edinburgh produced by Sir Colin Buchanan and Freeman Fox and Partners. As in Washington, D.C., they are seen as a way of getting express coaches from the fringes of the city, through the suburbs, to the centre, though they would be instead of motorways, not part of them. Whether these busways are ever built remains uncertain. The consultants were commissioned by the former City Engineer to give their stamp of approval to one of the most destructive sets of motorways yet proposed for any city in Europe, and although these highways were modified in the course of the study, enough of them remain to have brought the whole exercise into disrepute.

The place that looks most set to pioneer this new approach to urban road building is Boston, Massachusetts. It is not a city with a go-ahead image—the Georgian proportions of Beacon Hill and the creeper-covered façades of nearby Harvard give the opposite effect. Nevertheless it was the first city in the United States to have a subway and it was also the first to take the technocratic procedures of classical land-use transportation planning and their results and throw them firmly out of the window. This reassertion of political control over runaway technomania was the work of Francis Sargent, a progressive Republican Governor of Massachusetts. In a pattern since repeated in Toronto, he first put a moratorium on the construction of freeways costing $1,000,000,000 and then bypassed the professional highways establishment by setting up a Boston Transportation Plan Review under a trusted outsider. In this case it was Professor Alan Altshuler, a distinguished political scientist, who subsequently became Secretary of Transportation for the Commonwealth of Massachusetts.

One of the problems faced by the review team was access to Logan Airport, across the harbour from Boston. Over the previous decade the use of cars to get to and from the airport had become established, large car parks had been built and the conventional wisdom was that there was no alternative but to go on feeding this process with a $600,000,000 six-lane freeway tunnelled under Boston Harbour and multi-storey car parks at the airport itself. Altshuler stood that idea on its head and showed that a two-lane tunnel at a third of the cost, to be used solely by airport limousines, buses, trucks and emergency vehicles, was a practical alternative and one that would be available to everyone. Governor Sargent and the Mayor of Boston agreed.

Having talked about buses running along tracks, the time has come to have a look at trams. They have virtually vanished in Britain but are enjoying a revival on the Continent and in

North America. The explanation is that trams, like buses, have a capacity well suited to the densities of modern cities.

Arguments about which form of transport is better invariably continue far into the night. Each has its advantages and disadvantages even when one discounts the fact that, as passenger flows creep up, the greater size of the tram is useful, and that when they sink down, the ability of buses to share their kind of 'track', and its costs, with lorries and cars comes into its own. Putting these characteristics aside the smooth riding of modern trams, their freedom from smelly fumes and the existence of conventions about their right of way over other vehicles are all advantageous.

In Germany, Switzerland and Belgium the question of abandoning them never seems to have come up and development has been insistent and steady. Larger, articulated vehicles with capacity for up to three hundred people have been introduced and are now generally managed just by a driver, often a woman. Obviously no individual could handle the change of such large numbers of passengers and so the selling and cancelling of tickets has been transformed. Flat fares, tickets sold in bulk at discount, track-side ticket automats and on-board automatic cancelling machines, together with plain clothes inspectors, have therefore all made their appearance. Thanks to such innovations boarding speeds have been maintained at the rates possible with a conductor and bilking kept in check. Ways have been found to combat congestion too. In towns such as Brussels and Antwerp, short lengths of tunnel have been built to enable tramways, renamed pré-metros, to dip under the most impassable of city-centre streets and so maintain service in the face of rising car use. In Bremen, on the other hand, trams use streets converted into precincts, thus avoiding congestion without the expense of tunnelling.

Cities as tightly packed with people as Rome are obvious candidates for high-capacity trams and it is no coincidence that they are being reintroduced on the streets to serve the hordes of pilgrims expected for Holy Year in 1975. The trams will run on lanes out of bounds to other traffic and will be accompanied by a hugely enlarged bus fleet. The progress of both forms of transport will be helped by the total exclusion of visitors' cars from the antique city.

The excellent service that can be given by street trams when they have priority over other traffic is apparent in Amsterdam. Line One, which goes out to the western suburbs, has increased its patronage by half, thanks to a mixture of tram-only lanes in the inner city and rights of way between the carriageways of suburban boulevards. Beyond this there is the possibility of creating what are best thought of as supertrams or light railways that do not run on the streets at all. This is being done on Tyneside where short lengths of tunnel and a fourth river bridge are being built in order to send new life coursing through underused and decaying nineteenth-century railways. Possibilities for light railways of this kind exist in Edinburgh and Birmingham as well but advocates of them will need to arm themselves with more than a romantic attachment to steel wheels and rails if they are to answer the claims of busmen that such railways would be far beter converted into busways. The great advantage of the bus over the tram is that, in addition to speeding along the former railway, it can turn off it and pass the houses, shops or workplaces lived in or visited by its passengers. Assume that any busway might be used, not just by municipal single-deckers, but by fleets of minibuses run by other operators too, and it could speed the passage of very large numbers of people.

Recognition of this possibility has only jelled in the last couple of years and at the time when the Tyneside Passenger Transport Executive was comparing the relative merits of busways and tramways, it was possibly less obvious. For this and other reasons the Executive opted to convert British Rail's existing North Tyne Loop into a thirty-four-mile light railway linking Newcastle, Gateshead and the other towns on Tyneside. Whitehall was impressed by their arguments and at the end of 1972 the Government agreed to pay three-quarters of the £65,500,000 cost. It was a brilliant coup for Tony Ridley, head of the Executive, and previously one of the architects of the motorways plan for Greater London. It should be added that the supertrams, which are due to begin operation in 1979, share part of their tracks with British Rail goods trains, something that would have been out of the question for buses. Passengers will be helped to get to and from their front doors by making interchanges with other forms of transport—walking and bicycling as well as buses and cars—as smooth as possible. The ideal is to be able to walk across a platform or, if there is a change of level, to step on to an escalator and find the other vehicle, whatever it may be, right there. Tyneside is aiming to do this and precedents for it can be seen at many places on the Continent. One is Rijnhaven Station on the Rotterdam Metro where the trains stop literally on top of a bus station.

Trams coming into use in the 1970s are likely to surprise anyone who has only experienced pre-war or 1950s vehicles. The new Tyneside cars will be ninety feet long with a flexible joint amidships and seat eighty people. Acceleration will be twice that of suburban electric trains, top speed will be fifty miles per hour and at peak times a tram will pass through the middle of Gateshead and Newcastle every two or three minutes. The rattles, bangs and draughts of trams of old will be eliminated by careful design and aircraft-like doors that plug into their openings rather than sliding across them. The new street cars being built by the Boeing Airplane Company for Boston and San Francisco will be correspondingly modern.

British Rail should have woken up to all of this several years ago, seconded some of its staff to Frankfurt or Essen, and then started making a case for light railways. A shift to dependable, comfortable, light-weight carriages (it is hard to see why the Tyneside trams should weigh thirty-eight tons) and to simple, unmanned stations would conserve energy, reduce labour costs and free railway property for development.

Having missed that opportunity, it is time for the railwaymen to go to Lille in France, to Morgantown, West Virginia in the United States and to Toronto in Canada to see examples of developments that may enable tracked transport systems to return the challenge of the busmen. These show it is possible for trams run by computers to come at one-minute intervals at any hour of the day and night and eliminate waiting.

Driverless trams or mini-trams or intermediate capacity transport systems, as they are variously called, may turn out to be another expensive nonsense. It is so easy to be seduced by the glamour and show biz of high technology. The brilliant brochures show streamlined vehicles racing through futuristic cityscapes. Carefully selected facts slip off the slide-rule tongues of super salesmen. American politicians are heard to say that 'if mawd'n technalogy can put a man on the moon, wha mawd'n technalogy must be able to solve the praablems of the cities'. Huge sums of public money are subsequently devoted to startling hardware, only for it to turn out, a few years later, that a new law, a different tax or a revamped version of something tried and true would have done the job far, far better.

It is necessary to keep these things in mind when looking, for instance, at the VAL (Métro à véhicules automatiques légers) being built in France to link Lille with its new satellite Villeneuve-d'Ascq. At one end of the five-mile long automatic tramway is the centre of old Lille and at the other one of the faculties of a university with a 1974 enrolment of 40,000 students. Two other stations are located in suburban Lille, two in dense residential areas in the new town, one at the new town centre, and one more surrounded by another university faculty. The VAL's two-car trains will pass through all these places on sturdy viaducts and will be capable of carrying one hundred and four passengers, seventy-two of them seated. At peak times the VAL will carry about six thousand passengers an hour in one direction. Electric motors and rubber wheels (some tram!) will make the twenty-two-ton articulated vehicles quiet inside and out and eliminate local fumes. The cruising speed of the trams will be thirty-seven miles an hour, giving a travel speed, including stops, of twenty-five miles an hour. Engins Matra, the prime contractors, compare this with the ten miles an hour of a city bus which is a bit unfair. Buses running on the fifteen-mile-long busway system being built in Redditch New Town in England are forecast by the Department of the Environment to have a service speed of thirty miles an hour.

Like the trams themselves, the VAL stations will be unmanned and will be more like lift lobbies than conventional train or tram platforms. Passengers will buy a ticket from an automat in a small booking hall, pass through an automated turnstile and wait in a room equipped with sliding doors in the wall adjacent to the track. These will remain shut until a tram arrives and stops. The doors of the vehicle and the station will then open simultaneously like those of a lift. Gone will be the days of cold, wet and windy platforms.

It may be a brave new world or it may be 1984. More will be known in 1975 when the VAL is due to be commissioned by the Établissement Public d'Aménagement de la Ville Nouvelle Lille-East, the public corporation charged with building the new town. I have my doubts about it all. The analogy of the lift is not entirely reassuring. Those who use it are no doubt thinking of the plushy cabins and marbled lobbies of Madison Avenue skyscrapers. Lifts inside blocks of municipal flats in Glasgow and London have an altogether different atmosphere. People do not always behave in them with the propriety expected by the engineers. Sometimes they even piss in the corner. This could be an unwanted side effect of automation.

In the United States several VAL-like transport systems are in use or under development. All are rubber-tyred trams driven by computers, not humans. Tampa Airport in Florida has one, Dallas–Fort Worth Airport has another of a more sophisticated kind. So far the only one in a town setting is the Federal Department of Transportation's three and a half mile system at Morgantown. It has been used for extensive tests of the computer controls which can operate the vehicles safely at thirty miles an hour with only seven and a half or fifteen second gaps between them (ninety seconds is considered good going on a modern underground). I will come back to systems of this kind later on because they are, Tampa excepted, better thought of as push-button taxis. At Morgantown, for instance, the six-ton, twenty-passenger cars (there are seats for eight) pull off on to bypass tracks at stations, enabling other vehicles to go through non-stop. This seemingly simple variation in station design makes a world of difference to the traveller. Assuming the tram cars carry only three or four people at off-peak times, they can be programmed to stop only where those on board want them to. Since braking, stopping and accelerating are very time-consuming, trams of this kind can get passengers to their destination quicker than those of the VAL type without having to travel as fast.

Something very different is going on in Toronto. The driving force there is Governor William G. Davis of Ontario who is a New World Joseph Chamberlain, a believer in civic enterprise. In *Victorian Cities* Asa Briggs says that Chamberlain pushed through the municipalisation of gas and water because he saw his task 'as that of governing Birmingham in the interest of "the people", all the people'. Davis has likewise set up an Ontario Transportation Development Corporation because he believes that 'a variety of transportation facilities will put people first'. Historians may vote that there the similarity ends, since one of Chamberlain's greatest monuments was Corporation Street: 'a great street, as broad as a Parisian boulevard' which necessitated the destruction of acres of dilapidated artisans' dwellings, while one of Davis's crowning achievements was the stopping of the Spadina Expressway, its modern and comparably destructive equivalent.

In place of freeways Davis has staked his reputation on elevated tramways carrying vehicles supported, not on wheels, but on magnetic fields. The principle is well established enough and known to any child who has played with a pair of bar magnets and found that while opposite poles attract, like poles repel. This same repulsion is used to keep a magnetically supported vehicle a fraction of an inch above its track, thus assuring it a frictionless ride. Forward motion is imparted by linear motors, another innovation.

The contractors for this remarkable new technology are Krauss-Maffei of Munich and they are due to have a two and a half mile demonstration track ready for the opening of an exhibition in 1975. The vehicles are not initially expected to be driverless but will be highly automated and may evolve to a fully-automatic operation with off-line stations. One of the most interesting aspects of the 'mag-lev' trams is that they are seen not just instead of freeways but in place of additions to Ontario's excellent subway network too. Freeways are out on grounds of equity and disruption to the environment. Subways are out because they are too costly and can carry more people than wish to move along the inter-suburban routes where public transport is most needed in Toronto.

Governor Davis summed up the arguments for the new transit in November 1972 when he said:

> What we are discussing is a modern intermediate capacity transit system that is attractive in appearance, smooth and quiet in operation, comfortable, safe and pollution free. The major advantage is that it is sufficiently economical to permit it to be installed in a relatively short period to provide a far-reaching network of rapid transit for the Metropolitan Toronto area and also for Hamilton and Ottawa.

At that time a fifty-six-mile system for Toronto was estimated to cost (Canadian) $13,400,000 a mile, compared with between $25,000,000 and $30,000,000 for a mile of conventional subway. On these figures are pinned the hopes that it will be possible to build two miles of overhead tramway for every one of underground railway.

A map of the proposed network tells another aspect of the story. Five routes are envisaged but two of them, instead of going to the centre of the city like all the subway lines, cross the central and northern suburbs linking them to the airport.

As at Lille, so at Toronto, great uncertainty hangs over Governor Davis's dream. Is it another example of technology in search of a market? Much will turn on the frequency of services provided and the extent to which stations on the new transit system can be put at the centre of sought-after destinations.

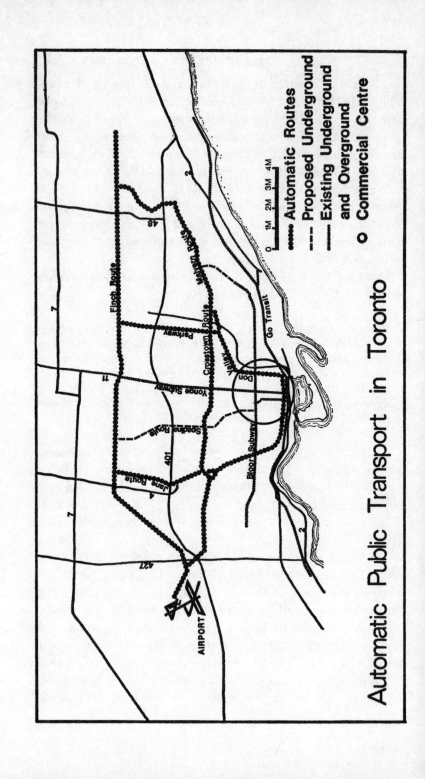

Automatic Public Transport in Toronto

Happily Toronto has a good record in both these respects. The existing subway offers a service that is second to none and every encouragement has been given to developers to build blocks of flats within easy walking distance of suburban stations. In the case of the intermediate transit system, the Governor has said he hopes to see terraces of houses with gardens built around stops. Given a busy airport at one end, a large new town at the other and medium density houses around the stations in between, magnetic trams capable of carrying 20,000 people an hour in each direction could, with patience, even show an operating surplus. Chamberlain's Corporation Street 'improvement' did, though it took sixteen years to do so—and in those days interest rates were three and a half per cent.

It is now over a decade since *Traffic in Towns* was published and throughout that period repeated efforts have been made to employ 'Buchanan principles' to reconcile the growing use of cars with good living conditions. Such efforts have been a failure, as one or two unusually perceptive people said they would be right from the first. A comparison of Buchanan's report with Nottingham's slimmer and less well-known *Zones and Collars* helps to show why. Both contain principles capable of being applied on a town-wide scale and both are concerned with trying to reconcile mobility with safe and healthy streets, but at that point all similarity ends. Whereas *Traffic in Towns* started with the assumption that through and local traffic must be segregated, *Zones and Collars* assumes that the first job is to disentangle public and private transport. All other differences flow from that parting of the thoughtways.

This divergence is nowhere clearer than in the treatment of what Buchanan apologetically called environmental areas (a nasty name) and Nottingham calls zones. In *Traffic in Towns*, as might be expected in a report commissioned by Ernest Marples, a public works contractor turned Minister of Transport, such areas were conceived as a desperate, last ditch defence against a mounting army of vehicles that the Ministry insisted must be accommodated. In the Nottingham report, on the other hand, environmental areas are not just defences against short-cutting traffic but containers, where cars are held in queues and only allowed to trickle out in such numbers as guarantee that no congestion builds up on main roads and other bus routes. Given this situation, traffic is kept in check and the 'need' to build new roads is greatly diminished. Highway budgets can be spent instead on houses, swimming pools or hot lunches for old people.

This alteration is not, of course, the result of new technology or new planning techniques but the imposition on the technocracy of new human values. Improve conditions for pedestrians and dig the buses out of congestion, Nottingham City Council told its officials and after some preliminary hiccuping by the City Engineer, they buckled to. Councils in other cities can do the same.

6 Dial-a-Ride

Take two familiar and well-tested kinds of equipment—the small bus and the telephone—put them together and shazam! you have a form of transport that is a low-cost car for the car-less and a car without parking problems for the car-ridden. The prospective traveller rings a dispatching office, places an order for a trip, gives his name and address and at the time appointed a minibus with a radio telephone on board is waiting at the door. Some riders will already be in their seats and others will be picked up in turn at their front doors, on the way to the shops, the works, the hospital, the station or whatever. Services of this kind are already operating in Britain at Maidstone, Eastbourne, Harrogate and Carterton in Oxfordshire and single adult fares at the end of 1973 were twenty, twelve, ten and six pence respectively. In the United States and Canada dial-a-ride got under way at Peoria, Illinois in 1964 and by 1973 services in twenty-two towns had proved themselves to be capable of attracting not just more riders than conventional bus services, but car owners as well.

Dial-a-ride is a bus and taxi hybrid. It gives a better quality of service than a bus but undercuts taxis in cost. Naturally, it attracts the antagonism of both. In Ann Arbor, Michigan, both the transportation authority and the Ford Motor Company were taken to court in 1971 by local taxi operators for having the effrontery to announce a dial-a-ride service. Fortunately for the people of the town, first Washtenaw County Circuit Court and then the Michigan Court of Appeals found against the taxi men. The residents of East Kilbride near Glasgow are less fortunate. An application by a cab company to start a service there was rejected by the traffic commissioners who feared that the regular bus services would be harmed.

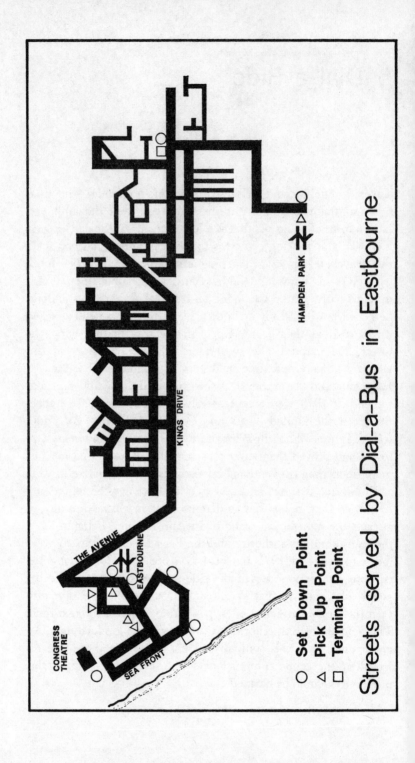

○ Set Down Point
△ Pick Up Point
□ Terminal Point

Streets served by Dial-a-Bus in Eastbourne

The evidence is that dial-a-ride *can* attract passengers away from fixed-route buses, though this is based on situations where the traditional services were poor. Thus the Regina Transit System in Canada, which put on some dial-a-buses and took off some fixed-route services found that it had increased its passengers by fourteen per cent. Across the border in the United States the same pattern of events occurred at Batavia, a small town of 18,000 people in upstate New York. There bus patronage increased by thirty per cent when a high-quality dial-a-ride service at sixty cents replaced conventional buses at twenty-five cents a ride.

Denis Freeman, a taxi operator in Maidstone in Kent, found something perhaps more surprising. His dial-a-ride services have increased his taxi business by thirty per cent. Freeman says the explanation lies in the dramatic presence of his bright orange minibuses in the city, all of them emblazoned with the name and telephone number of his firm, and the arrival of customers at the railway station who cannot or will not wait for the half-hour dial-a-ride service and so take one of his taxis instead. Is this a freak occurrence? It seems not, because taxi patronage has also increased in Ann Arbor in the period since the taxi men's law suit.

The moral of this would seem to be that both bus and taxi companies should get in on the new act as quickly as they can, but for this to be possible some institutional sound barriers need to be broken. For bus companies, at least in places where there is full employment, finding drivers may be a problem. Assuming this obstacle can be overcome, the bus operators will have to cope with the traffic commissioners who licence their services and who are obliged to 'have regard for the public interest'. This is likely to cause difficulties since the commissioners can be extremely conservative in interpreting their remit. At Abingdon in Berkshire, for instance, they insisted that dial-a-buses should tour through the town even when there were no passenger requests!

Taxi operators are likely to find the new market even more

difficult to enter because the bus companies are almost certain to oppose them, even though they may be unwilling to venture into dial-a-ride themselves. Denis Freeman, a dynamic and enterprising man, says he is crippled by antiquated Road Traffic Acts that enable the bus companies to stop him from charging competitive fares and from putting people down and picking them up wherever they want. His flat fare was twenty pence at the beginning of 1974 and his minibuses were able to stop at only two places in the middle of Maidstone. Yet at Harrogate a bus company operated service was licensed to charge ten pence and to stop on demand anywhere in the town centre.

The fears of the busmen are understandable. Their industry is based on big vehicles for which the Government pays half provided they are used predominantly for conventional stopping services at low fares. Yet this structure is geared exclusively to moving masses of people to work. Clumsy, one-man operated buses are at best inconvenient and at worst dangerous for housewives with children and shopping, the elderly and the infirm. New laws and licensing regulations are needed to release the opportunity opened up by the bus-plus-telephone and to ensure competition between fixed-route buses, dial-a-ride services and taxis. Even under present conditions this kind of competition could only be beneficial for the public. Where it is intended to introduce Nottingham-style schemes to limit wasteful use of cars it is essential.

In small towns where limits on the use of cars are unnecessary conventional bus services are likely to give way entirely to dial-a-bus and taxi services and this has happened in Batavia in the United States. In the much larger town of Regina (population 140,000), however, the two kinds of service co-exist. In fact nearly half of Regina's 'telebus' passengers transfer to a fixed route bus. A similar combined service is being investigated by Eastern Counties Omnibus Company for a rural area near Peterborough in England. Dial-a-ride vehicles would collect villagers at present without any bus service and transfer them to buses running along a main road and vice versa. Another form of co-

existence is to have fixed route buses serving busy routes to
the town centre, leaving suburban travel to be covered by dial-
a-ride. A third combination is to have fixed-route services at rush
hours and non-routed ones at other times.

In places where dial-a-ride is already working there tends to
be a mixture of customers who book by the week to go somewhere at the same time every day, others who book at least thirty
minutes before they wish to depart in order to guarantee being
picked up at a chosen time, and then those who ring up at
short notice. Magnetic flags stuck on a wall-mounted street map
marking the addresses of all the pre-booked customers enable
dispatchers to plot the routes of one or several minibuses. Drivers
are then given lists with the addresses of sequences of passengers
on them and radio-telephoned only the addresses of late bookers.

Many patterns of routing are possible. The commonest is for
all the passengers to be taken to and from their houses and one or
two stops. However, services can equally well be run from many
addresses to many destinations and it may be no coincidence that
Batavia's B-Line service, which is financially the most successful
dial-a-ride system in the United States, has this pattern. All
parts of the town are served every twenty minutes and about
100,000 people a year ride in one or other of five small buses. A
single trip cost sixty cents and five-day commuter tickets cost
four dollars in 1973. The B-Line carries packages as well, special-
ising in hospital supplies and deliveries from drug stores to houses.

With time, repetitive patterns may emerge in the demand for
dial-a-ride services with the result that loop-shaped routes running out from, say, the town centre begin to establish themselves
with variations occurring only as drivers slip down a side road to
collect or deliver a passenger. The City of Oxford's Abingdon
service, the first to get under way in Britain, has evolved like
this. After starting as a dial-a-ride, the radio telephone was removed and the service turned into a stop-anywhere one but with
a fixed route. Abingdon is only a small place. In bigger towns
this kind of fixed route 'hail-stop' service is unlikely to be
adequate.

From the customer's point of view dial-a-ride is convenient and easy to understand. From the transport operator's point of view the attraction is flexibility. Vehicles can be small or large, luxurious or plain, frequent or occasional, depending on what the traffic will bear. Not only can routes be planned to satisfy demand trip by trip, but the level of service can be adjusted without the customers being affected or even being aware of the change.

In most cases the dispatchers, who sit at telephones and book calls, work out routes manually and speak to their drivers over the radio, but computers and teleprinters may be used to reduce the manpower needed as the number of buses in use grows. It is even possible to give customers numerical codes so that they can use their telephones not just to dial the dispatching office but to give their order direct to a computer. At slack times electronic wizardry can enable customers to ring through the dispatching office automatically and speak to the driver himself.

Ordinary buses do not have overheads of this kind and are therefore cheaper to operate but the difference appears to be slight. At Regina fixed route buses cost (Canadian) $1.14 per revenue mile while running telebuses costs only two cents more. Furthermore as the telebuses attracted more riders at higher average fares their introduction reduced Regina Transit System's deficit. Regina's cold winters, which can freeze cars solid, helps to explain the success of dial-a-ride in the prairie capital. Long-established conventions of subsidising one-third of the cost of public transport and of giving pensioners free travel passes, at a total cost of (Canadian) $1,000,000 in 1972, are no doubt important too. Yet dial-a-ride has achieved results that suggest there is more to it than this. Wallace Atkinson, General Manager of Regina's public transport, put it this way at a conference at Ann Arbor in 1972 :

Many people who ride the telebus were never on a bus in their lives before. We are getting people who could not start their

cars on a cold morning and took the bus and then continued
to take it. We are getting the young children who had to be
driven everywhere by their parents but who can now safely
ride the telebus. There are children on the system who are
going to day nurseries. How many three- and four-year-olds
can ride a regular transit system safely? We have handicapped
people who cannot walk to a bus stop. We have people with
cystic fibrosis, muscular dystrophy, asthma, and other handi-
caps so that they cannot walk to a bus stop, cannot stand in
the rain, or cannot walk on a dusty day. We have a door-stop
service for these people. We are also catering to all sorts of
other special needs. If the system has any trouble, we can call
the passengers at home and tell them what happened.

In both the United States and Britain the *eminence grise* behind dial-a-ride is the Ford Motor Company. Ford had the
imagination to see that demand-responsive public transport could
result in sales of vehicles and of electronics made by Philco, its
subsidiary. The company therefore gave free advice to some of
the early starters in the field and now offers it for a fee in the
United States. In Britain, on the other hand, where development
is less advanced the company's transportation planning office at
Warley in Essex still gives its expertise free.

Ford's research has made it clear that the number of trips
per hour handled by a dispatcher-plus-driver team is crucial to
the economics of dial-a-ride. Using trips per square mile served
as a basis of measurement, Ford put the frontier of economic
success for dial-a-ride at ten an hour for transatlantic operating
conditions, a rate regularly achieved in North America at only a
few places including Regina, where the rate was twenty-one trips
an hour in 1972.

How can this level of business be achieved? Examination of
conditions in Regina suggest that, without limits on the use of
cars, low fares are influential and it could be that the residential
density of the town—about thirteen persons to the acre, which
is considerably more than the average for most American towns—
is significant too. Accessibility to telephones is bound to be important though dial-a-ride operators can install free ones. Denis

Radio Taxis (Denis Freeman's firm) have done this at a super-market and a hotel in the middle of Maidstone. West Yorkshire Road Car Company, who run a 'chauffeur coach' (yet another name for the bus and taxi hybrid) service in Harrogate, are aware that many potential passengers do not have phones and invite them to book in writing if they cannot call in on foot or use a pay box.

Philip Oxley, who is Ford of Europe's Mr Dial-a-Ride, acknowledges that the low level of telephone installations in Britain—about four out of ten households have one—is likely to limit the market but takes comfort in the high rate of increase in subscribers. There are also great variations in the distribution of telephones. Two-thirds of the households in the areas served by dial-a-ride in Maidstone have them.

Finally there is marketing. One ingenious opening exploited by the operators of the B-Line in Batavia is to contract with local shopkeepers and even bankers to provide free dial-a-rides down-town. In the running battle that goes on between out-of-town and down-town merchants in the United States, dial-a-ride with its door-to-door service and absence of parking problems is an answer to a down-towner's prayer. The time-table for the Harrogate service reveals a variation on the same thinking: 'By courtesy of Marks & Spencer Ltd we also pick up and set down in their layby outside their grocery department in Oxford Street. Use chauffeur coach for those heavy groceries—straight from the store to your door!'

Carrying express goods is another possibility already exploited in Batavia and one that Ford is researching. If dial-a-ride why not dial-a-load? With goods vehicles used in towns in Britain currently doing one mile in four empty, the sharing of lorries would reduce overheads for shippers and, assuming that fewer vehicles would be needed, noise and disturbance as well.

Dial-a-ride is still in its infancy in Britain but in Canada and the United States it has reached take-off stage with a large litera-ture backed up by ten years of practice. A vivid picture of pro-gress can be obtained without moving from an armchair by reading *Demand-Responsive Transportation Systems,* United States Highways Research Board Special Report 136, which is a report of a conference at Ann Arbor in 1972; *Dial-a-Bus: Guidelines for Design and Implementation* produced by the Transportation Development Agency of the Canadian Ministry of Transport; and *Dial-a-Ride in North America 1973* by Roger Slevin of the Centre for Transport Studies at Cranfield Institute of Technology, Bedford.

The immediate future can best be seen on the ground at Ann Arbor in Michigan (population 100,000) where the residents voted a $1,500,000 subsidy in 1973 towards a town-wide 'Teltran' system. This was a six-fold increase in public support for communal transport and amounted to a tax of fifty dollars for every household. (The townspeople also voted $800,000 towards an eighty-mile network of cycleways, prompting Karl Guenther, Ford of America's dial-a-ride manager to say:

> There is a coalition in Ann Arbor right now between what I call the bicycle freaks and the transit freaks. They have motivated a large bloc of the community to stop additional road improvements in this current budget year. This is a fantastic development. It suggests how important public attitude is and that the people in the community must want something before politicians cause it to happen.

The effect of the subsidy was to cut fares on the ordinary buses from thirty-five to twenty-five cents (with free transfers) and dial-a-ride from sixty to twenty-five cents. Use of dial-a-ride accordingly increased by half in the sector of the town served, producing four hundred rides a day from an area of just under two and a half square miles.

Town-wide 'Teltran' involves a fleet of forty-five dial-a-buses and fifteen fixed route express vehicles, offering an integrated service that enables people to travel between remote points in the town with a maximum of two transfers. Such a trip would start with a telephone call that would bring a dial-a-bus to the traveller's point of departure. He would then be carried to an interchange with one of several express bus services starting on the fringes of the town, passing through the centre and continuing out again into other suburbs. The passenger would then transfer to another dial-a-ride vehicle and be dropped off at his exact destination.

Local trips to schools and shopping centres in the outer suburbs may be made without transfer and another group of dial-a-ride services tour through the inner suburbs and downtown. This is by far the most complex system yet attempted and the meshing of the dial-a-ride and the fixed route services calls for great skill on the part of both dispatchers and drivers if the expresses are not to be kept waiting. Computers are to be used to help plot compound trips and travellers who ring up to book a ride are given details of their transfer points as well as the time they are to be collected.

Ann Arbor has also pioneered a new kind of ticket designed to put the cost of travelling by dial-a-ride on the same footing as going by car. This is a fifteen-dollar unlimited-use monthly pass. Holders of these passes may take members of their families with them free of charge. Given this kind of tariff, dial-a-ride is indeed a car for the car-less.

Some thought has also been given to ways in which dial-a-ride might evolve and the most likely prospect appears to be a move towards automatic, rubber-tyred mini-trams for the express leg of any journey. As at Ann Arbor, these advanced dial-a-buses would tour the streets where people wanted to get on and off but instead of transferring their passengers on to express buses for the long-haul stretches of trips across town, or to an airport, they would climb on to overhead guideways where the driver would hop off, leaving the vehicle to continue under automatic control.

Americans call this hybrid 'dual-mode transport' and the Department of Transportation in Washington made it the subject of three research contracts worth a total of $1,500,000 in September 1973. One went to General Motors for the development of an ordinary internal combustion powered minibus that could be driven on the streets by a driver and be electronically

controlled on guideways. Rohr Corporation will develop a bus
that will be gas turbine powered on the streets and electric
powered on the guideways. Transportation Technology Inc.
will work on one that would sit on an air-cushion-supported
pallet on the guideways. The Department sees transport systems
of this kind coming into use by 1980 in medium to large urban
areas.

Dual-mode systems have a lot to be said for them. They get
people to and from their front doors. They are economical in
fuel, involve a sharing of rides and are a development of a known
kind of service rather than a new technology searching for a use.
Furthermore they necessitate only limited investment in overhead
guideways yet would offer a town-wide transit service at all
stages in the growth of the guideway network.

Engineers have dreamed about automatic highways for years
but have never faced up to the risks that would be inevitable and
the problems of responsibility that would result if privately owned
vehicles of differing standards of maintenance were to travel
under automatic control on public highways. Dual-mode transit,
based on a standard fleet of vehicles owned and maintained by
a single public or private corporation, would obviate these difficulties. To my way of thinking, this is a very promising vision of
the city transport of the future—an evolving system of small-
scale shared vehicles running for much of the time on ordinary
streets but moving on to modest elevated guideways for those
parts of their journey that *Traffic in Towns* envisaged would take
place on gigantic urban motorways.

Wallace Atkinson of Regina Transit says that whenever people
are told about dial-a-ride their reaction is one of enthusiasm.
Residents are even beginning to design services and put them to
their local councils or bus companies. This has happened in
England in the small Sussex town of Burgess Hill. The advocates
of the service envisage that a single minibus would make five
tours through the various sectors of the town in the course of
an hour and charge a flat fare of five pence per loop.

Minibuses that go to the doors of their passengers may make it necessary to rethink ideas about designing towns around busways and bus routes. For the past few years thinking amongst town planners has been moving steadily in that direction. The Stockholm underground is now a long-standing example of rail-oriented development. Runcorn shows how a new town can be arranged around a figure-eight busway and is in mid-development. The process was taken a step further in Britain in 1973 when the Department of the Environment issued a circular to all local authorities (Number 83/73), stressing the need for them to provide for public transport in designing the layouts of all new and redeveloped residential and industrial areas. The circular also endorsed standards for accessibility to bus services long in use on the Continent. These specify that there should be no more than four hundred metres or five minutes' walk between any house or place of work and its nearest bus stop.

In *Public Transport on Tyneside: A Plan for the People*, the Tyneside Passenger Tranport Executive argues that the same thinking could be applied to the management of traffic in existing estates. Direct routes would be created for buses and short-cutting cars prevented from using them by inserting short stretches of bus-only roads along the way.

Dial-a-ride services, with their ability to operate in conventional suburban layouts, make it necessary to think this over very carefully. The designing of towns round direct routes for public transport will still be necessary and will contribute to keeping down the cost of services. But in places where houses are thinner on the ground, where the pattern of demand is more scattered, and in those places where women are trying to get home with children and shopping bags, door-to-door service will be necessary too.

It is early days yet to see how dial-a-ride and fixed-route buses will fit together in Europe but interest in the new mode is growing. On the Continent Volvo and Mercedes are getting involved in it and services are in use in the Netherlands. At Frankfurt Airport minibuses, each one with a destination placard on it, take groups of passengers to different parts of the surrounding region.

Are they dial-a-buses or shared taxis? The one merges impercept-
ibly into the next. All that is certain is the need to remove obsolete
laws that hinder the introduction of such services in Britain. Once
they are in operation, hospitals, clinics, and all public authorities
that need to transport individuals from door to door should support them. Limits on parking and other restraints on the use of
cars in towns may then be introduced in the knowledge that an
array of bus, dial-a-ride and taxi services can take their place. For
those without cars the advantages are obvious. Those with cars
will be saved not just parking problems but the chauffeuring of
children and elderly relatives and friends.

According to Wallace Atkinson this is already happening in
Regina:

> Everybody is riding. We have children as young as three
> years, senior citizens, and business people. The heaviest riding
> is coming from the high-income families (average home
> $40,000 and average income $25,000). Over half of our
> passengers come from families that own two or three auto-
> mobiles. The other half comes from one-car families. I guess
> the average car ownership in the area is about 1·6 to 1·7 per
> household. We have taken pictures at 10.00 a.m. on a week-
> day at a three-car home where the garage doors were opened
> and two cars were in the garage and one was on the street.
> The cars stay home unless there is some special need to go
> across town. I might add that parking in Regina is fairly cheap
> (about $15 per month) and it is free at the government build-
> ings.

But what about the problems of the poor if a cheap conventional bus service is replaced by more expensive dial-a-ride?
Atkinson has an answer to that too:

> Maybe I should have started out by saying that in Saskatch-
> ewan we live in a 'welfare state' . . . There are poor in our
> community, and there are people who need assistance. The
> people on welfare, the people who really cannot afford the
> fare, and the handicapped people are given a pass that is paid
> for by the State. They pay nothing on the system, but we get

the full value for the pass from the State. The in-between areas where there is high demand from low-income groups will have both fixed-route service and telebus because the demand is high enough to provide both. People in those areas will have a choice of fixed-route service or deluxe service. Anyone in those areas unable to walk to a bus stop will get a telebus pass paid for by welfare funds. We think this is the way to go.

7 Getting on the Right Track

Many people believe that building underground railways is virtually the only sure way to improve mobility in large cities. They see them as safe, dependable, blessedly free from the delays and frustrations of traffic jams, and capable of being built without destroying the existing fabric of cities. The capacity of railways to move huge numbers of people—up to 64,000 an hour in a single direction—is reckoned to stand further in their favour. In fact such Mississippian flows are rare and the 24,000 people going in both directions in peak hours on the busiest sections of London's Victoria Line are more typical. Yet even that number, if they rode in cars at average occupancy rates, would need a motorway twenty lanes wide.

Advocates of undergrounds take further confidence from the fact that of the world's hundred odd cities with a population exceeding one million, virtually all are building a new 'rapid transit' system or extending an existing one. At Munich, Mexico City, Milan, Melbourne, it is everywhere the same; tunnelling is under way. Even North American cities have joined in, with Montreal and Toronto in the lead. The cities of the United States, with what their detractors see as characteristically car-crazy conservatism, held out longest against the new wave of thinking, but by 1972 the wedge-nosed trains of San Francisco's much-troubled Bay Area Rapid Transit (BART) District entered service and digging finally started in Washington, D.C. in the same year.

However, it would be a mistake to assume that all this activity signals unanimity about the good sense of building new underground systems in modern cities. Opposition to them is particularly strong in the United States and Canada but it may be heard in Germany, the Netherlands and Britain too.

I have referred to one aspect of this criticism elsewhere : the gradual thinning down and spreading out of settlements as increasing numbers of people obtain the wherewithal to buy themselves more house-space and perhaps a garden too and as manufacturing and then service industries set up alongside them. This fundamental urban process has vital implications for traditional underground railways. It draws away many commuters who might otherwise wish to travel into the centres of cities. It means that fewer people live close to railway stations. And it leads to a flurry of inter-suburban travel, not just to get to work but for shopping, seeing friends and having fun. Radially disposed railways could not be less suited to serving these new patterns of travel.

Put this set of changes beside the escalating cost of digging undergrounds, not running tunnels, which can be dealt with by ingenious mechanical moles, but stations which have to be dug largely by hand, and the case for constructing completely new systems begins to look thin. Needless to say railway planners are not oblivious to these changes and have tried to respond to them. San Franciso's brand new seventy-five-mile-long BART is an example of one of the answers they have come up with.

BART extends across an immense and sprawling urban region with about two and a half million residents. Freeways criss-cross the entire area and over the years motorists have grown accustomed to getting about at fifty to sixty miles an hour. In order to compete with this performance, the BART trains are designed to do a maximum of eighty miles an hour, which gives them an overall speed, including stops, of forty to fifty. But for such speeds to be possible it has been necessary, in turn, to space the stations out at between two and four miles. The result is for very few stations to be within the inner residential areas of San Francisco where the buildings are tight-packed, car ownership is low and where improvements to public transport are badly needed.

BART is not an urban railway at all but a suburban one designed to whisk well-heeled commuters from their split-levels and ranch-types in Alameda and Contra Costa Counties across the bay into San Francisco. Little use will therefore be made of the system outside rush hours, though this could begin to change as it is connected up to airports, sports stadia and exhibition grounds.

Nevertheless BART will affect the residents of San Francisco. By making it easier for suburbanites to get downtown it is encouraging the growth of a Manhattan of the West that is pushing up rents and driving out small businesses. These will in turn tend to move into nearby residential areas, pushing rents up there too.

Across the bay in the suburbs a different set of conflicts is apparent. The basic problem is competition between the inexpensive commuter bus services run across the Bay Bridge by AC Transit and BART's more expensive rail fares. As might be expected the bus company is being urged to abandon its services and to act as a feeder to the subway even though this will involve its passengers in greater expense and, in some cases, inconvenience. Local bus services designed to take people to hospitals and shops and visiting are under threat of disruption too. In Milan tram services have been reshaped to conform to a new metro in exactly this way. During the first eight years after the metro was opened, over eighty miles of routes were swept away and passengers on all forms of public transport dropped by one-third.

I have purposely painted a black picture and chosen the extreme case of the Bay Area but conditions in the United States are much as I have portrayed them. Huge sums of Federal money are poised for commitment to new subways that will satisfy the needs of only a tiny amount of all travel in their regions—the most optimistic forecast for BART is seven per cent—and cater for already privileged suburban minorities. It is against this background that it is necessary to set the $1,400,000 that BART had cost when the first stretch opened for service, the probable $4,000,000,000 cost of Washington's ninety-seven-mile network and the $7,000,000,000 set as the cost of a rapid-transit system for Los Angeles. With extensive freeways already in existence in all these cities, small wonder the subway critics insist that large new fleets of buses, operating along roads specially made for them and in lanes set aside for them in roads already in existence, would be less expensive, more speedily available and more useful. Small wonder, too, that they point out that subway cars cost at least three times as much as buses.

In Europe conditions seem on first sight to be more favourable to new undergrounds, partly because densities tend to be higher than in the United States, even in new suburbs, and partly because there is greater scope for using town planning powers to steer development round stations. On the other hand the centres of many European cities are often places where people live as well as work and are frequently treasure houses of history and architecture. Experience suggests that neither are likely to survive the rent and property booms set off by new undergrounds. Amsterdam, with its remarkable expanse of seventeenth-century burghers' houses, is typical of cities where the social and architectural character are threatened by the ousting of residents to make way for commerce. As it is, the number of people living in the central area fell by over a quarter to 75,000 between 1960 and 1968, while employment barely changed at all. Vienna is on the danger list too. The life and beauties of Lyons and Marseilles are less celebrated but the centres of both contain lively mixtures of flats, shops, offices and cafés. The metros that are under construction will replace this variety with the uniformity of America's Middle Western central business districts, alive by day and dead by night.

Most cities in Britain have already gone that way. The centres of Manchester and Birmingham are now little different from those of Denver or Detroit. The square mile of the City of London has for inhabitants only a few hundred caretakers and cats (though if a merchant banker's gossip is anything to go by, the cats have been notable for their failure to keep down an ever-growing mouse population).

In Munich there has already been a reaction against the social and economic effects of the two railway systems opened to coin-

cide with the 1972 Olympics. So great has been the displacement
of central residents that previously flourishing schools have found
themselves with empty classrooms. Popular discontent with this
and other issues led the mayor to set up a special group of ad-
visors—the *stadt entwicklungsferat*—and in 1973 he was recommended by it to cancel further railway improvements designed
to increase accessibility to the centre and to substitute for them
transit links that would aid travellers going between suburbs, and
traffic management measures designed to throttle back on the
number of motorists visiting the city centre. This set of proposals
was not to everyone's liking and a counter-plan, advocating
further highways to service Munich's expanding commercial and
financial centre, was put to the Bavarian State Government by
a study group at Munich Technical University.

Paradoxically, decisions to build radial underground lines are
in many cases taken to protect the older parts of cities from
highways and parking lots and to prevent them from 'dying'.
Only in Zurich was the erroneousness of this kind of thinking
exposed before it could do any serious damage. The residents
first voted against a skein of radial motorways that would have
trussed up the town as tight as a capon on a butcher's slab and
went on to reject an underground that would have transformed
its ancient centre and incited a house-building splurge in the
suburbs.

The Swiss have a reputation for being hard-headed and practical so it can be taken for granted that the citizens of Zurich
were not behaving like ostriches. They want their town to prosper
but they have their own ideas about what prosperity is. They
want the pace of development to be comfortable; they like their
old city centre streets and they consider that improved trams connecting many parts of the city will distribute accessibility, and
therefore property values, more satisfactorily than an underground serving only a few. Judging by what has happened in
San Francisco and Munich, the good citizens of Zurich would
appear to be more than usually sagacious. Or perhaps it is just
that the enviable Swiss tradition of putting important issues to

the vote has given expression to a wisdom that is stifled in less democratic countries.

Undergrounds form only a small part of the world's urban railways. What the Germans call *stadtbahn* or city railways and what countries with an Anglo-Saxon history call suburban railways are far more common and have been the object of a great revival of interest ever since it was realised that they could be converted into undergrounds in all but name and at moderate cost by tunnelling between one-time termini on either side of a city centre. Examples of this kind of over-and-underground can be seen at Brussels, Paris and Munich and others are under construction or planned at Melbourne in Australia, Liverpool, Philadelphia in the USA and Manchester.

The history of Manchester's Picc-Vic link (it is destined to connect Piccadilly and Victoria main line stations) shows how thinking in this city region of 2,800,000 people moved away from shiny new undergrounds and towards improved suburban railways during the 1960s. The story started with a study of a monorail from Ringway Airport into the city. Taylor Woodrow, licensees for the French 'Safège' monorail, were the instigators of this project because they were looking for sales. Initially there was a good deal of enthusiasm for the idea because monorails looked so modern. Truffaut's film, *Fahrenheit 451*, with its crosscutting between some uncomfortable Le Corbusier-style architecture at Roehampton and the Safège prototype in France should have made the enthusiasts sceptical. Monorails are just railways with funny tracks. The suspended cars may appear modern, but the kind of service they offer is limited to what is possible from vehicles shuttling to and fro along a track. The Manchester monorail project accordingly died a slow death and was succeeded by an official study into different kinds of rail transport. This led to a proposal for an eleven-mile underground costing fifty million pounds. A monorail was knocked out of the running for being too costly and too visually obtrusive. Meanwhile Barbara Castle's 1968 Transport Act had gone through Parliament and led to the setting up of a Passenger Transport

Authority based on Manchester. The new body reviewed the situation once more and came to the conclusion that a Picc-Vic tunnel just over two miles in length would be preferable to an underground because it would enable trains from forty-five miles of lines, fanning out across the whole region, to serve three new stations under the city centre. The project therefore went ahead steadily until it ran into a public expenditure cut-back in 1973, but it is expected that it will be built if it can be reframed as a series of smaller, self-supporting schemes rather than a single and very costly one.

Melbourne, a place that is as much a creature of Victorian commerce as Manchester and rapidly approaching it in population, is also pouring new wine into its old railway bottles. Spencer Street and Flinders Street, the two main line termini, are already linked by a viaduct but an underground link is being built too, to provide a loop and so enable suburban trains to enter and leave the city on the same line without stopping and backing. When completed the new tunnel will also serve three convenient new underground stations, while Flinders Street will have its capacity for trains raised from 103 to 176 an hour. Given this encouragement, commuting into the centre is expected to increase by forty per cent and commuting by rail by seventy per cent between 1964 and 1985.

Both Manchester and Melbourne are buying what are in effect extensive underground systems and, to their credit, they have found a way to get them on the cheap. Whether they are being as prudent in permitting mountainous pile-ups of commercial development to happen in their city centres is much less sure. Owners of the property involved are bound to benefit. Commuters may just have longer journeys than would be the case if their jobs were located in the suburbs.

Cities that already have undergrounds are in a different situation though they too are faced with the choice of improving service to the centre or trying to make it easier to get between the suburbs. London Transport has so far opted for serving the centre. First the Victoria Line, now the Fleet Line and, once it is completed, a proposed third line from Wimbledon through Chelsea to north-east London will all pass within about a thousand yards of Piccadilly Circus. The exception to this is the extension of the Piccadilly Line to Heathrow Airport where 60,000 people go to work every day.

In Paris the RATP is equally centre minded. Huge sums are being poured into a network of long-distance express metro lines (the Réseau Express Régional) which run under the middle of the city, crossing at Chatelet not far from Notre Dame. The scale of the public works involved is titanic, since the trains are full-sized ones and could theoretically run on to Lyons or even Brussels.

Extensions are also being made to seven of the ordinary metro lines so that people who have moved out to new suburbs such as Vitry and Bobigny can commute back into the old city. Automatic train control is being used to squeeze in additional trains (intervals of eighty or even fewer seconds are envisaged) but the prospect of everyone having a seat is still remote. It might be less so if some places of employment were spooned out of Paris and put down in the vicinity of suburban metro stations. This is being done at La Défense but the policy is not being pursued consistently.

La Défense, like Versailles and the Champs Elysées, is the architecture of *la gloire*. It is a vast vertical city sitting on top of the express metro, adjacent to a station on a suburban railway line between the western suburbs and the Gare St Lazare, and due to have a line on the ordinary metro extended under it. Eventually over fifty thousand people will work there, mixed up with several thousand residents and visitors to a national exhibition hall. If the scale of the place is overpowering and the immense parking dungeons a cause of self-defeating traffic jams, the principle of planting commercial development close to existing and proposed urban railways is absolutely correct.

In the London region Croydon fulfils a role comparable to that of La Défense, though it says something about the role of government in Britain and France that Croydon's transformation was the work of a dynamic borough councillor who saw an opportunity and, to Whitehall's considerable relief, seized it, while La Défense was a project conceived and promoted by Paul Delouvrier, the Prefect of the Paris region and a central government officer.

Other less blockbusting examples of decentralisation on to suburban railway stations can be found scattered over the London and Stockholm underground systems, yet the approach is not one that is suitable only to urban regions with radiating patterns of railways. The Dutch have shown that it is equally applicable where a constellation of towns and cities are linked by a criss-cross of lines. An example of Dutch practice can be seen at Utrecht where a wholesale market and convention hall, the Hoog Catharijne (High Catherine) centre, has been built next to the city's main station. Businessmen from Amsterdam, Rotterdam, The Hague and other cities all over the country visit the market and because it is where it is, rather than beside a motorway, they have the maximum inducement to go by rail. Once there they are able to make use of a hotel and a sports centre that are in the same cluster of buildings and enjoy the canal-side delights of seventeenth-century Utrecht without walking for more than three or four minutes.

The railway services that link the towns of west Holland—the Dutch call them collectively the *Randstad* or ring-city—are scheduled at almost underground frequencies and they serve an area similar in size to that served by London Transport. The great difference between the two systems is in the arrangement of the lines. London's all lead to the City and the West End where they create a single zone of maximum accessibility and a Matterhorn of property values, whereas those in the Randstad provide equivalent accessibility to a collection of lesser peaks.

The desirability of adapting radially organised rail systems to permit intersuburban movement and to improve accessibility to suburban centres has so far been recognised in few places. Toronto is one and I referred to its plans for a grid of magnetically levitated tramways in a previous chapter. Boston too, or more properly the Massachusetts Bay Transportation Authority, which runs an eighty-mile subway and light railway network and serves a regional population of 2,800,000, is bent on similar objectives. Existing lines are being upgraded and extended outwards but a circular transit route through Brookline and East Cambridge is also under study. This route was put forward by Alan Voorhees, about the only American consultant who plugged away at the need for public transport during the 1960s. Boston's circle line will be about three miles from the city centre and serve innumerable medical centres and colleges, including Massachusetts Institute of Technology.

Developers are bound to some extent to be attracted to points in the suburbs where a ring route crosses the radials because people will be able to get to them from all four sides. Further impetus to development can be given by the stick of city centre parking restrictions and the carrot of 'development bonuses'. Both Toronto and San Francisco allow such bonuses, which means that developers are allowed to build up more voluminous and therefore more profitable buildings on sites over or next to railway stations than elsewhere.

In Toronto numerous blocks of flats have been put up along the Yonge Street Line since it was opened in 1954 as a result of an inducement of this kind that is operative up to 1,500 feet from stations. The result is one of the most remarkable examples of co-ordinated development in the world and the Toronto Transit Commission proudly takes visitors to the top of a skyscraper in the middle of the city to show it to them. Yonge Street stretches away in front of the viewer's eyes and at right angles to it rise up a succession of mountainous ranges of buildings, each one corresponding to a station and a cross street.

In the San Francisco Bay Area the bonus rules are slightly different but no less effective. Developers are allowed to add twenty per cent to the floor area of buildings that have direct connections to a station or ten per cent at sites that have no direct access but are within 750 feet. R. R. Stokes, the General Manager of BART, was able to claim as long ago as 1970 that these inducements had provoked the development of buildings worth $850,000,000 within walking distance of his future turn-stiles.

The extremities of the Stockholm underground show how town planners and architects approach the same problem. Clusters of flats, shops, libraries and clinics, each one surrounding a square, were completed at Vällingby Station in 1954 and Farsta in 1966. Then in 1971 a regional shopping centre of unprecedented size was opened at Skärholmen. The developments differ markedly in scale and detailed design but the philosophy is the same at all of them. Flats, stacked up at first in towers and later in five-storey slabs are clustered near the stations to increase the numbers living within walking distance of trains and shops. Then came rows of houses on the ground and beyond them villas.

However, not all the 'sleeping towns' of Stockholm are so rigorously planned. On the railway lines leading out to the prosperous districts of Saltsjöbaden and Djursholm the style of building is more like that of the garden suburbs that grew up at Harrow, Pinner and other more sought-after stations on the London Underground in the 1930s. At such places many railway commuters find it is too far to walk to the station and so they go there by car and bicycle or by bus. Furthermore, those who can afford to choose seem to prefer this kind of low, loose-knit, arcadian suburb to those planned by architects. It is something that needs to be borne in mind.

One of the great myths of the 1960s was that skyscrapers alone made it possible to get lots of houses into a limited space. In fact it was a matter of architectural fashion. Le Corbusier had woven a magic spell round the idea of shimmering towers set in velvety parkland in the 'twenties and 'thirties and it captured the imagination of countless architects. Unfortunately Le Corbusier's 'radiant city' was little more than the single-minded exploitation of the potential of the lift and such places are as uncomfortable as those shaped too closely round that other late nineteenth-century transport technology—the private car.

Research done by Lionel March at the Cambridge University

Centre for Land Use and Built Form Studies has helped to show that a given amount of house room can be got on a site in several ways. One is to pile it up in one corner in a tower of flats. Another is to lay it out in, say, four parallel rows of houses and gardens with each pair fronting on to a street. A third is to take those rows of houses and gardens and set them along the edges of the site, leaving a park in the middle that may be shared by all the residents overlooking it. Revolutionary? No. Several squares of houses were built on exactly these principles off Ladbroke Grove in London in the 1870s and, according to people who live in them, the combination of a small private garden leading by way of a gate at its far end into a communal, but not public, park is close to ideal. For children it provides a selection of playmates and room to roam and for their mothers knowledge that their young are not cast loose amongst the unknowns of the city. John Nash had done a similar thing on a much grander scale at Regent's Park in 1810. The estate and its surrounding terraces are now widely held to be one of the finest pieces of town making in Britain but strip the terraces of their palatial pediments and porticos and they are nothing but ribbon development ringing a park.

The subject of densities is one that can lead to so much misunderstanding that I have used the term as little as possible. Less precise but more familiar concepts, such as terrace houses with gardens, are more meaningful to all but those who work in town planning. If houses of this kind are arranged round not only the park space that ordinarily goes with the houses in towns, as at Ladbroke Grove, but also a school and its playing fields, spaciousness is possible at a density as high as one hundred persons to an acre. In a square mile surrounding an underground station it would therefore be theoretically possible to build houses and schools for 64,000 people, none of them more than five minutes' walk from the trains.

Groups of houses have been built on exactly these principles in the London borough of Merton and Richard MacCormac describes them, and the theory underlying them, in the *Journal of the Royal Institute of British Architects* for November 1973. How far or how close to practicality it would be to build extensive tracts of a town in this fashion may be judged from the fact that there are about two-thirds as many people per square mile throughout the entirety of Kensington and Chelsea with their mixture of rich men's palaces and poor men's slums. The purpose of the exercise is not therefore to press the case for obliging everyone to live at one hundred persons to the acre, merely to show that ways of organising houses that are popular with householders and well understood by builders can be used to achieve densities that are conducive to walking. Arranging the houses around the edges of sites is the essence of it.

Yet no matter how conscientiously towns are built up round their underground and suburban railway stations, many passengers will need to use other modes of transport at the ends of their journeys. I have described in other chapters how the lot of cyclists can be improved, how never-stop systems can be used to extend the range of pedestrians, and how the effort of interchanging between railways, trams and buses can be reduced. Self-drive hire cars could also be made available at suburban stations.

Opinion differs in the transit industry about the extent to which having to change 'horses' deters travellers. At Munich the transport planners have organised both railways and trams with as many lines radiating directly from the centre as possible, in the belief that the deterrent is serious. At Toronto interchange is thought to be acceptable so long as passengers are required to expend only a minimum of mental and physical effort and are not obliged to wait. So firmly does the Toronto Transit Commission hold to this view that nearly all its bus and tram routes inter-connect with the subway which, in the case of the Yonge Street Line, has a train every six minutes even as early as 5.30 in the morning. (I am indebted to David Copsey for this and other information. It appears in a Cranfield Institute of Technology report called *The Wider Aspects of Transport Technology*.)

So far I have discussed interchange solely in terms of steps and stairs and waiting times, but being able to pass from bus to train or train to bus without having to buy a second ticket is as important. Making transfers of this sort easy for season ticket holders was one of the main justifications for the formation of a transport community of previously separate operators at Hamburg. Offering a similar service to single-trip travellers is less easy if it means that buses need to sell tickets covering underground rides as well. Flat fares are one way round this problem but they only work in small towns and if councils are prepared to subsidise them. Without subsidy flat fares are bound to have to be pitched at a level that will drive away short-distance travellers. Travel passes that entitle their possessors to go by bus, underground and suburban railway as much as they like are a better bet. They were pioneered in small towns in Sweden and then taken up by the Stockholm Transport Company. By the winter of 1972/3 sales of subsidised fifty-kroner (about five pounds sterling) passes were selling at a rate of over 300,000 a month and petrol shortages and price increases caused a surge in sales the following winter. Similar passes have been put on sale in London and the West Midlands but never at a price to make them really attractive.

The object of all these contributions towards easier travelling is to turn urban railways into something that can be perceived as a town-wide service rather than a set of trains negligently lashed together with buses, trams and taxis. Railways will have to evolve in this direction if they wish to survive.

Toronto's belief in high-frequency services outside rush hours has already come up. It is more common to find ninety-second or two-minute intervals at peak times expanding to ten or fifteen minutes at other times and particularly towards the end of lines. In 1969 Max Mross, the then head of the Hamburg Transport Community, took a look at his transit system from the point of view of a passenger and said there ought to be a train every few minutes throughout the day. And he said this could only be achieved without incurring insupportable wage costs by introducing driverless trains. Lines have been successfully automated in Paris, London and Philadelphia but never operated without a man on board. San Francisco's BART has tried to go a step further and merge trains under automatic control and has encountered difficulties that are too embroiled in industrial politics for it to be clear whether they are temporary or permanent. Even if one assumes that the technological problems can be overcome, as I imagine they will, the safety of passengers who might be trapped in trains broken down in tunnels and the fears that some women have at being alone or, worse still, almost alone, all need to be carefully weighed. It is less risky to reduce labour costs by means of unmanned stations, particularly ones that are in the open, and this has been done on the modernised suburban railway that runs out from Philadelphia to Lindenwold. Ticket selling, money changing and ticket cancelling are done by automats under the eye of television cameras at all twelve stations. A police force of seventeen provides additional surveillance and telephones are provided for passengers who need information or assistance.

But reducing station staffs does not make the trains come more often. Despite its efficiency the Lindenwold Line offers no more than a ten-minute service during off-peak times and an hourly 'owl' service at night. That is a far cry from Max Mross's goal of a train every two or three minutes.

With driverless minitrams already in operation in a few places, and coming into use in several others, cross-fertilisation to conventional railways seems certain though it may be slow. Roger Maasthagen, a senior engineer with the Stockholm transport undertaking, cautioned me against expecting fast progress in this field in 1970. 'Mr Bendixson,' he said, 'I would like to explain something to you. Railway engineers are very conservative men, but underground railway engineers are by far the most conservative of them all.' Nevertheless William Maxwell, the executive member in charge of engineering for London Transport, gave a paper making a case for driverless underground trains only four years later.

Pending fully automatic trains, much can be done by the improved marketing of conventional railway services. Since it was opened in 1969, the fourteen-mile-long Lindenwold Line has steadily increased its off-peak patronage by providing parking space at stations (9,000 places in 1972) and by negotiating with bus companies to provide special feeder bus services. The result was a daily ridership of 42,000 on weekdays and an operating surplus of $600,000 in 1972. Since then more trains have been put into service, a new station opened near a main highway interchange and a dial-a-ride service got underway at Haddonfield, one of the suburbs served by the 'hi-speed line'. Underlying all these developments is a determination to see the travelling public, not as a mass but as a sum of many small groups. Shoppers, sports fans, theatre and concert goers and, of course, commuters are therefore all thought of and catered for separately, a philosophy that results in parking fees being dropped at some stations after ten in the morning to encourage off-peak travellers and the scheduling of enough trains to assure shoppers of room to put their parcels on the seat beside them rather than on the floor. Assuming this kind of methodical attention to customer needs is backed up by the development of hospitals, shopping centres, hotels and office blocks close to stations, it may become possible to run a five-minute service from six in the morning until eleven at night without dispensing with train drivers and without making an operating deficit.

Something can also be done about a problem that enthusiasts for urban railways tend to overlook—noise. Older undergrounds all too often inflict ninety decibels on their riders, obliging them to shout conversation at one another. People in buildings overlooking tracks suffer too where undergrounds come out of their tunnels and bang and squeal their way through the suburbs. Continuous rails, noise barriers and improved electric motor drives, forced ventilation, and plug instead of sliding doors can all bring marked benefits. Given improvements of this kind, interior noise levels can be reduced to between 72 and 75 dB(A). Exterior noise levels will also drop and can be reduced further by using one-

or two-car instead of ten-car trains. In the United States the Urban Mass Transportation Administration believes that inside noise can be got down as far as sixty-five decibels and has awarded a contract to Garrett AiResearch Manufacturing Company to build an experimental transit car to demonstrate this. Another object of the project is to show ways of achieving a marked reduction in operating costs.

Underground railways are for public transport what motorways are for private transport—the most expensive way to get things moving. For this reason, if for no other, it pays to look very hard at arguments for pouring millions into new lines or systems designed largely to get commuters into city centres. Better bus and tram services or short tunnels between historically separate suburban rail lines are likely to be more effective and less expensive. In cities that already have undergrounds money is likely to have wider benefits if it is spent on modernising and adapting existing lines rather than on building new ones, particularly if such modifications embrace redevelopment at suburban stations and circular linkages between stations on adjacent radial lines.

The idea of a city with not one but many centres may still be uncommon but it is by no means new and, as Peter Hall argued in *The World Cities* in 1966, it does help to reduce congestion. In large metropolitan areas there is really no choice. Decentralisation is a fact. The importance of urban railways is that they can, in combination with town planning controls and development bonuses, be used to give form to this process.

8 Moving Goods

No single aspect of road transport arouses more ill-feeling than the pounding of houses and the stinking up of streets by heavy lorries. Everyone is affected and most people feel helpless. The nonchalance with which the road mammoths are parked wherever their drivers please is merely the last straw. Road haulage interests can say until they are blue in the face that diesel fumes are less noxious than petrol, that trucks form only a small proportion of all traffic (one in ten vehicles in Britain in 1971) and that we would all die without daily deliveries of a hundred and one commodities but it will avail them nought. A broad-based body of opinion is determined that goods movement can and must be handled in less objectionable ways. A belief that the railways could be doing a far better job is also widespread.

It is not hard to see how this situation has arisen. Increased economic activity, even the publication of philosophy theses, leads to increases in the movement of goods. The construction of atomic power stations and motorways calls for huge quantities of steel and cement, the purchase of television sets and other household appliances by millions of families puts other kinds of consignments in motion, while the cultivation of exotic appetites ensures that more goods travel ever-greater distances. This mounting exchange has its crazy side—the export of British coal to Belgium and the export of Belgian coal to England—but it also means Seville oranges in Southport and Oxford marmalade in Florence. Even Britain's modest economic growth has therefore had its effect. The tonnage of goods transport per head rose from thirty-three in 1965 to thirty-seven in 1971, a twelve per cent increase in a mere six years, and it could be up to fifty tons a head by 1981. Amongst the other countries of the

European Community the rate of growth has been, and is likely to continue to be, even faster.

Had the railways been the prime movers in this explosive process little resentment would probably have arisen. In fact it has coincided with a decline in the use of rail for goods shipment and a meteoric rise in road haulage.

Estimated ton-miles of inland goods traffic in Britain

	1955	1965	1971
Rail	21,400,000	15,400,000	14,900,000
Road	23,000,000	41,000,000	50,400,000

The ton-mile is not yet a household term but it is invaluable in measuring freight because it embraces both mass and movement. Thus a 1,000-ton goods train going 400 miles from London to Edinburgh would do $1,000 \times 400$ or 400,000 ton-miles.

The fall of rail and the rise of road transport has been caused by many things, among them the decline in coal mining, that historic industrial companion of the railways. The railways themselves contributed to the process by converting from coal to diesel fuel while householders exchanged their grates for gas and electric fires under the influence of smoke control legislation. Coal has gone on being burnt, of course, but in giant power stations built next to the mines, allowing energy to be transmitted as electricity via the national grid. At the same time there has been a growth in new freight traffics which never were sent by rail and which emanate from factories built next to main roads.

Why do company transport managers opt so extensively for road haulage? To start with it is because so many consignments go only from one side of a city to the other or from a warehouse to a series of shops. Lorries also provide a chauffeured, door-to-door goods service. You can give a shipment to a driver at the outset of the haul, tell him where to go, and by when, and know exactly who to blame if something goes wrong. The railways with their origins in shifting coal and ores and their convention of marshalling trains by shunting do not offer this kind of smooth and speedy chauffeur-driven service.

Carried forward by the tremendous growth in their business the road hauliers have invested in more vehicles and, with an eye to increasing productivity and profitability, bought larger and more obtrusive ones. Thus in ten years up to 1971, the number of juggernauts on British roads capable of carrying twenty to thirty-two tons, and which weigh as much as five family-sized cars when *empty*, increased from 13,000, to 65,000. Simultaneously the number of modest-sized trucks capable of carrying between two and a half and eight tons declined in number from 330,000 to 189,00. The hauliers quite rightly say that had they not used bigger vehicles they would have been obliged to use much larger numbers of smaller ones and to charge more for their services. They ignore the sleep that has been lost, the roads that have been destroyed, the buildings that have been cracked and the obstruction that has been caused by the growing use of giant vehicles.

None of these forms of disturbance is easy to measure but the Transport and Road Research Laboratory has examined the incidence of undesirably high levels of traffic noise and estimates that between nineteen and forty-six per cent of townspeople are already affected and that on present trends the proportion could rise to ninety-three per cent by 1980. In the United States the Environmental Protection Agency reported on noise to the President and the Congress in December 1971 and forecast that land badly affected by noise from freeways and airports could increase from about 2,000 square miles in 1970 to about 3,300 square miles by the end of the century, if no action was taken to stop the process. In all these trends heavy lorries play a dominant role because when noise is a nuisance it is the noisiest sources that cause the most disturbance.

On the assumption that whatever else is done large numbers of heavy goods vehicles will continue in existence in Britain—how could it be otherwise in a country that has over 220,000 miles of roads and about 11,500 miles of railways serving a mere 3,000 goods and parcels stations—action against their noise is needed urgently. This means persuading the nine member countries of the European Community to take joint action. The British Government has not been idle and has declared its intention to see the permissible noise level for the most powerful and therefore noisiest juggernauts lowered from 91 decibels in 1973/4 to 88 dB(A) in 1975/6 and to 80 dB(A) in 1980/1. This would mean that by 1981 a new lorry would make no more noise than an average passenger car does now. Unfortunately the achievement of these standards is held up by a controversy within the Community about 1980/85 lorry weights. At the beginning of 1974 the French were saying that they were not prepared to discuss the British noise proposals unless the UK Government agreed to a thirteen-ton axle loading. With Britain, Germany, Holland and Italy all advocating a ten-ton standard, the European Commission put forward a compromise of eleven tons, but this has succeeded only in creating a stalemate. Until this *impasse* is resolved the lorry makers will be free to go on making vehicles that emit 91 dB(A). And as this standard is established by measurements made at a distance, anyone standing close to a juggernaut is liable to be subjected to one hundred decibels, or about the level of a big, three-engined jet at take-off. This is on the threshold of pain. It explains why it is common to see people who are waiting to cross a road screwing up their faces as heavy vehicles accelerate past them in low gear.

I do not intend to argue pros and cons for the Common Market but the stalemate over vehicle noise touches a fundamental issue. It is a conflict between the so-called efficiency of Eurobeer, Eurobread and Euroanythingelse made the same for everybody in order to cut production costs, and the democratic good sense of allowing individual nations to set product standards that accord with their own priorities. It will be perfectly clear where my sympathies lie and why I think that the Treaty of Rome needs to be rewritten and given other objectives than the standardisation of everything from pins to power stations. In the meantime it is necessary to keep up the pressure at Brussels in order to get a decision on Euronoise and to get on with other measures that will be needed anyway. Extremely noisy vehicles will be with us for a number of years irrespective of what the European Community does and additional ways need to be devised to reduce the nuisance they cause.

The opportunities that exist are of three main kinds. There are those that are applicable everywhere, either because they affect short and long hauls or because they involve the modification of roads and buildings. Then there are ways of making distribution in urban areas more efficient, thus reducing the number of vehicles needed. Finally, and tied to the second possibility, there are ways of civilising long hauls.

As I have said earlier, the first priority within towns is to manage traffic so that bus and taxi services are improved. In the first generation of schemes designed to do this scant attention has been given to goods vehicles. They have been left to fight for positions with private cars, but there is no reason why this should always be so. In places where cars are being held in queues to avoid creating congestion elsewhere, and where buses and taxis are being given a clear passage, there is no technical reason why trucks should not be afforded privileges too. It is a matter of enforcement and various ways could be devised to achieve it. The main benefit of letting lorries share in the better running conditions created for public transport is that they will make less noise and emit smaller quantities of fumes than if they are grinding and bumping along in jams.

However the last thing that is desirable is for trucks of all sizes to be able to go anywhere. Powers already exist under the Road Traffic Regulation Act 1967 to enable local authorities to ban vehicles of particular classes from specified places. Oxford, Exeter, Gloucester and Norwich use them to keep vehicles over three tons unladen weight out of their medieval streets unless they have a destination there and these places are satisfied with the results.

The indiscriminate parking of lorries can also be controlled, and following a successful pilot scheme in Tower Hamlets in 1972 the Greater London Council decided to make similar orders covering larger areas. In June 1973 the Council announced that vehicles over two and a half tons unladen weight would be forbidden from parking on the streets of the London Borough of Bromley between 6.30 p.m. and 8.00 a.m. Lorries are obliged either to park within commercial premises or in one of seven public carparks.

Further powers for bringing juggernauts under control are contained in the Heavy Commercial Vehicles (Control and Regulations) Act 1973. It obliges all local authorities to establish networks of through routes for vehicles of over three tons unladen weight or zones from which they are excluded. English and Welsh authorities had until April 1974 to comply with this law and Scottish ones an extra year's grace. The outcome is expected to be a national network of about 30,000 miles of lorry routes. This legislation, which is often called the Dykes Act, after the MP who introduced it as a private member's bill, also prohibits 'heavies' from parking on verges and footways, but as parking for loading and unloading is an exception, lorry drivers will no doubt continue to block footways in preference to roadways.

Off-street lorry parks, now backed by the Government with £10,000,000 for site purchase, following the recommendations of a Department of the Environment working party report in 1971, are another device for taming the juggernauts. The parks already in use provide guarded compounds, cafés, sleeping accommodation and diesel fuel and tend to be located in industrial areas, close to docks or on the fringes of towns. They are essential companions to the prohibition of street parking though their establishment should not preclude the designation of certain streets in industrial areas as places where lorries may be parked. I will return later to their potential role as trans-shipment points from juggernauts to town delivery vans.

This battery of controls will, if fully used, bring cowboy road haulage to an end. Big trucks will be confined to a limited network of routes and obliged to go to road 'stations' when away from their home depots and not picking up or setting down goods. The operation of them will thus be more akin to that of a railway wagon, though they will still have a much more extensive network to ply than a corresponding railway goods vehicle.

In practice there are several snags to this arrangement. One is that villages and towns along designated lorry routes will continue to be pounded by the passage of long-distance heavies. Another is that the channelling of heavy commercial vehicles along certain town roads will tend to increase the level of annoyance to those who happen to live and work beside them.

In the Government's view, the trunk road and motorways programmes are the best hope for coping with the first of these problems. The then Secretary of State for the Environment expressed this view with conviction in a speech in May 1973 though his own figures hardly supported his optimism. He said:

One of the aims of our current programme of strategic roads is to achieve environmental improvements by relieving a large number of towns and villages in this way. Of the five hundred and twenty towns in England with a population over ten thousand about one hundred have by-passes or high quality relief roads and by the end of the 1980s another one hundred and fifty will have been completed.

Warming to his subject he went on:

Some of the effects of such relief can be measured and expressed in terms of reduced levels of noise and pollution, but the main benefit is to the well-being of local inhabitants: the relief from stress through being rid of noisy, smelly, intrusive traffic which they feel should not be there.

Look at the figures more closely and it becomes clear that by 'the end of 1980', which means 1990, more than half the towns in England with more than 10,000 people will still be in the thrall of the highwaymen and under stress from 'noisy, smelly, intrusive traffic'. This is a result of a belief, held by the central governments of all countries in Europe and North America, that motorways are the sole method of handling inter-city road movements. Yet such roads are pure highway engineering. They were conceived in the 1920s and 1930s when traffic was light and their role is to increase the speed and safety of vehicles using them. They achieved this objective by a concentration of resources in a few corridors and by neglecting the effect of traffic on non-road users elsewhere. Thus it was not until 1970 that a White Paper on road transport policy, in fact *Roads for the Future: The New Inter-urban Plan for England*, contained a section entitled 'Environment and Amenity', but it was only window dressing.

Motorways remain the standard inter-city road improvement. Their imagery of modernity precludes any questioning of the premises that underpin them. Speed, safety and capacity remain king. No one in Whitehall asks whether other kinds of roads would bring greater benefit to larger numbers of people both on the roads and off them. Continued reluctance to ask this question will ensure that juggernauts will still be roaring through two hundred and eighty towns in England in 1990.

What alternatives are there? One is to build roads that are less expensive than motorways in order to ensure that greater lengths of them are built for any given budget. In 1972 rural motorways were working out at about £1,300,000 a mile while simple twenty-four-foot wide, two-lane bypasses were costing about £250,000 a mile. If the one was substituted for the other, towns could be relieved from the evils of through traffic at five times the present rate. Two-lane bypasses would not be speedways, which means they would reduce fuel consumption, and the ubiquity of them would mean that good average speeds could be maintained over a large number of routes. People everywhere would gain relief from persecution by whatever long distance trucking could not be put on the railways.

Yet even if every item of through goods traffic could be by-passed round towns, most lorry trips will start and end within them. In the long term premises generating very large numbers of goods shipments may be located outside towns and near railways or main roads but in the meantime something needs to be done about people living in buildings overlooking trunk routes. In some cases, and I know of one not a thousand yards from where I am writing, residents have obtained reductions in their rates to compensate them for objectionable traffic. A more positive approach has been adopted over aircraft noise. In France air passengers are now taxed to pay for the resettlement of people living within the range of insupportable airport noise and for sound-proofing buildings that remain in use. In Britain grants are available, under restrictive conditions, to pay for sound-proofing round London Airport. These are important precedents, as is the Land Compensation Act 1973, which empowers public authorities to give grants to householders whose homes are adversely affected by noise from new public works. The definition of public works now needs extending to cover buildings blighted by the canalising of juggernaut traffic under the Dykes Act.

Huge quantities of goods go only short distances in Britain. In 1971 the average length of haul by lorries weighing under five tons unladen—the typical high street delivery vehicle—was twenty-one miles, while amongst the heavies weighing over eight tons unladen the average haul was only forty-one miles and down nine miles from what it had been four years earlier. The average length of haul by railways, on the other hand, was about seventy miles.

The explanation for the shortness of all these trips is partly that the country is small but it is also to do with the nature of a developed economy. So much of the goods in transit are boxes of biscuits going to grocery shops, lavatory cisterns being delivered to plumbers' merchants and bundles of annual general reports going from printers to company headquarters. Consignments of this kind cannot be handled except by road. Reductions in the nuisance caused by short-distance consignments must therefore be achieved within the context of road haulage.

One indication of the scope for improvement is the extent of empty running. In Britain as a whole, trucks ordinarily do about a quarter of their mileage with nothing on board, while if figures from a city as large and dense as New York are anything to go by, utilisation in large cities may be far lower. The United States Secretary of Transportation reported in 1972 that goods being moved in one day into a single square mile of Brooklyn in 4,200 trucks could have been accommodated in twenty-eight of them.

The consolidation of goods going to the same location is already established practice for shop chains such as Marks & Spencer. Until a few years ago several hundred manufacturers used to deliver their own goods in their own vehicles to the firm's two hundred and fifty-one stores. This not only led to trucks blocking one another and other vehicles if several arrived at once, but also to difficulties in distributing the goods round the shops. The shortcomings were particularly serious for food-stuffs and led Marks & Spencer to consider transit depots. The idea looked promising and another firm was asked to set up a trial depot to receive goods in bulk one afternoon, co-ordinate them and dispatch them early the following morning. The experiment was a success. The number of lorries delivering goods to a medium-sized store fell from one hundred and twenty to twenty a week and, coincidentally, vehicle unloading times also fell from more than one hundred and twenty to twenty minutes. A series of depots has since been set up to receive, co-ordinate and deliver eighty-five per cent of the food sold by Marks & Spencer.

In Holland this kind of approach has been extended from single firms to city-wide delivery systems and in 1973 twenty-seven trans-shipment depots jointly owned by groups of road hauliers were in use. Just as Marks & Spencer, incoming consignments going to several destinations are divided up and re-loaded on to local distribution vehicles, often with other goods on board.

It is no coincidence that the Dutch are becoming the hauliers of Europe. They are good organisers, are willing to try new ideas and as individuals they have the free-booting resourcefulness necessary in road haulage. Britain's role as the carrier of the world's goods by sea in the last century rested on similar human foundations.

Trans-shipment depots are starting points for several reforms to road haulage in towns. The first step is to give them a second role as off-street parks for heavy vehicles, thereby emphasising their role as truck stations. The good sense of this was noted by the British Government working party on lorry parks in 1971. Some of the Dutch trans-shipment depots take this logic a step further by embracing rail sidings as well as road connections. A further refinement would be to use quiet, low-energy-consuming vehicles for local distribution and for deliveries to pedestrian precincts. One kind of vehicle that might be suitable is a hybrid combining a battery and a constant-speed diesel generator. Development work on such technological cross-breeds is going on in the Soviet Union. They have a greater range than all-battery vehicles but emit little noise and only small amounts of fumes, because the diesel operates continuously at its most efficient speed and is heavily shrouded.

In Britain the hauliers have repeatedly pooh-poohed the idea of trans-shipping goods from one kind of vehicle to another on the grounds that the labour costs would be prohibitive. No account has been taken of savings through being able to off-load goods more quickly, using fewer vehicles and being able to schedule the timing of movements to avoid congestion or other hindrances. The hauliers ingenuously revealed their ignorance in a report, *Lorries and the World We Live In*, commissioned from them by the Government in 1973. Discussing trans-shipment the report says : '. . . It was unexpectedly found in Holland that, as well as conferring environmental benefits, trans-shipment centres, when properly organised, could provide a means of keeping down costs. The system can thus be sensible both environmentally and commercially.'

Dan Pettit, chairman of the working party, and his colleagues were furiously criticised for saying that the potential for shifting goods from road to rail was 'marginal' and for mooting the idea of special roads for lorries, but if one overlooks their reluctance to give up any of their profitable long-haul traffic to the railways, their report is full of valuable information.

Oxford seems likely to be the first town in Britain to set up a Dutch-style town trans-shipment depot, thanks to an initiative by National Carriers Limited, one of the two operating divisions of the National Freight Corporation (the other is British Road Services and together they account for a tenth of the country's haulage industry). Following the creation of a precinct in Queen Street that is out of bounds to deliveries between 10.30 a.m. and 5.30 p.m., and anticipating the establishment of another one in the Cornmarket, National Carriers offered to receive goods during those hours for delivery at other times. These deliveries are made in medium-sized trucks.

The use of small containers is an integral part of the goods consolidation process. Marks & Spencer use a range of them designed to fit both their shops and their lorries and suitable for handling by machine. Such containers are reusable and lockable to reduce pilfering. The benefits are quicker handling in and out of vehicles, thereby speeding up loading and unloading, reduced packaging for manufacturers and reduced waste disposal for local authorities.

Trans-shipment still involves many unknowns but some of them should be revealed by a study promoted in the face of immense difficulties by the Chichester Environment Trust and Jennie Hinton, their secretary. The Department of the Environment is providing half the finance and a report is due by the end of 1974. The consultants are Nathaniel Lichfield Associates who compared the costs and benefits of better bus services and bigger roads in Stevenage and laid the foundations for the 'superbus' services now in operation.

If better public transport can be provided for people by dial-a-ride, it seems reasonable to assume that better goods delivery services can be provided by dial-a-van. The Ford Motor Company think so and announced a substantial programme of research in this field in 1972. The rationale is that the cost of putting a radio-telephone in a truck is offset by the increased work the driver can do because messages can be got to him while he is on the road. A customer, wanting a shipment fulfilled speedily, rings the dial-a-van control centre and gives his order. A truck dispatcher then looks at the location and loading of the firm's fleet of vehicles and radios a message to the one most suited to doing the job. Mileage is saved by avoiding a return to base and by doubling up in shipments. Already some experience has been gained of this kind of work by the operators of the dial-a-ride service in Batavia in the State of New York. This suggests that in small towns and country districts it may be possible to combine some kinds of goods and passenger transport. Another precedent for this is the post vans being used to take passengers in the Scottish Highlands and Kent.

If dial-a-van services are ideal for dealing with random and intermittent consignments, pipelines are at the opposite extreme and suitable only when flows are heavy and continuous. These conditions are sometimes found between main postal sorting offices and district offices in the heart of busy commercial areas and such a postal duct can be seen in one of the tunnels of the pré-metro in Brussels. It is about a metre in diameter. Paris has its famous and much smaller diameter 'pneumatique' postal pipelines, which can be used to express letters to any point in the city in a matter of hours. Only the unbelievable density of people and activity in Paris makes this practical.

Goods trans-shipment depots may provide an opportunity to apply this sort of technology to move merchandise to and from department stores, high street shops, warehouses and mail-order firms. Such pipelines might be of any size, be square, oval or round and designed to carry wheeled capsules that would be pushed along by moving air at atmospheric pressure. Collars of rubber or plastic at the ends of the capsules would ensure a nearly air-tight fit with the tube and bypass loops would enable the column of air to continue round off-loading points. Almost any degree of automation would be possible. A prototype of a 'Tubexpress' designed by Professor Robert Carstens of Georgia Institute of Technology is in operation at Stockbridge, Georgia and it has been used by containers travelling a total of 38,000 miles. The promoters are the Trans-Southern Pipeline Corporation of Houston, Texas.

Pipelines for bulky objects may not be science fiction, they are already in limited use for disposing of household rubbish in Sweden as well as for shipping oil and other liquids in many countries, but the dispersed structure of cities suggests that it will take time, if ever, before they play a major role in goods movement. Ready-mixed concrete going to building sites, milk going to dairies, sugar going to chocolate factories, not to mention paper to printers and a thousand other bulk commodities, are therefore likely to go on arriving by heavy truck for the foreseeable future. Prohibitions on the use of such trucks at night are one way to reduce the nuisance they cause, pending the development of quiet vehicles or changes in land use. Failing this noisy vehicles that need to be used in sensitive areas may be treated with 'hush kits'. For the most part, they consist of sound-absorbent lagging but some incorporate redesigned fans and air intakes as well.

Work is well advanced with the design of kits of this kind for existing heavies in the United States. Several experimental kits have been fitted to vehicles and test driven for long periods. They are designed not only to reduce external noise but to do something about the row often suffered by truck drivers. This can be as bad as a continuous ninety-two decibels, which leaves a man temporarily deaf after a long period of motorway driving. The kits are likely to cost about $500, or not more than four per cent of the initial cost of a vehicle.

It is time now to look at the road versus rail controversy and the movement of goods over longer distances. The future as the road hauliers see it holds an increasing number of juggernauts rumbling down an ever-more-extensive motorway network, either to provide direct door-to-door service or, where they are forced to take account of external costs, trans-shipment to smaller quieter vehicles for town distribution. This kind of future could mean an extra 20,000 vehicles of five tons or over unladen weight every year throughout the 1970s and an increase in the total fleet from 204,000 in 1971 to about 380,000 by the end of 1980. British Leyland alone hopes to sell 6,000 a year of its new 'Marathon' super-heavy and is calling the 280-horsepower monster the 'gentle giant' to soften up opposition to its 89 dB(A) roar.

The all-important question is how much of the long-distance component of this growing avalanche of goods traffic can be got on to the railways. Ministers of Transport have a nasty habit of looking at the tonnages of goods moved, including, for instance, the thirty-six million pints of milk delivered daily to British doorsteps, and of being very pessimistic because such a small proportion—only about seven per cent—goes over one hundred miles.

Total goods traffic in Britain in 1971

	Tons	Percentage	Ton-Miles	Percentage
Road	1,735,000	85	50,400,000	63
Rail	196,000	10	14,900,000	18
Inland Waterways	5,000	—	100,000	—
Coastal Shipping	46,000	2	13,100,000	16
Pipelines	54,000	3	2,000,000	3
	2,036,000	100	80,000,000	100

Thus the Minister told Parliament in 1973 that 'a fifty per cent increase in rail freight would . . . reduce goods traffic on the roads by less than eight per cent'. If the Minister had concentrated on ton-miles instead of tons, he would have found, according to British Rail, that trips over one hundred miles accounted for about one-third of the ton-miles carried by the road hauliers. Looking at the scope for a shift to rail from this point of view, he could therefore have said that a fifty per cent increase in rail freight would reduce long-distance goods traffic

on the roads by no less than forty-four per cent. Clearing that proportion of juggernauting from the trunk-road network is something worth doing and it says something for the persistent highway bias of the Department of the Environment that this particular set of figures is not acknowledged.

The financial value to the railways of shifting traffic from
road to rail on this scale would be considerable but the extent
to which it happens is tied up with the future of British Rail. To
some extent that future was clarified in November 1973 when
the Minister for Transport Industries outlined a five-year £891
million investment programme—a sixty per cent increase over
previous levels. This made it clear that the advocates of run-
down had been defeated.

Only a month before a similar decision had been reached in
Japan to authorise the Railway Construction Council to build
five more *Shinkasen* or high-speed passenger lines. Yet hardly was
the decision made than the Premier asked the Council to investi-
gate ten more lines. Assuming all go ahead, Japan will have
about 7,000 kilometres of new passenger railways by 1985. New
lines are also under construction in Germany and Italy, and in
France, the SNCF is expecting the go-ahead for a new line from
Paris to Lyons. In the United States too an attempt has been
made to revive railways by setting up a semi-national corporation
to invest in them. With about four times more fuel needed to
ship a ton of goods by road than by rail, these moves were given
additional significance by the oil crisis.

However, the real issue in road–rail competition is not investment—important as that is—but what kind of goods service the
railways offer. For at least a decade they have concentrated on
customers with complete train loads of oil, cement, coal, motor
cars or other commodities to move, and on standard road/rail
containers carried on liner trains. The advantage of the liner train
to both the customer and the railways is that no time is wasted
on shunting wagons from one train to another in a marshalling
yard. The snag is the limited number of origins and destinations
available to prospective shippers of goods. The ability of con-

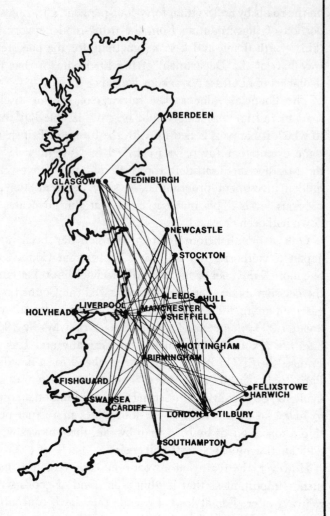

- • Single Terminal
- ▪ Two or more Terminals

Freightliner Routes

tainers to go by road and rail is intended to offset this difficulty but it has so far failed to do so because of the competitive rates charged by the road hauliers. Meanwhile British Rail is continuing to run down its ancient wagon-load system and in the twelve months up to November 1973 the board scrapped 40,000 wagons and closed down thirty freight depots. In abandoning antique equipment the railways are undoubtedly correct but in opting out of the business of moving truck loads of goods between a wide variety of points they are guaranteeing that they will never play a major role as a freight mover and never make substantial encroachments into the huge receipts of the road hauliers. These amounted to £3,540,000,000 in 1971, compared with the £260,000,000 earned by British Rail.

The locating of new factories and industrial estates on sites beside existing railways or within reach of short new spurs is one way for British Rail to start winning business from the hauliers. Grants to firms to help buy the special wagons that may be needed for their goods are another and the Minister of Transport said that both were under consideration when he announced the railway investment programme at the end of 1973. Both policies were introduced in Germany in 1969. Something also needs to be done about marshalling. The United States Department of Transportation, announcing a contract in 1972 for the development of a computer model to improve the allocation and management of freight cars, said that the average wagon moves loaded for only about seven per cent of the time. For the rest it stands empty, waits at loading docks or is in a repair shop. It is a record that makes the trucking industry seem a paragon of efficiency.

Developments under all these headings would enable the railways to handle truck-sized consignments to many destinations more speedily and efficiently than is possible today. However, nine times out of ten it would still be necessary to transfer the goods to and from the roads at the start and finish of their journeys. Liner train depots have huge travelling gantries to do this job and their cost means that two full train loads of big boxes must be handled a day to break even. This is why there are so few of them. Cheaper methods of transfer are needed. The piggy-backing of road trucks that are just driven on to the end of the train by a ramp is the ideal and is increasingly practised in Germany. It is not possible in Britain with conventional trucks because small-scale tunnels and bridges do not provide room for both a rail wagon and a lorry. This loading gauge, as it is called, is nine feet wide by thirteen feet high in Britain, compared with ten feet two inches by fifteen feet three inches in Germany.

One answer would be to design special lorries expressly to go on trains. The lorry makers have been forcing a reconstruction of towns, roads and lanes to accommodate their juggernauts for the past twenty years. It is time to put the boot on the other foot.

In Germany the number of trucks piggy-backed by ordinary goods trains increased from eight thousand in 1967 to ninety-seven thousand in 1972. Stimulated by this progress the Deutsche Bundesbahn introduced its first *rollende Landstrasse* or rolling road service between Cologne and Ludwigsburg near Stuttgart in 1969. This route runs parallel to one of Germany's busiest autobahns and is served by trains made up of flat cars with tiny wheels that can be loaded or unloaded with trucks in twenty minutes. By the middle of 1970 over a hundred lorry and trailer combinations were being carried every week and in 1972 a thrice-weekly international service was in operation between Cologne and Verona. If the Channel Tunnel is built, and loading gauge problems can be overcome, there will be a comparable opportunity to piggy-back goods in and out of Britain from as far away as Glasgow or Cardiff.

Yet the railways will have to go further even than this in their efforts to compete with the hauliers. They will have to forget all those arguments about the efficiency of the railways resting on the ability of one man to drive a locomotive pulling thirty, fifty or a hundred wagons. What is the use of that kind of efficiency when the customer has not got a train load of cement to send but wants to ship a wagon load of tape recorders from

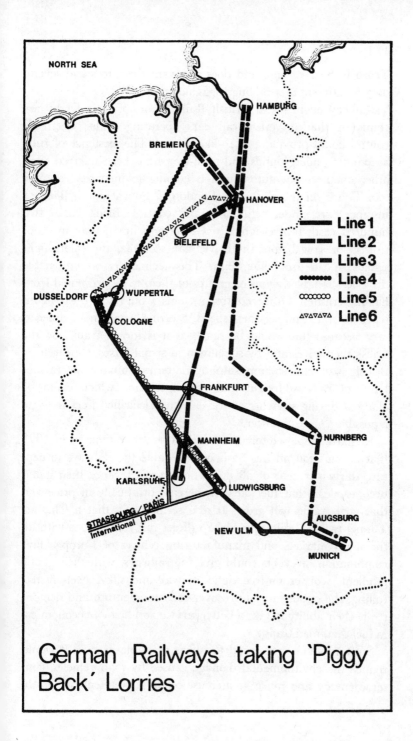

NORTH SEA

HAMBURG

BREMEN

HANOVER

BIELEFELD

Line 1
Line 2
Line 3
Line 4
Line 5
Line 6

DUSSELDORF   WUPPERTAL

COLOGNE

FRANKFURT

MANNHEIM   NURNBERG

KARLSRUHE

LUDWIGSBURG

STRASBOURG / PARIS
International Line

AUGSBURG

NEW ULM

MUNICH

German Railways taking 'Piggy Back' Lorries

Truro to Scarborough and does not want them to stand several days in different marshalling yards along the way?

Railway engineers at British Rail's laboratories at Derby are confident that driverless rail cars operating under electronic control could provide a lorry-like service. The existence of fully automatic undergrounds and mini-trams has been referred to in other chapters but automation is coming to inter-city railways too. Trains on the electrified London to Bournemouth line, for instance, are under semi-automatic control. Black boxes two hundred yards before signals give electronic instructions to trains to stop or slow before the driver can see what the colour-light signals ahead are telling him. This technology would enable driverless freight wagons or groups of them to be prevented from having crashes. Other control systems would tell the wagons when to start and set their speed. Steering would not be necessary because this would be done, as it is for all trains, by the tracks themselves and by signalmen in signal boxes. Research by British Rail into sodium/sulphur batteries, suitable for various kinds of railway freight and passenger cars, which could be charged during stretches of travel along electrified lines indicate a possible source of power.

Richard Hope, editor of *Railway Gazette*, estimated in 1973 that automation on this basis could enable the railways to capture thirty per cent of all domestic ton-miles. Since then it has become clear that fuel oil will increase drastically in price and that coal traffic will grow. It also seems likely that a Channel Tunnel will be built, opening up direct rail connections with all the main markets and manufacturing centres of Europe. This combination of events could give the railways, with their gentle gradients, congestion-free rights of way and silky, steel-on-steel rolling, the opportunity to recover their momentum and demonstrate their ability to give a better service and be more economical in fuel than road transport.

Shifting goods from road to rail is desirable because it would reduce the environmental damage caused by road vehicles, conserve energy and make greater use of the investment tied up in the railways. However, William Gissane of the Birmingham Accident Hospital has exposed another reason for clearing heavy vehicles off motorways. This is that forty per cent of all car occupants who die in motorway accidents do so following a collision with a lorry. With lorries weighing up to thirty-two tons and cars weighing about one it is not surprising. In crashes involving both, cars get pulverised.

No discussion of goods transport would be complete without some consideration of canals, though, as the figures given on p. 172 show, they play at present only a very minor role in Britain. One reason is that the country has a set of secret waterways, better known as the sea which take big ships. Yet for some reason —can it be the bad publicity of Masefield's 'Dirty British coaster . . .'—no one pays any attention to the potential of coastal shipping to relieve inland routes. My own feeling is that it would be better to concentrate on coastwise traffic and leave the canals as far as possible in the hands of holiday makers and fishermen. The exception to this is estuaries such as the Humber and the Thames, where there are opportunities to use barges that can be lifted on to mother ships to cross the sea. British Waterways Board took delivery of its first vessel of this kind in 1973 and is basing it at Grimsby. It is a BACAT or a Barge Aboard Catamaran, that can carry eighteen canal barges with a fifteen foot beam. The country's few major inland waterways are clear candidates for this ingenious form of transport.

Congestion-free urban roads, quiet lorries, the post-officing of goods in cities and the transfer of shipments to the railways— these are the main ways in which the juggernaut invasion can be civilised. Over a much longer period there is the prospect that growth in the volume of goods in transit will tail off as Europe's industrial societies evolve into post-industrial ones. There are signs of this in the United States but it still leaves a vast volume of merchandise in circulation.

Ten years ago the prospects for these changes were dim and

particularly for the rejuvenation of the railways. At that time all attempts to pursue sane policies were shipwrecked at the outset by a belief that the railways must be made to pay their way. Since then the idea has dawned that the roads do not 'pay' either. If a British Roads Board was set up tomorrow under the chairmanship of a Doctor Beeching it would immediately have to set about axing half the country's minor roads. And if it started charging interest on the grants offered to local authorities to build roads, that would be instructive too. At present the city and county engineers are given interest-free presents to pay for their concrete wonders. Interest is charged, of course, but it is marked down as another item in the national debt. Roads are therefore thought to be 'profitable' whereas railways are known not to be.

Nevertheless the rate of increase in the deficits of Europe's railways is daunting. According to a 1973 report on transport policy by the Common Market Commission, 'the aggregate deficits of the national railways of the Six, after deduction of costs met by the States, rose in 1971 to 1,400 million units of account [about £700 million] ten times as high as in 1960'. Even the most blinkered train enthusiast will realise that such a progression cannot go on. Greater efficiency is necessary.

A key to this increased efficiency is the setting up of combined road and rail trans-shipment depots on the fringes or in the suburbs of cities. As in so many ways the railways with their liner train depots in the midst of cities are locked into an obsolete nineteenth-century urban context. Industry has moved out to the suburbs. The hauliers have picked up their depots and followed it. The railways must follow suit.

9 'Taxi!'

Few laymen include taxis and hired cars in their thoughts when they are talking about public transport. Few transport planners do either and a Martian examining their plans would conclude that public transport means buses, trams and undergrounds. The imagery and the status of chauffeured transport presumably explains why it is kept on a separate mental shelf in this way. Taxis are aristocrats whereas buses are proles.

So deeply seated is this attitude that die-hard egalitarians tend to oppose suggestions that taxis should be given advantages over cars in order to make them speedier, and thus less expensive. Seeing them as chariots of privilege, they are dedicated to eliminating them; the last thing they want is to slow up the rate at which taxi meters clock up fares and so win their drivers additional customers.

There is a basis for such attitudes. Surveys of the passengers using taxis and hired cars show that those with high incomes use them more than those with low ones. Nevertheless taxis can be life-lines for the poor and the elderly who do not have cars, as well as being a convenience for the rich. Without them, getting to stations with suitcases or going to funerals, for example, would be well-nigh impossible for many people. Taxi drivers themselves are the best judges of the social backgrounds of those who hail them and all those I have ever talked to have confirmed that they do not cater exclusively for the 'carriage trade'.

Fortunately the reputation of taxis as a high-class form of transport, coupled with the excellent service they offer, augurs well for them. Indeed some transport experts, particularly in the United States, argue that taxis and hired cars (and developments of them), will be the main forms of public transport in the future. They have even begun to evolve a jargon to describe individual forms of collective transport. Public automobile service is one. Para-transit is another, though I must confess that this label always conjures up for me a picture of an underground carriage gently floating down to the ground under the shroud of a vast parachute.

The exclusion of taxis from most reckonings of public transport, coupled with the fragmented organisation of the industry —big companies like the well-known Yellow Cab Co. in the United States are exceptional—means that facts about them are not abundant. Those that are available make it clear that in a period when car ownership has been increasing and the use of buses declining, more taxis have been coming into use. In Britain the number nearly doubled between 1965 and 1970, giving a total of 25,000 and in London the number increased from 6,400 to over 8,000 in the same period. More recent figures are not yet available for the country as a whole but in London 2,000 additional taxis entered service between 1970 and the end of 1972. This expansion is probably linked to the jumbo jet era, in which case something similar may have occurred in Edinburgh, Dublin and other European tourist centres. Facts about the number of hired cars in service are even more elusive, since their owners are not obliged to register them, but they are estimated to have increased in London from a very few in 1960 to 20,000 in 1970. Assuming that they came into existence in the rest of the country at only half the rate they did in the metropolis, there may have been about 80,000 in use in 1970, or about as many as buses.

The extent that taxis are used is surprising. A few years ago Martin Wohl of the Urban Institute at Washington, D.C., reported that as many as 850,000 people a day were carried by taxis in New York and that Yellow Cabs carried half a million in Manhattan alone. To put these figures into perspective he compared them with the 400,000 passengers who travelled on the suburban railway services in and out of Grand Central, and the four and a half million people who subjected themselves to the city's awful subways. The use of taxis in London is less intense—no doubt because bus services are better and parking easier—but still substantial. The Maxwell Stamp Committee, set up by the British Government to report on the taxi trade in 1967, estimated that a quarter of a million people go by taxi on an average week-day and that hired cars carry an additional 300,000. This compares with the five million odd who use the buses and two and a half million who go by tube.

In the United States 170,000 taxis were in use in 1970 and carried 2,400 million passengers, or slightly more than a quarter of all public transport riders. Each vehicle covered about 40,000 miles in a year and carried an average of 14,000 people, which works out at 47 passengers a day over a 300-day year. The fares collected exceeded in value the total for all bus and urban railway tickets. The scale of these earnings has whetted interest in the role of taxis in the economy of cities and as providers of jobs for the urban poor. A picture has emerged of taxis as an important avenue of economic advancement for ghetto residents as well as being a valuable form of public transport in places where buses have become virtually extinct. Everything turns on whether there is freedom to ply for hire. If there is, households that are too poor to own cars may be able to buy and run car-cum-taxis. Such vehicles are used to ferry members of the household and their friends and neighbours to suburban factories inaccessible by conventional public transport, to carry home bargains available only at remote supermarkets, and to earn an income as taxis. Any resulting increase in car ownership in a poor district gives rise in turn to a demand for petrol and repair work and is a stimulus to men to go to technical schools to learn automotive engineering. Taxis-cum-private cars may thus be a path towards higher incomes and improved skills and an escape route from poverty.

An argument for helping the car-less to buy cars may seem out of place in a book that is otherwise dedicated to making do with fewer of them but the paradox is intentional. One reason why so little progress has hitherto been made towards taming the car is that solutions have too often involved forcing one group of people to go back to conditions of travel that affront their self-esteem, while preventing another group from achieving a status they strongly desire. If this assessment is correct, it follows that those with cars can be best weaned away from them by providing more prestigious and convenient alternatives to the increasingly ubiquitous car while still giving those who have never had a car a chance to own one. The taxi and the hired car are unique in catering for both possibilities at the same time.

It is relevant too that drivers of taxis and hire cars are increasing in number and that, according to the Stamp Committee, they have been prepared to work up to twelve hours a day during a period when many kinds of jobs have been hard to fill. Indeed, labour shortages in other branches of public transport have led to the introduction of underground trains without guards and buses without conductors. Michael Beesley of the London Graduate School of Business Studies, one of the few English economists who has studied personal forms of public transport, uses facts of this kind to question the conventional wisdom that high labour costs of running buses make it impossible for them to earn their keep. If that is so, he asks, why has an even more labour-intensive form of public transport been able in London to overcome rising costs without changing its methods of production, except by going for additional business in the suburbs where running conditions are less congested.

This helps to get into perspective the yelps and screams of bus managers concerned about the difficulties of paying adequate wages to the drivers of their 70-seater vehicles and of recruiting men to jobs which may go from six in the morning until six at night. Productivity in the taxi trade, measured by the number of seats available per driver, is much lower than in the bus industry, and the hours of employment are apparently as arduous, yet the supply of labour has increased.

One reason for the success of taxis appears to be that the

organisation of the trade is the exact opposite to that of municipal transport. The taxi trade is almost pre-capitalist. It lacks powerful, large-scale entrepreneurs and the powerful, large scale trades unions that are necessary to counterbalance them. In London, for instance, one in three cabs belongs to a 'mush' who has mushroomed from being an employee into an owner-driver and the rest of the drivers are nearly all self-employed journeymen who work for a commission or increasingly pay the cab owner a flat rate to take out his hackney. Both forms of contract give the journeyman a share in the risk of the business and a sharp interest in its success. They also give him the taxation advantages of being self-employed. If the welfare state has sapped self-reliance there is no evidence of it in the London taxi trade. There has been a strong trend towards one-cab proprietors ever since the end of the hard times of the early 1950s.

Michael Beesley stresses the importance of small-scale entrepreneurship and correspondingly weak trades union organisation in permitting conditions of work in the taxi trade to evolve. He illustrates this by showing how the number of drivers doing four or fewer shifts a week in London increased from six and a half per cent in 1952 to twenty per cent in 1968. This huge increase in part-time drivers enables peaks of demand to be met without having men idle at other times and is something that many bus managers would give their eye teeth to introduce but cannot. They are the operators of large, bureaucratic and inflexible semi-monopolies and are faced by large, bureaucratic and inflexible unions with monopolistic control over conditions of work.

Michael Beesley concludes (in the *Economic Journal* of March 1973) that difficulties over adjusting working conditions in the bus industry stem not so much from labour restrictions as from an inability to test new ideas. A lack of information about what might or might not be possible results and with it a stalemate over innovation in conditions of work.

Another advantage of the taxi trade is that it is a line of business in which it is possible to grow old gracefully rather than retire with a deadening thud. This can be seen in London where a proportion of the 'mushes' are in their sixties and seventies. (They have to undergo annual medical examinations after the age of sixty-five.) As a man gets on he is able to farm out more and more shifts to journeymen, thereby reducing the strain on himself without losing the stimulus of driving and the pleasure of talking to old cronies at cabmen's cafés.

Freedom to get into the taxi and hired car business is as important outside the ghettoes as within them, and is as valuable to taxi users as to taxi proprietors. Where there is freedom it is customary to find large numbers of vehicles in use, relatively low fares and a high level of patronage. Where entry is restricted by government regulation, response to growth and change in the demand for travel tends to be slow and the evils of monopoly all too evident. Where restrictions are maintained in the face of rising demand, then pirate taxis—in the United States they are generally called 'gypsy cabs'—spring up.

Recent events in New York illustrate the effects of restricting the number of vehicles allowed to operate. Under a long-established licensing system, 'medallions' giving a right to ply for hire, and designed to be displayed on cabs, are issued by a municipal taxi commission on payment of a small fee. During the 1960s, however, the commission put strict limits on the number of medallions it issued, giving them scarcity value, so that by 1970 they were changing hands at about $22,000. As there were then 11,779 in circulation they had a total market value of over $250 million, a sum that had to be borrowed by all the taxi proprietors and which was therefore reflected in the fares charged.

Given these conditions, it was inevitable that gypsy taxis would spring up. Not only was the demand for cabs growing as public transport became more disreputable and dangerous, but there were sections of the community—blacks, elderly and poor people, for instance—who were ill-served, and rough districts of the city such as South Bronx that rarely saw a medallion-carrying cab at all. By 1972 it had happened: the *New York Times* reported that 16,000 gypsy cabs were in operation, almost all of them driven by blacks or Puerto Ricans, and South Bronx was back on the taxi map. The authorities were powerless to stop them or judged it better not to try. The monopoly value of the medallions collapsed, though they are still in use, and a two-level taxi system had come into existence.

Something similar occurred in London in 1960 when mini-cabs first appeared in the streets, arousing fierce antagonism amongst the established cabbies and causing a number of nasty incidents. Their arrival was not due to any limits on the number of taxis operating in London since none exist. Control over entry, as exercised by the Metropolitan Police, is aimed at maintaining the quality of service. The quantity of it is left to be determined by the market. Quality control is focused on the ability of drivers to find their way through the urban jungle, and on their vehicles. Novices have to demonstrate that they know the quickest routes between all the streets and main public buildings in the inner boroughs. This mental encyclopedia is called 'the knowledge' and takes twelve to eighteen months to acquire. Vehicles have to comply with prescribed standards of safety and design, hence the famous London cab that can turn on a sixpence and in which it is said one may comfortably wear a top hat!

This police control over the quality of service is accompanied by Home Office control over the level and structure of fares and while it may have slowed down the rate of increase in the number of hackney cabs in service, it was not the only reason for the emergence of minicabs. A new market for personal travel was emerging amongst people living outside the traditional hunting grounds of the hackneys—families on holiday going to airports, groups from the suburbs out for an evening and wanting to be able to drink freely, and even hospitals in a hurry to deliver blood. Customers such as these had no hope of flagging down a passing cab on a nearby corner. They wanted to be able to telephone for service and in many cases preferred the comfort and speed of a saloon car to the stately, spartan and (at least in the case of older models) noisy grandeur of top-hat cabs. Furthermore, in the 1960s the minicab operators were able to buy mass production cars for £500 to £700 instead of batch-produced Austin or Beardmore taxis for £1,300 and the drivers of them were able to get on the road with no more qualification than a driving licence, a certificate of insurance and a street directory. Fares were unregulated and could be adjusted from job to job and this remains so.

In the period since 1960 the two kinds of taxis have settled down and learned to live together. The hackneys have prevented their rivals from using the word taxi and, by dint of frustrating them from giving any indication that they are for hire, have effectively stopped them from finding fares in the street. The hire cars have in consequence learned to rely more and more on the telephone and on pre-arranged bookings, to cover districts of London outside the central area and to carry passengers further than the top-hat cabs.

A completely different and far less satisfactory situation prevails in most provincial cities in England. The number of taxis that may ply for hire is restricted and fares are controlled. Licensing is often in the hands of municipal transport committees, bodies whose first loyalties are to their buses. The result is a reluctance to issue additional licences and in turn an increase in the value of the licences already in existence. These have to be purchased from a retiring operator by anyone wishing to enter the trade, thereby restricting entry to individuals able to borrow several thousand pounds. Hire cars can be expected to increase in number to fill some of the gaps created by this situation but as they cannot ply for hire, this is likely to be of small comfort to travellers arriving by train and hoping to find a cab waiting at the station. As the following table shows, this problem is serious in Manchester and Liverpool and judging by the very large number of residents per taxi may be much worse in Birmingham. In Newcastle upon Tyne, on the other hand, where the taxi fleet was allowed to grow the market value of a licence was only £500 in 1970.

City	Residents per taxi	Taxis	Cost of Licence 1971
Birmingham	6,000	175	not known
Liverpool	2,500	300	£2,000/2,500
Manchester (and Salford)	2,300	384	£3,000
Newcastle upon Tyne	1,800	not known	£500
London	800	10,000	—

(The figures are Michael Beesley's)

Taxis and hire cars are obviously a boon to those without their own transport. Another advantage is that one public car can do the work of many private cars in the course of a day, thereby reducing the space devoted to parking. This emerges from some facts gathered in London by the Stamp Committee. They found that a top-hat taxi makes on average twenty-two trips a day and carries thirty-three people and covers eighty-four miles and that the average hire car, large limousines excluded, does nine jobs and covers one hundred and five miles. The average private car, on the other hand, carries only six persons a day and is driven only twenty miles. For the rest of the time it just sits around, getting in the way.

Some awareness of the merits of taxis and hire cars has begun to emerge in the last few years. The first sign was when taxis in Paris and London were allowed to use lanes of roads and whole streets otherwise reserved for buses. This is a precedent of some importance. It demonstrates a recognition that taxis are more important than cars and that more than one standard of public transport is necessary in cities. Kungsgatan in Stockholm exemplifies this new thinking but it has parallels in cities in several countries. This Swedish street is in the middle of the city, it is lined with shops and abuts a large pedestrian mall. Closing it to traffic was impractical because numerous buses used it. Yet something needed to be done to provide more room for pedestrians and to reduce the dominance of traffic. An answer was found in widened pavements and a ban on all vehicles except buses and taxis.

Privileges have been conferred on taxis in other ways in Munich and Rome. In the Bavarian capital, cab ranks have been located at points round the great central precinct where they are convenient for people who want to go to other parts of the city. Parking for cars is in all cases further away. (More surprisingly, the same arrangement can be found in the little cathedral town of Hereford on the borders of England and Wales. Just as much as in vast Munich, greater use of a small fleet of taxis in such little places could release space wasted on parking for private cars.) In Rome, certain small shopping streets near the Corso are reserved for people on foot and taxis. Not many cabs use them so they are generally peaceful; nevertheless, anyone collecting a wedding dress from one of the fashion houses or needing to be taken home because they are sick can be picked up at the door. Most cities have streets suited to this kind of treatment. Jermyn Street and Beauchamp Place in London are typical. Both are lined by luxury shops with dazzling windows. At present they are cluttered up with parked cars and inconvenient both for people on foot and taxis. Widening their pavements and confining access to taxis would almost certainly benefit the shops and demonstrate that public rather than private cars are appropriate in certain places.

On first sight it may seem revolutionary to exclude cars from inner cities and to rely instead on buses, taxis and hired cars but things have evolved in that direction by themselves. Already taxis account for twenty-two per cent of all traffic circulating in the Loop, or central business district, of Chicago. (It gets its name from a loop of elevated railway of Piranesian proportions and gloom.)

Circumstances in London appear remarkably similar. In the central area taxis make up fifteen per cent of all traffic but within Mayfair, the heart of the West End, they account for between thirty and forty per cent of it. Idiotically, a large part of their usefulness is lost through having to proceed at a snail's pace. One measure of how much productivity is lost emerged from the cab drivers' strike in 1966 which allowed the speed of the remaining vehicles to increase by between forty-four and seventy-eight per cent, depending on the time of day. It may seem Irish to use data gathered during a taxi strike to make a case for taxis, but the figures show with startling clarity the benefits of getting rid of some vehicles. Wipe out a corresponding number of private cars and the benefits would flow to users of buses and taxis. There must be some danger that the taximen would take advantage of any monopoly granted to them and push fares to exorbitant levels but it appears small. Sufficient of their customers could use buses, undergrounds, bicycles, mopeds and telephones for it to be a risky move. Strikes over regulated fares are a more real danger but in London's case the Home Office has since 1966, acknowledged that rising costs must be promptly covered by increases in revenues.

As a general rule privileges should not be granted without payment and there seems no reason why taxis should be an exception. At present they are at best no noisier and fumier than other cars; at worst they are powered by hammering diesels as noisy as three-ton trucks. Any measures to give them special rights of access should therefore be accompanied by others to reduce their emissions. Noise from older vehicles can be muffled by fitting hush kits (see p. 171). New vehicles should be obliged to conform to emission standards more severe than those for ordinary cars. Some information about air pollution in Chicago's Loop may help to explain why. As much muck from vehicles and heating flues is poured into the air there in two days (in technical language 'the emissions load per square metre') as in 365 days averaged over the country as a whole. Improving the quality of the air in places where people and vehicles are thickest on the ground is therefore a first priority and concentrating on intensively-used vehicles such as taxis is an effective low-cost way of doing it.

So far I have concentrated on the taxis we are all familiar with and on ways to get greater use from them. I have also suggested that they are a key to limiting the use of private cars in cities. What are the prospects for this? Far more is certain to be involved than quiet taxis with privileges to enter parts of city centres that are out-of-bounds to cars; far more even than unrestricted freedom for taxis to multiply.

Wilfred Owen of the Brookings Institution in Washington looked at this question in a paper on cars in developing countries for the Organisation for Economic Co-operation and Development. One point to emerge is the extent that public transport is already based on cars and other small vehicles in the Third World. Of course buses are in use too but where they are organised on a large scale as municipal concerns, they appear again and again to be outclassed by the compact vehicles run by their more adaptable and smaller rivals. The success of five-to-fourteen seat urban transport is thus as much a matter of organisation as technology but the two are closely interwoven. Owen illustrates this with facts gathered in Teheran, the capital of a country which the Shah of Iran promises will be in the same industrial league as Britain, France and Germany within twenty years. Public transport in Teheran is in three parts: a fleet of 1,655 buses which carry 700 million passengers a year; 11,000 taxis which carry 290 million passengers; and 2,000 so-called collective taxis that carry 100 million people a year.

Owen draws particular attention to the collective or 'jitney' taxis, consisting of large American saloon cars running, like buses, on fixed routes. 'Jitney' was an American nickname for the nickel or five-cent piece at the time of the First World War. As it was also the fare for the original shared taxis in the United States the name got transferred to them. Anyone who has visited the cities of the Middle East, Latin America or Mexico will be familiar with other names for this ubiquitous form of transport: *dolmus* in Istanbul, *collectivos* in Rio de Janeiro and *service taxis* in Mexico City. In some cases the cars have signboards that indicate where they are going; in others the townspeople just seem to know the routes that are covered and have obviously acquired this knowledge by question and experience. One of my favourite memories of jitneys comes from Ankara, a city I explored in my twenties. I had not been there long before my eye was caught by the much-chromiumed Chevrolets and Plymouths that patrolled the main avenues of the city, sometimes speeding along but on occasions loitering so as to enable the driver to give what to me, with two years' National Service behind me, could only be interpreted as a hand signal to all and sundry to fuck off. Later I learned they were driving jitneys and had two seats to fill.

In Teheran Owen found that the patronage of collective taxis had increased five times faster than that of conventional taxis in the five years up to 1972, a period that saw the use of buses decline by half. He therefore considered the effect of substituting an enlarged fleet of the successful jitneys for the dying buses and found that an increase in the jitney fleet from 2,000 to 14,000 would do the job. But what about congestion? Needless to say all the streets of Teheran are already busy and jams common during rush hours. The addition of 10,000 jitneys could therefore be expected to make things even worse. Owen's answer was to look more closely at the city's 160,000 private cars. Why not see what would happen if the users of all those cars went by collective taxi? On the assumption that each car was carrying six people a day and that each jitney could carry one hundred, he estimated the big switch could be handled by 10,000 more jitneys.

The outcome of the exercise is that a city such as Teheran, with a population of three million, could be supported by a system of 35,000 collective and individual taxis or about one-fifth of the vehicles now involved in carrying people. Reductions, in some cases dramatic ones, would follow, in the space needed for highways and parking, in congestion and fuel consumption and the scale of investment required to keep the city moving. This is not a purely theoretical matter even though I have outlined it in theoretical terms. Wilfred Owen is a consultant to the World Bank, an organisation that is financing urban transport in developing countries and concerned to find economical solutions. To turn the theoretical into the practical might necessitate providing jitney substitutes for only one-third or one-half of the private cars instead of all of them as implied in the Teheran exercise. The savings in resources and reduced congestion would still be enormous and they are there to be grasped as much by richer countries as by poorer ones.

Fixed route taxis are rare but not unknown in Europe and North America. Two services were found by the Stamp Committee in Paris, both linking terminals of the Metro at the nineteenth-century gates of the city to fashionable residential districts further out. The Committee also found that all the *portes* had once been so served.

In the United States jitneys can still be found in Atlantic City, New Jersey and running along Mission Street in San Francisco but, as in Paris, today's services are a shadow of those of the past. The grandfather of them all is believed to have been a Model-T Ford that began to cruise along a main road in Los Angeles in 1914 and to steal away passengers from street cars (trams) running out towards Long Beach. The idea caught on famously, being taken up by men laid off other jobs during the depression that accompanied the opening stages of the war, and within a couple of years 62,000 jitneys were cruising through cities all over the country. A trade journal called *The Jitney Bus* was founded as early as March 1915.

It was a short-lived blossoming. The seeds of the jitney's doom had been sown even by that pioneering Model-T in Los Angeles. The powerful electric street-car industry was determined not to lose passengers to its young rubber-tyred rivals. Anti-jitney ordinances were passed in city after city and the monopoly of the street railways was re-established. *The Jitney Bus* prudently renamed itself *The Motor Bus*. The monopoly of the tramways is now only history but it lives on in the defensive apparatus of ordinances built up against the jitneys. They are still enforceable by latterday transit operators and Arthur Saltzman writing in *Technology Review*, July/August 1973 (a Massachusetts Institute of Technology publication) says :

A resurgence of jitney operations cannot take place in the United States unless the restrictive regulations are removed from the law books. Undoubtedly the established transit operators and regulatory agencies would fight to preserve their monopoly. The jitney kind of public transport is still an anathema to most transit operators: the mere mention of jitneys by this author has been known to provoke them to lecture upon their evils.

In the case of Britain, present road traffic regulations preclude jitney services as effectively. Hire cars have no right to solicit custom except by advertising in the papers, by signs on buildings, popping little cards through letter boxes and other indirect means. Hackney cabs are equally hamstrung. They are not licensed to give rides to *ad hoc* groups, nor are their fare scales or taxi meters geared to being paid by several persons. And if a minibus owner applied to the traffic commissioners to run such a service he would be opposed by the bus companies already operating stage services on the same route or near it. At one time there was hope that a new Road Traffic Act would be passed in 1974 that would sweep away the gamut of antiquated regulations that stand in the way of innovations in road passenger services. As it turned out the Government bowed to pressure and limited the effects of the Bill to part-time minibus operators in country districts. But even these relaxations failed to survive when the Bill lapsed at the dissolution of Parliament in March 1974.

Needless to say, a battle went on behind the scenes in Whitehall over the drafting of even these limited concessions. The economists, as might be expected, were for removing controls and regulations in order to allow new operators offering new kinds of services to get into the market. The established national and municipal bus companies, equally predictably, feared that they would lose some of their passengers and painted terrifying pictures of the financial and institutional collapse that would occur if this was allowed to happen. They also argued that the labour to man services based on smaller vehicles would not be available, citing as evidence their own difficulties in getting staff.

Who is right and who is wrong? The expansion of the London

taxi trade and the growth of the hire car business everywhere
suggests that the busmen are not necessarily correct about labour.
Labour is available if the terms of employment are right. The
bus companies find recruitment difficult, not only because the
jobs they offer are arduous and the pay moderate but because the
work is out of tune with the expectations of younger people. There
is no independence, little scope for enterprise and none of the
tax advantages of self-employment. There are also the obstacles
to part-time work identified by Michael Beesley.

However, this whole argument leans much too far in the direction of official thinking in assuming that bus and taxi operators
of all kinds must inevitably find themselves struggling with congested roads and squabbling over a dwindling number of passengers like starving men competing for a few miserable crusts.

A different prospect emerges if one assumes that, an improved
and widened array of public transport services is promoted in
conjunction with limitations on the use of cars. This would provide plenty of scope for buses as well as jitneys. Buses with their
large capacities would serve busy, radial routes at all times but
work some others only at rush hours. Jitneys, minibuses and dial-
a-ride services would cover the more lightly-travelled, criss-cross
routes, the night hours, and cater for travellers willing to pay
more for a faster and more personal service at all times and on
all routes. Drivers might go from one kind of vehicle to another
in the course of a day.

It is necessary to go back and look again at Teheran in order
to understand how jitneys, like the dial-a-ride minibuses described earlier, could play an important role in our cities. Teheran
is a loose-knit and sprawling place, a Los Angeles on the cheap,
and like it or not so are the suburbs of all western cities. Modern
European suburbs are more tight-packed than those in California
but they in no way resemble the streets of two- and three-storey,
brick-built houses that grew up around the tram lines and urban
railways of nineteenth-century western cities. Jitneys are attuned
to the urban terrain of the twentieth century. They can cross it
speedily, stopping exactly where their riders want them to. A

bus doing the same trip would stop about four times a mile. The good service offered by jitneys, coupled with their low overheads and, in developing countries, the economy of using sweated labour, account for their popularity and their low cost.

Establishing the probable costs of riding by jitney in a European or American city, assuming that labour would not be sweated, is fraught with difficulties. Much would depend on the level of patronage. This would in turn be influenced by the extent of limitations on using private cars. Fares would undoubtedly lie between those of buses and taxis and might vary with the time of day. Experience in Hong Kong, where wages are low, is that a five pence bus fare would cost between seven and fifteen pence by jitney.

Experiments conducted first on a single route and then throughout a sector of a large town are needed to replace speculation by fact. Nottingham would be a suitable place since the jitneys could operate along routes where the use of private cars is to be limited by traffic collars. Assuming that the shared cars were painted uniformly and brightly, or had some other distinctive marking, they could be given the same privileges as buses without creating problems of enforcement. Any risk of the jitneys capsizing the finances of the buses could be eliminated by combining the introduction of the shared taxi services with increases in parking charges in the city centre.

All debate about the potential of jitney cabs and the exact form that their services would take in cities where they are unknown is bound to be cloaked in ignorance until experience is built up. It could turn out that fourteen-seat, light buses of the kind found in Hong Kong or that five-seat public cars as used in Teheran would be better. It could be that jitneys are really only needed at rush hours and that at other times they should offer taxi or dial-a-ride service.

Answers to these questions are badly needed. Taxis and jitneys are among the more promising forms of future passenger transport. Jitneys, in particular, are an alternative to private cars that does not involve packing people wholesale into buses and trams.

(As Americans put it, they take the 'mass' out of mass transit.) They are suited to the loose-knit layout of suburbs and the patterns of movement in them. They are a way to save both fuel and land and, last but by no means least, they can be got into service quickly and inexpensively.

This is a tremendous list of advantages and it explains why shared taxis are so much used in developing countries. Obstructive and obsolete regulations prevent their playing any role in Western countries. The laws may be intended to protect bus services but their main effect is to eliminate a genuine rival to private cars.

Central government in Britain should commission a handbook on jitney services, suspend the obstructive provisions of the Road Traffic Acts and offer financial assistance to local authorities interested in promoting experiments.

10 Gee-Whizz Technology

Every now and then a new technology is born that makes a big difference. Someone puts a flanged wheel on a rail, kicks an internal combustion engine into life or switches on the apparatus necessary to send a first, flickering telephone message. The trouble is that ideas of this sort come up all the time and it takes a seer to tell the winners from the losers. How many people, for instance, would have said in 1900 that the petrol driven car was going to vanquish the steam and battery-powered models that at that time seemed equally promising as successors to the horse?

In the event, the various contenders fought it out in the market place and we all know which won. We do not know, however, how much weight to attach to the strength and drive of individuals such as Henry Ford and the Duryea brothers. Is it possible that if one or other of them had gone into steam the history of the motor car might have been quite different?

Today we may be on the doorstep of yet another era in the history of transport as important as that ushered in by say, the first canal or Herr Benz's pioneering horseless carriage. The technology this time consists of car-like cabins running under electronic control on elevated tracks criss-crossing entire city regions. It is an idea that was conceived out of the frustrations of mass motoring; its sire is the taxi and its dam the computer. If someone with sufficient determination takes it up, this form of transport could be a reality in dozens of cities in as little as fifteen years.

Europeans tend to focus on the physical characteristics of the new transport concept. Thus in Britain it has been labelled auto-taxi and cab-track, while the Swedes call it *spartaxi* (rail taxi) and the Germans *cabinentaxi.* The Americans, on the other hand, are more concerned with the kind of service that would result and use the label 'personal rapid transit' or PRT for small-cabin systems and 'group rapid transit' or GRT for ones with vehicles big enough for twelve or more passengers. Serious study began to be given to this breed of technology in the mid-1960s. It was pioneered in Britain by Leslie Blake, a visionary engineer at Brush Electrical Engineering, a Hawker Siddeley subsidiary. Following a swords-into-ploughshares shake-up in government research, his project was taken up by a Transport Research Assessment Group based on the then Road Research Laboratory at Crowthorne, Berkshire, and a detailed technical report on it was published by the Royal Aircraft Establishment in 1968. Since then the project has gone through several vicissitudes but work is continuing on a group transit system called minitram. The Advanced Systems Division of the since renamed Transport and Road Research Laboratory is in charge of the project.

In the United States automatic transit first obtained respectability from a series of reports and studies commissioned by the Department of Housing and Urban Development in Washington during the Johnson Administration. One was a lucid general discussion called *Tomorrow's Transportation* published by the Federal Government in 1968. One of the other studies included a cost-benefit assessment of various forms of transport that considered not just speed and cheapness but air pollution, 'the intrusion of automobiles into the city', accessibility to 'key areas' and the mobility of ghetto residents. The outcome was a proposal for a four-hundred-mile small cabin system for Boston. This research was done by General Dynamics Corporation and was published in *Scientific American* in July 1969 as 'Systems Analysis of Urban Transportation'.

Since then driverless vehicles have moved out of the laboratory and begun to appear in an early, experimental form. Leading engineering companies such as Boeing Airplane and Otis Elevator in the United States, Messerschmitt Bölkow Blohm, Krauss Maffei and Siemens in Germany, Société Matra in France and Hawker Siddeley in Britain have moved into the field. In Japan the Ministry of International Trade and Industry and the Society for the Promotion of Machine Industry are involved.

The term horizontal elevator is sometimes used to describe the new technology and it helps to convey the idea that the cabins are without drivers and that doors in both cab and station wall open simultaneously when they arrive at stops. However this is of only secondary importance. The systems I intend to focus on in this chapter have vehicles that are distinguished by their ability to share guideways, to negotiate their way through webs of routes and steer off into side-tracks when they need to stop, leaving other cabins to pass by unhindered to other destinations. The result is a much higher level of throughput and a much better level of service from a single track than is possible with systems in which the vehicles stop on the main line and block everything coming up behind. In fact transport systems of this kind are automatic highways. Intervals between vehicles may be as little as a few seconds or even fractions of a second and, as on roads, a journey involves a continuous sequence of points of converging and diverging traffic, where life or death decisions must be taken if crashes are to be avoided. This is where computers come in. Hierarchies of them are programmed with logical sets of instructions that enable decisions ordinarily made by drivers to be taken automatically.

But hold on : I am getting carried away! The sheer excitement of streets and cars that work without drivers invariably sends one's mind racing along pure technological avenues. One must first of all ask whether such hardware is worth having and look at the assumptions underlying it. This means considering the climate of opinion about cars and highways in the mid-1960s and looking at the early literature of personal rapid transit.

A good source is the article in *Scientific American* already mentioned on p. 200. In a concluding section Hamilton and Nance, the co-authors say :

In general, the results of our analysis make clear that, even with the most optimistic view of what might be achieved through improvement of the existing methods of transportation, such improvement could not satisfy the real needs of our cities in terms of service. Automobiles, even if totally redesigned for safety and smog-free steam propulsion, have the irremediable drawbacks that they must be driven by the user and are unavailable to a substantial percentage of the population. Buses and trains, however fast, comfortable and well scheduled, are unavoidably limited in average speed by the necessity of making frequent stops along the line to let riders on or off. All in all, our study suggested strongly that the course of gradualism is not enough : at best it is merely an expensive palliative for the transportation ailments of the cities.

On the other hand, our tests of the new-technology approach, particularly the personal-transit type of system, showed that it could provide really dramatic improvements in service. The personal-transit system would offer city dwellers a degree of convenience that is not now available even to those who drive their own cars. The city and its suburbs could be linked together in a way that would bring new freedoms and amenities to urban living—for the ghetto dweller now trapped in the city's deteriorating core as well as for the automobile-enslaved suburban housewife.

It is an eloquent case. The car is assumed to have set new standards that cannot be ignored. Social justice is prominently considered. The physical nuisances of cars are dealt with. If the paper was being drafted today it would no doubt argue the advantages of light-weight, congestion-free automatic cars from an energy conservation point of view as well.

Nevertheless, something of a reaction against the new technology has set in during the last few years. 'Transpo '72', an exhibition promoted by the Department of Transportation at Washington, was a turning point. Three contractors displayed systems that they talked about as personal rapid transit, but as someone pointed out, they would have been more correct in saying they had reinvented the tram. The jibe was far from being the whole truth but neither was it a complete misrepresentation and it was much quoted. Since then the label of group rapid transit has been coined to take the PR out of PRT. It was needed because it succeeds in portraying the new concept as an improvement on mass transit, with its cattle truck reputation, while not exaggerating the degree of personal service offered.

The change in title also symbolises a shift in opinion about what is likely to be practical in the first generation of automatic transit systems. Consideration of costs, of the safety of complex control systems and of inserting overhead guideways and their stations into standing cities has led to a withdrawal from the early objective of providing lines at every fourth or fifth street with stopping places at every four or five hundred yards. The systems on which most work is now concentrated involve vehicles for six, twelve and even more passengers but with off-line stops. Even this will mean a tremendous improvement in service over existing forms of public transport, and assuming such group transit systems are a success, they may well evolve towards full personal rapid transit in the 1980s and 1990s. Such a progression would involve no more than pushing out spurs, adding further off-line stopping points, introducing taxi-sized cabins and souping up the electronic controls. Vehicles of different sizes might even be mixed together. A further possibility which came up in the discussion of dial-a-ride is that group transit vehicles might be designed to run on ordinary streets with drivers and on guideways without them.

In the meantime the construction of networks with a coarse 'weave' means that many passengers will need to go by bicycle, bus or car to their nearest group transit stop. This will tend to deter some potential travellers, though the ability of the new systems to pass close to or through large hotels, office buildings, railway station and airport concourses and university precincts will win back others who would have to leave their cars at remote parking places.

So far the most authoritative cost estimates for group transit came from Denver where the voters gave their blessing to a transportation plan embracing nearly one hundred miles of routes

204

in September 1973. This was costed by the Regional Transportation District to work out at ten million dollars a mile complete with vehicles and stations.

At about the same time the Transport and Road Research Laboratory estimated that the cost of a small cabin system operating on a dense city centre network would be £1,250,000 a mile and in Germany the Demag-Messerschmitt consortium quoted a figure of 8 million marks (£1,066,000) a mile for their version of personal transit. These costs are not really comparable since the technologies they are based on differ in important ways but they make clear that group and personal transit systems are likely to be less costly than undergrounds but more expensive than buses and trams running on cleared ways in existing streets.

Costs of this order promise to confine investment in a first generation of driverless transit systems to corridors with considerable flows of movement along them and to a kind of service in which passengers are offered shared rides with perhaps twelve or fifteen others at busy times and cabins to themselves only at slack ones. This makes sense from an economic and resource point of view but it also means that people will be able to travel alone or in chosen groups at times when privacy is most desirable. Thus commuters will share cabins that will probably provide a stopping service but loving couples or nervous individuals who are travelling in the evening will be able to buy tickets and organise their riding to guarantee that their cabs do not stop anywhere between the start and the finish of their journeys. This is at any rate how thinking has evolved in the United States and it is the basis of the Denver plan. It is the old story of the Americans taking a theoretical idea, banging it around to make it serviceable and putting it on the market as a working proposition while everyone else is still dreaming.

American leadership in this field may, however, be challenged by the Germans whose reputation for daring innovation in transport is second to none. (Did they not perfect the first car? Did not the Third Reich bring the idea of the autobahn to its full maturity thirty years before any other country in Europe took such roads seriously? And what about Werner von Braun's rockets?) Given this tradition it is possible that the Germans will leap-frog group transit and plunge directly into systems offering personal service over closely woven networks of routes. The Federal Government is already sponsoring development work, three major firms are poised to go ahead and the Demag-Messerschmitt group have their little cabin-taxis running on an impressive test track at Hagen in the Ruhr.

The case for small cabin systems with many stops was argued by Brian Grant of the Transport and Road Research Laboratory at a University of Warwick conference in 1973.

The quest for radically improved public transport systems has logically led to increasing interest in the use of driverless vehicles which must of course traverse their own segregated tracks. The object is not simply to save the cost of the crew in a conventional vehicle (which can be more than 50 per cent of running costs): if they are driverless, vehicles can be of smaller capacity and run more frequently for the same running cost and yet maintain adequate line capacity. We can have smaller and cheaper stations, and more of them while decreasing vehicle weight and mileage per passenger. The labour content of the system will be low—and most important—practically independent of rush-hour loading. It should also be more economic to maintain an attractive off-peak service frequency. (*Advanced Transport Systems in British Cities: Urban Transport Research Group Symposium*, University of Warwick 1973.)

Further light is thrown on the same subject by the results of a study of personal transit in Hagen done by Demag-Messerschmitt. The town has a population of 140,000 now but is growing fast and is expected to reach 400,000 by the end of the century. Investment in some form of public transport is therefore bound to be necessary. One possibility examined by Professor Grabbe of Hanover Technical University is buses running on a network of busways and highways but they were found to be capable of attracting only about twenty per cent of commuters and to necessitate a complementary system of motorways. An eighty-mile network of cabin-taxi lines serving one hundred and eighty-two stops, on the other hand, was found to attract sixty-two per cent of all rush hour trips and forty-seven per cent of all other journeys. Such a personal transit system would cost 900,000,000 marks (£120,000,000), but as Demag-Messerschmitt are quick to point out, the investment would not only provide excellent public transport for the car-less but permit far less to be spent on highways than with other forms of public transport.

Needless to say, the figures for the attractiveness of various forms of public transport need to be viewed with the same scepticism as those in any transport study. Hidden behind them are all sorts of assumptions about parking, congestion, the cost of travel and the value of time. Still, they help to illustrate the point that people are likely to make more use of a form of public transport that comes to within a few hundred yards of their front doors, goes anywhere and involves little or no waiting, than of other less convenient systems. Whether the community cares to spend so much to provide such a good service is another matter and one that is being hotly argued in Germany.

Back in Denver the pros and cons of different forms of automatic transport have been debated for a couple of years and it has been decided to provide something that is more akin to a driverless bus service than driverless taxis. With this in mind a hundred and fifteen extra buses are being bought to improve traditional transit in the period up to the commissioning of its successor. And when group transit does start up the buses will be switched to feeding it or serving other less densely travelled routes.

This is an important pointer to the way in which other towns might move from buses to the new technology. Most places with a population of 100,000 or more have one or two bus routes that are very intensely used and which may be candidates for automatic transport. Even in a town such as Reading, for instance, which has a population of 132,000 there is an east-west flow of movement that necessitates a high-frequency double-decker bus service throughout the day. Furthermore this flow is bound to intensify as new housing estates are built to the west. Nottingham's free city-centre bus loop with its hundred thousand passengers a week exemplifies a different kind of opportunity but one that the Transport and Road Research Laboratory is keen to demonstrate can be handled by minitrams, its version of group transit. With this in mind the Laboratory has studied the potential of central Southampton and is now concentrating on Sheffield. The cost of moving into the era of automatic city transport becomes much less daunting when looked at in this way. A city, instead of investing hundreds of millions of pounds in an extensive network might spend ten million over several years replacing one or two of its bus routes with minitrams and avoiding investment in highways.

Automatic transport seems almost certain to catch on in the United States. Public opinion is ready for it. The engineering industry is itching to get in on the urban transport market. And, most important of all, the 1973 Federal Highway Act provides the beginnings of a flow of finance. The Act for the first time released highway taxes for public transport, raised the Federal contribution to urban transit projects from two-thirds to four-fifths and allowed the cities to switch funds from unwanted highway schemes to transit. Subsequent legislation, spurred on by the energy shortage, is certain to move further in the same direction.

In a previous chapter I referred to the experimental group transit installation at Morgantown, West Virginia and to the system at Dallas–Fort Worth Airport. Both have stations that are off the main lines and are able to offer services tailored to groups and individuals. Both are operational too and are therefore useful sources of information.

Morgantown, which is on the way to having three and a half miles of line, six stations and forty-five vehicles, will probably go down in history as the Stockton and Darlington of automatic city transport. It is a nondescript little town mixed up with a straggling university with hordes of students going to and fro between classes several times a day and a professor of industrial engineering who not only managed to get Washington's ear but $70,000,000 of its money as well.

Far more people are likely to see and use the pioneering system at Dallas–Fort Worth Airport. It started up at the beginning of 1974 and carries passengers and their baggage between a hotel, various car parks and other parts of the giant Texas airport. Twelve and a half miles of track used by sixty-eight rubber-tyred vehicles and punctuated by fifty-one off-line stopping places loop through this Mecca of technics. Most of the cars have room for sixteen seated and twenty-four standing passengers but some are specially designed to handle cargo or airport rubbish.

So much for exceptional installations contrived by wizard professors and technomaniac airport managers. Neither had to persuade electorates to tax themselves for the privilege of riding about in driverless vehicles. This is what makes the Denver plan important. The citizens there voted yes to a proposal for a ninety-eight mile group transit system with sixty-eight stations that is estimated to cost $1,600,000,000 and to take until 1983 to complete. This will cost them a half-cent sales tax, though it is expected that Washington will finance the greater part of the project. The good people of Denver, it should be added, own more cars per head than the citizens of any other major city in the United States including Los Angeles. They also suffer very nasty smog.

The Denver network will be elevated for most of its length but will dip into tunnels for over three miles to get through the city centre. Passengers will ride in groups of up to twelve in eight hundred cabins that will travel at a top speed of forty miles an hour. This will give the system a capacity of six thousand people an hour in a single direction, the equivalent of a three-lane freeway. Arrangements for bus-and-ride, park-and-ride and kiss-and-ride will be made at as many stations as possible.

Safety and security of passengers are confidently discussed by the Denver Regional Transportation District and stress laid

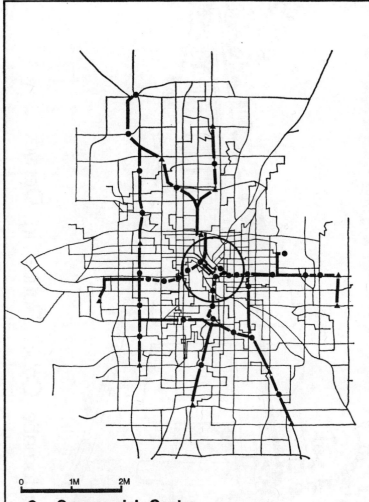

0	1M	2M

○ **Commercial Centre**

— **Routes for Automatic Cabins**

• **Station**

▲ **Station with Park and Ride Facilities**

— **Local and Express Bus Routes**

Future Public Transport in Denver

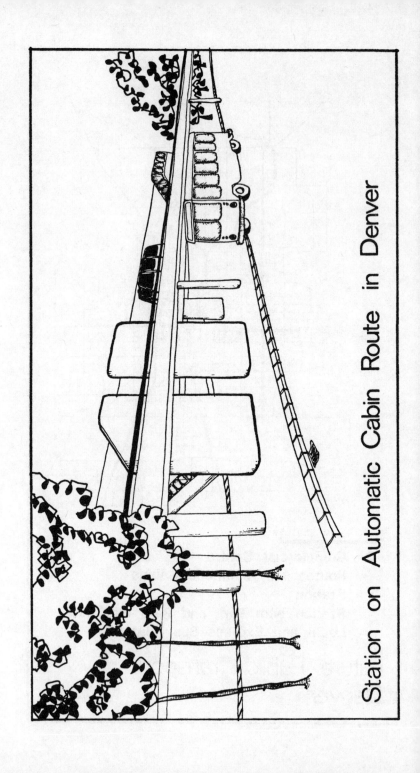

Station on Automatic Cabin Route in Denver

on the presence of an attendant at every station with a mixture of windows and TV monitors giving him a view of all parts of it. This is in notable contrast to the unmanned stations envisaged at Lille. Passengers in Denver are also promised two-way communication with the control centre.

Financial forecasts made on the basis of a thirty-five-cent average fare show an operating deficit of $7,000,000 in 1978/9 changing to a surplus of $11,000,000 in 1985 and of $16,000,000 in 1990. By that time income from group transit is expected to be offsetting losses on the buses and could be paying off the capital cost of the system. The high cost of maintaining electronic equipment of exceptional complexity on the BART subway makes it necessary to treat these figures with caution. On the other hand, it is increasingly clear that lack of federal financial support for BART in its early stages led to penny pinching that is only now coming to light.

I have said nothing so far about the land-saving implications of driverless transport but it could take two forms. Houses may be clustered around stops, as is envisaged along the magnetically supported 'Go Urban' system in Toronto. Or, with the prospect of people arriving at shopping centres, hotels or offices by transit rather than by car, the opportunity can be taken to cut back on parking space. Ford of America, of all institutions, is working on the second assumption at Fairlane, ten miles from the centre of Detroit, where the automobile men have turned property developers and are planning to link a group of large buildings by driverless transport. The company is developing a system of its own for which several applications are being investigated.

Fairlane is a suburban nowhere with a shopping centre, Ford's headquarters, other blocks of offices and a hotel, either planned or thrown down with the negligence of confetti in the midst of a desert of highways and 'spaghetti junctions'. According to the drive-in rule book each one of the buildings would be surrounded by a car park big enough to serve peak demand and too big the rest of the time. The property men recognised this as wasteful and propose to link all the buildings by a transit system so that the shopping centre car park, which is used to the full only on Saturdays, may be used by people working at the offices on week days and vice versa.

Ford's calculations show that this sharing will make it possible to eliminate five thousand parking spaces from a site about a mile square and devote the freed land to other more profitable uses. It is a pity Henry Ford did not come to this conclusion fifty years ago.

Work with driverless transport systems has been fraught with difficulty in Britain but Brian Grant of the Transport and Road Research Laboratory has quietly nursed the Laboratory's original project for 'cab-track' or automatic taxis into a proposal for 'minitrams' big enough for about twelve people and two prams. The evolution can be followed through a report called *An Aid to Pedestrian Movement* published by the City of Westminster in 1971 to another entitled *Opportunities in Automated Urban Transport*, issued by the Laboratory in 1973, which identifies Sheffield as a possible location for an experiment. Minitram, as at present conceived, involves overhead tracks smaller in scale than those of other group transit systems. The supporting columns have been trimmed to a minimum too. The result is a far cry from the titanic ironwork of turn-of-the-century systems such as the Chicago El and the Wuppertal monorail, and also from the massive concrete stilts at Lille and Morgantown. Such lumpish structures do not just affront the eyes, they are expensive too. At Morgantown they formed sixty per cent of the cost of the system.

The sensitivity to aesthetics shown by the Transport and Road Research Laboratory is necessary in a country where appearances are often all important, yet some critics of minitram think viaducts are unacceptable in any form in city centres. They look upon automatic transport as just another chapter in a long history of technomania and foresee travellers on overhead systems leering lasciviously into the bedroom windows of nearby houses, no doubt exposing themselves the while. A photomontage of a guideway passing over the heads of pedestrians in a traffic-free shopping street in Sheffield shows something that tends to be overlooked. Elevated public transport could make it possible to sweep cars and buses out of many city-centre streets to an unprecedented extent, thus freeing space for people on foot. This is a worthwhile gain particularly if it is associated with round-the-clock, high-frequency, public transport. However, it is a gain that needs to be set alongside the effect on the scene of overhead stations, which are bound to be far more unobtrusive than their associated guideways. Out in the suburbs these complications need not arise, since the vehicles could in many places run along the ground in fenced-in cuttings.

Trying to decide whether automatic group transit is a good buy raises complex issues. On the assumption that the main competition is buses in busways, it is necessary to juggle with capital costs (higher for minitrams), running costs (lower for minitrams), and levels of service (minitrams can run twenty-four hours a day and could be expected to attract more passengers including car users). And just to add further complexity, there is the possibility of starting off by building segregated ways for buses at a cost of about £400,000 a mile and of converting them to use by minitrams, with overhead guideways where appropriate, as patronage builds up.

Very little is known about these possibilities in Britain. The Transport and Road Research Laboratory, which is an arm of the Civil Service, is technocratic in style and bureaucratic in its cautiousness. Discussion of the prospects for the new technology has therefore been confined to the pages of a few technical journals and particularly the architectural press.

This is in marked contrast to the situation in Denver where the remit of the Regional Transportation District, which was set up in 1969, was to obtain acceptance for a transport plan by 1974 or dissolve itself. This remarkable get-on-or-get-out political style obliged the transport experts to leave their offices, explain to the community what was technically possible and then put together a package that would stand the test of the ballot box.

Meetings were held, the interest of the business community was curried, a newsletter was published, the media were cultivated and children were invited to design stations for the transit system, all in the pursuit of this two-way educational process. Cynics may sneer that the voters were hoodwinked by a skilfully conducted public relations exercise but they need to explain why participatory bally-hoo has failed to win support for less promising transport plans in other American cities.

No community in Britain is likely to get a chance to understand what automated transport would mean to them so long as the Transport and Road Research Laboratory remains in sole command of the programme. Worse still, there is every danger that, just as the development of personal transit was killed in Britain because a study was made of it snaking through the narrow streets of Soho and streaking across Regent's Park (it would have been as wise to propose using Westminster Abbey to test double glazing), so minitrams may not survive in Sheffield when the size of the stations comes to light.

Automated overhead transport needs to be looked at first of all in a grotty, semi-industrial suburban context such as the purlieus of London Airport and it needs to be put to the community as part of a plan to reduce traffic in the streets, create pedestrian precincts, turn parking lots into play-grounds and provide greatly improved public transport. The initiative must come from the local authorities, not from some remote arm of central government.

The new technology also needs to be brought out into the open. The Transport and Road Research Laboratory should hold public meetings on it in major cities. Hawker Siddeley and GEC–Marconi, the main industrial groups involved in research and development under government contract, should be told to get out and start selling their wares in order to get some feed-back from potential customers. The Minister of Transport should state his willingness to finance a limited length of test track that is integrated with other forms of public transport. The object would not be to let loose a flurry of overhead transit systems during the 1970s but to lay down some wine that could be drunk in the 1980s. By that time bus services based on priorities over other traffic, as in Nottingham, will be ripe for improvement and the resources to transform the busiest ones should be available. Quiet, fumeless automatic vehicles running overhead, on the ground and in tunnels where appropriate, could by then be exactly what is wanted.

11 The Future of the Car

Cars are a marvellous way of getting about, provided that you have one and the rest of the world does not. Once millions of people have them many trips by car begin to acquire the character of a ride by mass transit. One-way schemes are introduced, no-entry signs go up, turns are forbidden and circuitous bypasses are built—a whole apparatus of external controls is brought into play to canalise the growing floods of traffic and stop it from eroding life itself. At the same time car parks have to be expanded and opportunities for door-to-door travel limited. The balance of advantages then begins to swing back in favour of vehicles that are designed to be shared and to go to the heart of things. We are seeing this going on now. Dial-a-ride, bus-on-busway and shared taxi services that can enter precincts are the new frontier of public transport. The logic of this process is that cars will in future play a smaller role in the transport of individuals than in the past. Other modes of transport will be used more. Telecommunications will play an increasing role. Locations for homes and places of work will begin to be chosen with a view to reducing travel.

This will be an evolutionary process and the speed with which it occurs will vary from place to place, depending on the pressure applied by electorates and the imagination of city councillors. In very few communities will there be a switch from all-car to no-car transport, though this may happen at some holiday resorts. Elsewhere walking, bicycling and public transport will be used more and cars less. The slower the change the greater will be the cost to the community in congestion, pollution and frustration.

Many people may consider that changes of this sort are wishful thinking and that the grip of the motor industry on the imagination of the public and on Treasury officials is too strong. But fatalistic belief in the sanctity of trend forecasts is what got us into our present predicament of having too many cars, and inadequate public transport. It is necessary to shape the future, not to let it be shaped for us by blind forces.

Look what has been achieved by the United States Clean Air Act of 1970. After an initial uproar in Detroit and all sorts of special pleading about the cost of eliminating exhaust poisons, Japanese imagination and hard work provided an inexpensive solution. Exhaust catalysts that transform the muck in the tail pipe before it can coat human lungs may be fitted to cars in the United States for a few years but, because they increase fuel consumption, they will be quickly superseded by 'stratified charge' engines perfected by Honda in Japan. Tests of this new kind of internal combustion engine have established its superiority beyond all doubt. Thus the United States Environmental Protection Agency found that a 1973 eight-cylinder Chevrolet engine, fitted with Honda-designed combustion heads, was able to meet the stringent 1975 Federal Emission Standards without any fuel penalty. Since then Ford and Chrysler have taken out licences to use the Honda patents and General Motors are negotiating for one. European manufacturers are following suit.

The Japanese engineers succeeded in designing a clean engine where others had failed by going back to first principles. They looked into the combustion process, saw that noxious fumes were a by-product of rich fuel-to-air mixtures, and set out to reduce the richness while still keeping an engine that would fire easily. They did so by building little ante-rooms on to the combustion chambers of their engines and adding a third set of inlet valves to them. These additional valves admit small bursts of fuel-rich gas which go off like bombs in their ante-chambers and then rush out into the main chambers where they set off larger volumes of less explosive gas that burns more cleanly because it contains only small amounts of fuel.

An urgent need to reduce fuel consumption is leading to other modifications. In the short term motor manufacturers are stepping up production of economical models while fitting them out with stereo radios, leopard-skin seat covers and other sexy extras. Such frills ensure that buyers still pay what would have been the price of a 2,000 c.c. car even though they go for a model with a 1,500 c.c. engine. Meanwhile new models are being worked on in engineering laboratories from Detroit to Turin and elsewhere that will be marketed as cars like camels that hardly ever need a drink. Putting tigers in tanks is history. The new designs will be fitted with devices to warm up the inlet gases and make them burn more completely and gear ratios set to get more distance from every turn of the engine. Further reductions in fuel consumption will be contrived by paring weight and adopting smooth, wind-cheating profiles. Modifications of this kind will transform cars over a period of about five years, though the changes are bound to be more noticeable in the United States than in Europe. The 2,000-pound European car is already far more economical than its 4,000-pound, ten-miles-to-the-gallon transatlantic counterpart. Even so European car makers may be able to improve the fuel economy of the average family car by up to one-third.

The challenges of clean air legislation and the Arab intervention in the world energy market have been met by the motor industry with horror but adaptability. There have been lay-offs, cuts in production and retoolings but no one expects collapse. The diversification of the car firms into new forms of public transport has also begun. Ford is developing its own driverless minitrams as well as being involved in dial-a-ride; DAF in the Netherlands have become licensees for Krauss-Maffei's 'Transurban' automatic public transport system; and Volvo in Sweden are developing a new kind of electric trolley bus.

These reactions suggest that there is no need for governments to see themselves as the servants of the motor industry. Provided the motormen are given adequate warning of what lies ahead they can be expected to adapt. This opens the way to the most important development of all—a scaling down in the volume and a scaling up in the quality of vehicles produced. Avoidance of a

Europe with over one hundred and fifty million cars by the end of the century makes this essential. The voracious demands of cars for space mean that such a future would be accompanied by as yet unimagined disruption. Countries such as Britain, Holland, Belgium and Germany that are heavily populated and densely urbanised will be the worst affected. Popular holiday regions such as the Mediterranean coast will every summer turn into human hen batteries set in a deep litter of cars. The British are in the unhappy position of having advanced knowledge of these conditions because they are world-leaders in the race towards over-crowding by cars. The British Road Federation was kind enough to point this out in a Press release in 1971 :

Britain world-leader in congestion

Britain's roads are the most crowded in the world according to British Road Federation statistics published today. There are 62·6 cars, goods and public service vehicles for every mile of road, compared with 55·5 in Germany, 56·1 in Italy and 57·3 in the Netherlands. Roads in America (28·6), France (28) and Japan (24·7) are less than half as congested as roads in Britain.

Traffic in Britain has more than doubled since 1958. There are now less than $3\frac{1}{2}$ yards of trunk and principal road, including motorways, for each vehicle in Britain.

Yet trend forecasts produced by the Transport and Road Research Laboratory show that there are now only about half as many cars on the roads as there could be in twenty-five years' time.

Forecasts of vehicles and travel distances in Britain 1971–2010

	Vehicle Fleets		Annual Miles Travelled	
	Cars	All Vehicles	Cars	All Vehicles
1971*	12,100,000	15,400,000	108,700,000,000	137,500,000,000
1980	17,800,000	21,500,000	160,000,000,000	191,100,000,000
1990	22,800,000	26,800,000	204,000,000,000	239,900,000,000
2000	25,900,000	30,200,000	231,800,000,000	271,800,000,000
2010	28,100,000	33,000,000	251,200,000,000	298,700,000,000

* Actual figures.

220

Improvements to public transport and changes in town planning will help to arrest the eruption of this lava of steel but they alone will not be enough. Ways need to be found to make greater use of a much smaller fleet of cars. Fortunately they already exist. They are the sharing of rides on the one hand and the hiring of cars instead of owning them on the other.

Let us look first at the well-established habit of sharing rides. Facts about the numbers of people using cars for various kinds of trips in the United States suggest that journeys to work and shop offer the most, and holiday trips and pleasure drives the least, scope for it.

The occupancy of cars for trips with different purposes in the United States, 1971

Purpose of travel	Percentage of travel	Average number of riders in car
To and from work	34·1	1·4
Business	8·0	1·6
Shopping and other family business	19·6	2·0
Education, church or civic affairs	5·0	2·5
Holidays	2·5	3·3
Other social and recreational trips	30·8	2·5
All	100·0	1·9

Conditions in European countries may be somewhat different because commuting by public transport is more common but there is little doubt that the potential for sharing is still great. In French towns, for instance, only six out of every hundred trips by car are made with one or two passengers. The driver is alone on all the others. As conditions were almost identical in Stockholm in 1971, it looks as though passenger carrying of this order is a general rule.

The promotion of sharing is still in its infancy but privileges for cars full of people and arrangements for bringing potential sharers together are thought to be the right recipe. An experiment aimed at increasing the occupancy of cars crossing the San Francisco Bay Bridge above its very low normal level of 1·2 persons was designed on this basis. The bridge authority started off by announcing its plan to reserve three lanes for cars holding three or more persons and by issuing reply-paid post cards to users of the bridge, inviting them to send in details of their commuting trips. The information was then sorted by computer and groups of respondents with similar pathways were sent the names and addresses of one another. They were further encouraged to get together by the offer of toll-free crossings and a saving of about ten minutes through not having to queue to buy a ticket or throw a coin in a basket. The experiment successfully attracted groups of riders and hit the headlines when someone was observed crossing with a car full of immaculately dressed store-window mannequins.

Inducements to share can be introduced on highways and parking places at any point where different classes of vehicles can be physically segregated or charged different rates. Thus in Los Angeles it is proposed to admit cars full of riders to a busway being built along the San Bernadino freeway. In Nottingham shared cars could be allowed to use the bus-only lanes that will bypass points of planned congestion, though there could be problems of enforcement. It might be easier to give cars full of passengers privileges to park or to park cheaply at places where cars with only one occupant were either banned or charged a high rate. Supplementary licences that have to be bought by non-resident motorists wishing to enter inner cities could also be used to induce car-sharing. Licences of this kind are one of several measures that may be introduced in London in order to reduce by about forty per cent the 89,000 commuter cars that are daily driven into the city centre. Opportunities exist to induce sharing at the enclosed car parks of large industrial plants too. Full cars may be given the most convenient parking bays, allowed to leave by special gates or other privileges. Where parking space is limited, it may be restricted to cars with two or more riders.

Some study has been made of this last idea in Coventry, a

town that, in addition to being the cradle of the British motor industry, is a mini-Los Angeles, with huge numbers of people working in suburban plants. This leads to a criss-cross of movements to and from work, and because of the high level of car ownership, to congestion. The pros and cons of sharing are well set out in one of the technical appendices of the 1972 Coventry Transportation Plan and show that the main uncertainties are social and behavioural. Could workers depend on their mates to pick them up with the regularity demanded by the punch clocks at the works' entrance? Would executives refuse to join the scheme, thereby giving it a low-class image? The questions remain unanswered. Dealing with the quantities of data demanded and excreted by their computer unfortunately dominated the time of the Coventry planners.

Car sharing or pooling, as it is called in America, is a sufficiently unfamiliar idea for there to be a tendency to assume that it would be repugnant to drivers. This is bound to be true of some people but with the cost of motoring and parking going up and bus priorities eating into road space, sharing will become steadily more attractive for commuters who have journeys that are ill-served by public transport.

There may even be money to be made out of aiding people to share. Computer dating services that help boy meet girl in big cities have proved to be a commercial success. Commuter dating would be organised in a similar way. The basic equipment would be a telephone number, an office and, as business built up, access to a computer. Subscribers would ring up or send post cards stating the time and route of their journeys and a fee to cover the cost of the service. They would receive in return a list of perhaps five names and addresses of commuters with similar pathways from home to work.

Services of this kind have been organised by New York newspapers and one or two municipalities have set them up free. Honolulu in Hawaii announced its intention to promote car pooling in 1972 and at the end of 1973 the authorities in Washington, D.C. were working on a scheme in order to reduce the city's notorious smog. As a first step it was proposed to raise daily parking rates from three to five dollars in order to deter one-man one-car commuters. A computer-based car-pooling service was seen as a complementary measure and District officials believed it would be possible to group not just neighbours who happened to work close by one another but other compatible types such as single girls and non-smokers as well. (An offer to match girls and men might prove even more popular.) Cheap or free parking for car pools was under consideration as an added incentive.

Schemes of this kind were first mooted in the United States because of their potential for cleaning up the air, but latterly it has been realised that they have fuel-saving ability as well. Estimates made by the Federal Energy office suggest that if the number of people carried by the average commuter car could be doubled, 780,000 barrels of oil would be saved every day.

The promotion of car pooling to and from work does not presuppose that anyone is going to give up owning a car, merely that they are going to use it less. Some benefits would come from this and they should not be discounted. Rush-hour traffic would flow more easily, buses and those cars still in use would get about more quickly and parking congestion in city centres and at large industrial plants would be lessened. Air quality would be improved. Two unknowns, and ones that are bound to concern bus managers, are how many commuters would leave their services and go by car if they got the chance and how many wives, who now go shopping or visiting by bus, would use stay-at-home cars instead. Only experience will tell, but assuming that sharing schemes are part of strategies involving higher parking charges, bus priorities, pedestrian precincts and the introduction of dial-a-ride services, the main effect is likely to be not so much a decline in bus travel as a drop in the purchase of second cars.

This prospect will send chills running down the spines of car manufacturers but it could be to the advantage of everyone else. The further proliferation of second cars will result in a compounding of all the evils of motorisation. The encouragement of sharing would, on the other hand, ensure that household budgets would be less stretched and that housebound wives would have to wait less long before getting the use of a car. The cause of women's liberation would be well served, while the maintenance of good public transport would, at the same time, reduce the need for mothers to spend their time chauffeuring their children.

Second cars are still a comparative rarity in Europe. In Britain, for instance, only eight per cent of households were in this class in 1971 compared with thirty per cent in the United States. However Europe has reached a time when second cars are the fastest growing part of the market. If nothing is done to provide an alternative to them, transatlantic conditions can be expected.

Beyond the sharing of rides lies the more radical possibility of sharing the ownership of cars, in other words, renting them. Some people will see this as a veiled attack on private property and the thin end of a wedge of communism, syndicalism or some other suspect 'ism'. In fact the hiring of cars, vans and industrial plant of all kinds, is becoming increasingly common and for good reason. Just as few people bother to buy such expensive properties as hotel rooms or cinema seats because they do not use them sufficiently often, so in a context of improved public transport and rising car-running costs, hiring cars will make increasingly good sense.

In the United States self-drive hiring has recently been growing in leaps and bounds. One, probably exaggerated, estimate is that the share of the distance travelled by individuals in American metropolitan areas in self-drive hire cars will grow from nearly five per cent in 1970 to thirty-eight per cent by 1990. Over the same thirty-year period the self-drive fleet is forecast to grow from 320,000 to 5,000,000 cars, or fifteen per cent a year. Derek Riley of Eurofinance, a market research company, gave these figures in a talk in London called 'Financing Transportation Innovation' in December 1971.

Hitherto firms like Hertz and Godfrey Davis have catered predominantly for people whose cars have broken down and for travellers who have made long-distance trips by plane or train and want a car to get closer to their destinations. Leslie Fishman,

Professor of Economics at the University of Keele, argues that hire services of this kind should be made available in every locality at 'community garages'. Such depots would offer a choice of travel by bus, taxi, self-drive hire car and, where possible, train, with all of them charged for on the same basis. Fishman says it is essential for the cost of all modes of transport to be calculated according to the same financial rules to avoid biasing people's choice. As it is, the convention of paying periodically for the major part of the cost of running a car—hire purchase instalments, insurance and maintenance—and only the fuel costs when actually on the road, makes it seem cheaper to drive than to buy a bus or train ticket which is calculated on an 'average cost' basis. Average cost fares are ones in which the rate per mile contains a proportion of the cost of buying, maintaining, and amortising whatever the vehicle is as well as its fuel.

The full community garage concept put forward by Fishman and his co-author Stuart Wabe is described in 'Restructuring the Form of Car Ownership' in *Transport Research 1969*. It may only be practical to deploy it fully in new towns but chains of local self-drive car-hire depots based, for instance, on petrol stations, multi-storey and office car parks and garages could be established in existing towns. Whether or not anything of this sort happens will depend on the cost of running cars. If the use made of cars declines, these costs will go up steeply. This is brought out by the estimates made by the Automobile Association in 1973, updated to take account of petrol at fifty pence a gallon. They show how the cost per trip of using a car increases by about one-half as the annual distance travelled slips from ten to five thousand miles. (The costs given are in pence.)

Engine Capacity	Up to 1000 c.c.	1001 to 1500 c.c.	1501 to 2000 c.c.
Cost per mile at 5,000 miles per year	8·163	9·776	11·697
Cost per mile at 10,000 miles per year	5·212	6·260	7·360
Cost per mile at 15,000 miles per year	4·228	5·288	6·054
Cost per mile at 20,000 miles per year	3·737	4·502	5·349

Assuming that car owners do in future use their vehicles less and that parking and other charges increase too, there is bound to be a time for some people in some places when hiring becomes cheaper than owning. This time can be brought closer by introducing taxes that favour hiring against ownership. Purchase taxes on new cars may be increased. Tax concessions that encourage companies to buy cars for their employees may be removed. Domestic garages may be made the subject of special rates. Street parking charges may be introduced in inner cities, though they would need to be brought in slowly to avoid causing hardship.

On first sight this may seem a devilish thing to contemplate but the advantages of making greater use of a smaller number of vehicles are so great that things are already moving in that direction on both sides of the Atlantic. In the United States government departments in Washington and universities elsewhere have introduced car-sharing schemes in order to save parking space and their example is pertinent to virtually all large institutions. The first step is to rent a number of cars from a leasing firm and then offer them either on sub-lease or in lieu of salary to staff members who, for one reason or another, are obliged to commute by car. These commuters then drive to work in hirelings and park them at places convenient for colleagues who may use them during the day. The organisation of this sharing can be done as informally or formally as the scale of the operation and the style of the institution demands. A limited number of car keys may be issued to members of a car 'club'. Or the keys may be kept by someone with orders to issue them to certain users. Trips can be booked or not, whichever works better. Members of such car clubs who are able to do so travel to work by bus, car pool or bicycle, thereby reducing the sterilisation of land by parked cars, yet still have the use of a personal vehicle if they need one during the day. Rush-hour traffic is reduced. Car pooling is given a fillip and parking space freed for short-stay visitors or other purposes. (In central London half the available parking space is occupied by cars left stationary for eight hours at a time.)

A first attempt to offer this kind of self-drive hire car service to the general public was made in Montpellier in the South of France in 1971. The service was the brain child of an engineer called Philippe Leblond and was designed round a sophisticated coin-in-a-slot meter. Individuals joining the Société PROCOTIP, which was organised as a profit sharing co-operative, had to pay a monthly subscription of fifty francs (five pounds) in return for which they were issued with a key to the doors of all the club cars and a cassette shaped so that it could be plugged into the TIP (Transport Individuel Public) meters in the cars. These individually numbered cassettes were also designed to hold plastic counters which were on sale at tobacconists throughout the town for ten francs (one pound) each. After finding a car and plugging in a cassette holding two of these *jetons*, a club member was able to start up and drive for a total of twenty-two miles before reloading, though the rules of the club forbade leaving the town. The meter clipped segments off the *jeton* as the car proceeded and flashed a red warning light when the first one was nearly consumed. If the driver got to his destination with part of the *jeton* intact, it could be withdrawn in the cassette and used on another occasion. Another mechanism in the TIP meter made it impossible to withdraw the cassette until the handbrake had been applied and the windows rolled up.

Comprehensive insurance was part of membership but some check was obviously necessary to protect the co-operators from the cost and inconvenience of any too accident-prone member. This was contrived by ciné cameras in the TIP meters that automatically photographed the number of any cassette inserted, the time of day, the car number and the mileage at the start and finish of the hiring. If a car was found misused or crashed, the film in it was developed to find out who was responsible. If there were no signs of trouble the film could be left unprocessed.

By 1972 members of the co-operative had the use of thirty-seven bright blue Simca 1000s and Philippe Leblond's ambition was to expand this fleet to 150 cars. On an assumption that one car in co-operative use would replace fifteen to twenty privately owned ones, he calculated that a fleet of 600 TIP cars would be able to sweep 12,000 cars off the streets of Montpellier and thus eliminate the acute congestion found there.

Technologically speaking, the TIP cars were a success. The meters worked well, the amount of damage done to the vehicles was acceptable and the two students who kept the cars clean, took them to garages for petrol and redistributed them around the town drove the cars for only seven per cent of their total mileage. However, as important to the success of the project as technology was an array of guaranteed parking places where members of the club could expect to find and leave vehicles. By 1972 there were fifty-seven such parking places at seventeen points around the town, but the propensity of Frenchmen to park anywhere irrespective of prohibitions meant that they were by no means always available to the co-operators.

This was the Achilles heel of the system and the trouble was aggravated by ambivalence on the part of the police towards the TIP parking places. Should they treat 'transport individuel public' as 'transport individuel', in which case they could do nothing to help it, or should they treat it as 'transport public', in which case they were under an obligation to give it special assistance. Michel Frybourg, head of the French Government's Institut de Recherche des Transports, said in 1972 that this point of law would have to be clarified before self-drive urban hire cars could be successfully introduced in France. Or, if the decision went against them, they could be forgotten about. Unfortunately no decision was made and in 1973 the experiment was discontinued. At its peak the co-operative had about a hundred, mainly professional and post-graduate student members who were collectively using each vehicle between seven to twelve times a day and driving it a total of seven to fifteen miles.

At the last report the Société PROCOTIP was working on further schemes with the municipal authorities at Orleans and Rouen and the grapevine had it that off-street parking places were to be tried at Orleans. While it is obviously cheaper to station self-drive hire cars at the kerb, it is easy to see the advantages of off-street parking. It sidesteps the policing issue and is compatible with measures to widen pavements for pedestrians and eliminate space used to park private cars.

Members of the City Council at Montpellier were divided in their view of the self-drive experiment. Some believed that as the club members were all middle class, any action favouring the TIP cars would lose them working-class votes. Others saw the public cars as one element in a package for improving conditions for pedestrians and bus passengers and for city-centre trade through eliminating congestion and making it easier to get about. Thus Georges Cayzac, the councillor then in charge of traffic control, said in 1971 : 'If the scheme works, we look forward to the day when we can ban all vehicles except buses, taxis and TIP cars from the city streets.'

A lot has been learned from Philippe Leblond's pioneering project though unknowns still remain. We now know that people will hire cars the use of which is confined to a large provincial city (Montpellier has a population of 200,000) and that they make trips ranging from two to six miles. And we have M. Leblond's word that under the conditions found in Montpellier the income from a fleet of a hundred and fifty TIP cars would have covered operating costs and interest on capital. We have also been given a glimpse of a way in which cars could be made to work in harmony with buses and trams rather than obstructing them.

All the sharing schemes so far described have made use of ordinary cars. This keeps down costs but it makes no contribution to a more fundamental problem—the sheer unsuitability of maid-of-all-work cars for so much of the work they are asked to do and for so many of the places they are driven in. Alain Bieber raised this question in *Analyse et Prévision* in October 1971 when he asked 'Should We Urbanise the Motor Vehicle?' His thesis is that the history of the twentieth century has led the 'architecture' of cars to evolve in a way that is more and more in conflict with present-day road conditions and environmental concerns and that the grand touring tradition in car design is the origin of the trouble. He has in mind here the world of F. Scott Fitzgerald and Sinclair Lewis—of powerful, long-bonnetted machines, the open road and heroes and heroines with scarves trailing out behind them in the wind. Londoners who drove in evening dress down what used to be called the Bath Road to have dinner at Skindles by the river in Maidenhead were part of the same milieu. They could only have gone in open Bentleys. Bieber argues that these origins in part explain the continued emphasis on high performance in car design, even though speed limits are increasingly the rule and the typical trip is not a race down to Skindles but a matter of ferrying children to school, collecting groceries at the supermarket, or the daily grind to and from work. And to complete his case he shows that cars are increasingly used for prosaic urban and suburban trips and less and less for touring.

At the time Bieber's paper was written, the Americans seemed bent on turning their already massive cars into veritable tanks in the pursuit of passenger safety and in compounding the gas-guzzling effect of this weight increase by adopting wasteful air pollution control devices. The changed energy situation has since sounded the death knell of the passenger tank but conflict remains between the kinds of vehicle that are desirable for long-distance and urban driving. Furthermore, this is not exclusively an American problem. European big cars are out of place in the confined space of cities and little Minis and Fiats, though not out of scale are dangerously fast to be mixed up with pedestrians, as well as being too noisy and smelly to be allowed to rev-up a few yards from rooms in which people are working and sleeping. Out on the open road the roles are reversed. There the big cars provide good protection for their riders while the occupants of little ones are at excessive risk through being mixed up with vehicles that are much heavier and faster than theirs.

Bieber sees a resolution to these conflicts in having different kinds of vehicle for town and country driving and in switching from owning to hiring to enable motorists to choose machines appropriate to their purposes. Small, quiet, low-speed cars would then be hired for use in towns; spacious, higher speed tourers could be used for long-distance journeys; vans would be obtained for moving furniture or equipment; and camping cars for holidays. The potential for choice is endless and underlines the desirability of abandoning ownership. The private car, despite its reputation as a symbol of freedom is a set of chains confining motorists all too often to vehicles that are ill-suited both to their needs and to the places in which they are driving.

The logic of this argument has been accepted and put into practice in a few places. In certain retirement colonies in the United States electric golf cars are in use as town cars. They are small, quiet and slow and are used only on roads within their home colonies. Their practicality seems to have been discovered by accident. They were bought for caddying at golf courses and then found to be invaluable for shopping and visiting round the town. Elderly people in particular are overjoyed by the ease of getting in and out of them and the simplicity of their controls.

In Europe a former Amsterdam Provo called Luud Schimmelpennink is promoting special battery electric cars for renting in large cities. The Dutch Minister for Public Health and Environment presided at the inauguration of the first batch of these *witkars*, or white cars, at Amsterdam in March 1974. Schimmelpennink hopes to open 150 stations manned by 1,200 cars in Amsterdam over the next few years. In the meantime the City Council has promised to find sites for fifteen stations. The thinking underlying the *witkars* is similar to that of the Montpellier TIP cars but it goes further. Hiring is used not just to provide urban motorists with a less space-hungry alternative to private cars but to introduce vehicles that are compatible with pedestrians and city living. Phallic projections, wedge-forms and other products of the sexual phantasies of the designers of conventional cars are rejected in favour of a mobile gold fish bowl that is intended to make drivers feel exposed and fragile. The outcome, to eyes brought up on the childish inanity of conventional automotive styling, is an ugly duckling of a car. Its boxy upright proportions, designed to give all-round sight-lines and easy entry to two riders, could not be more different from those of British

Leyland's wedge-shaped Minissima, unveiled as a one-off eye catcher at the 1973 Earl's Court Motor Show, and subsequently paired with the pubic hair of a girl called Christy in *Men Only*.

Schimmelpennink has in Amsterdam an almost ideal place for the experiment he is conducting. The inner city is a compact place with 75,000 residents, only one-quarter to one-third of whom have cars, yet 30,000 vehicles are brought in every day by outsiders and dropped down on their front doorsteps. Schimmelpennink has also found allies amongst the city-centre shopkeepers who tried building car parks to attract customers, only to find it an expensive mistake. Now they realise that it is time to improve public transport and the pleasantness of the streets and have formed several committees to support the *witkar* project. One of these groups is based on the Damrak square and includes de Bijenkorf, the Harrods of Holland.

Much will turn on whether battery power proves to be satisfactory for the kind of use that is made of *witkars* in Amsterdam. Trips are on average expected to be about a mile in length and never of more than three miles; and between every pair of trips the little cars will spend a period at a station where their batteries will automatically receive a booster charge. Their reserves of energy will therefore be whatever remains of the charge put in over-night plus a series of boosts. If the worst comes to the worst and a car approaches energy exhaustion (after the equivalent of forty to sixty minutes' town driving), a red light will come on, warning the driver to go to the nearest *witkar* station and pick up a fresh mount. However this is expected to be a rarity.

Simulation tests done with the help of the Technological University at Delft suggest that the power storage characteristics of the *witkars* and the expected use made of them should be in balance. Furthermore there is some room for manœuvre by changing the type of storage cell used.

If *witkars* prove successful, they could transform the market for electric vehicles. Hitherto electricity has come into its own only in the case of delivery vans on stop-start rounds with milk, bread and post. Repeated efforts have been made to promote electric cars but the impossibility of creating maids-of-all-work capable of doing three hours at a continuous seventy miles an hour on motorways as well as town ferrying has ensured that they are never more than rich men's toys. Right now electric buses are the fashion, but they are no more promising than all-purpose electric cars. The massive size of their batteries makes them unwieldy and their lack of range makes them inflexible, though hybrid designs with generators on board may reduce these drawbacks. Urban hire cars are different. They would circulate in known places where battery charging points could be provided and would be used for short, slow, stop-and-start trips that on first sight seem ideal for electric power.

The battery charging stations essential for electric hire cars result in fundamental differences between the operation of Schimmelpennink's bubble-mobiles and the Montpellier TIP cars. Members of the Amsterdam co-operative, who pay a joining fee of about eleven pounds, are obliged to book their cars into a destination before they can take to the road. The club member inserts an identification card into a computer terminal at his departure station, chooses a destination station with the help of a map and, using a code number, tells the computer about that too. He then pushes a button to say whether he intends to make a direct or an indirect trip. The computer checks the member's account to see if it is in order, calculates whether there will be room to park at the chosen destination and, assuming all is in order, releases the key of the front car in the charging rank. The member drives off and the remaining cars are automatically moved forward to create space for arriving vehicles. If there is no space at the member's preferred destination, the computer will then hunt for a slot at the next most convenient stop.

All this is highly technological and I have my doubts about the practicality of it—at least to start with. Machines can so easily go wrong and there have already been reports of unreliability from Amsterdam. The strong points about electric hire cars are their low maintenance costs, their small size (four nose-to-tail bubble cars at a charging station occupy the space of one normal parking bay), their lack of noise and fumes, and their potential for replacing much larger numbers of private cars. These advantages could be gained without elaborate computer booking. An attendant at every charging station could check membership cars, telephone to reserve destination parking spaces, issue keys and keep the cars clean. He could be a tobacconist as well, to reduce costs, and could play some part in the business of redistributing cars to meet expected patterns of demand.

Sharing rides and renting cars are neither of them unfamiliar ideas. Many neighbours club together to go to work and football matches and for other purposes. Hiring cars is big business. Both are practical and sensible propositions, both could lead to major economies in the consumption of resources, yet neither find their way as a matter of course into the transportation plans of local authorities. This is because the questions the planners ask themselves have a built-in capital investment bias and neglect the husbandry of existing resources. The resulting plans favour the expensive against the cheap and the disruptive against the unobtrusive. They reflect the thinking of highway engineers, not transport entrepreneurs. The outcome is plans to build highways that turn forecasts of car ownership into self-fulfilling prophecies.

Economic changes that will make motoring more expensive, coupled with a need to eliminate the waste and environmental hazards of mounting traffic, make it essential to promote the sharing and hiring of cars. At present it is illegal to pay for shared rides and there is confusion about who is responsible in the case of accidents. This illegality needs to be removed and the extension of all third-party insurance policies to cover paying passengers should be made obligatory. Insurance companies have no reason to fear such a move, since vehicles with several occupants are less prone to accidents than those with only one. It may be that passengers act as a mollifying influence on drivers or that people who are willing to share are, by definition, less aggressive and so less accident prone. Either way, some American insurance companies offer reduced premiums to commuters who share their cars.

Hiring vehicles instead of owning them promises other benefits Hirers would get a choice of vehicles tailored to their changing needs, the amount of space devoted to parking could be reduced and changes would occur in the technology of vehicles. Robustness and long life would replace planned obsolescence as design criteria and would help to stabilise runinng costs. Greater emphasis on safety could be expected and opportunities would be created for pollution-free urban cars.

The scope for sharing and hiring is bound to differ from place to place, with the former being more promising in remote villages and the latter being better attuned to the denser parts of towns and cities, though there would be plenty of overlap in between. In places where public transport is poor the objective would be to reduce the need for second cars. In places where it is good the aim would be to give people a genuine choice between owning and not owning cars. Unless this opportunity is seized the forecasts of the trend men of an end-of-century fleet of cars that would occupy one hundred square miles in Britain when parked, and five to ten times as much space in Europe, will come to pass. No amount of tinkering with the technology of vehicles will lessen the oppressiveness of this army of steel. The terms of tenure between man and motor must change.

12 Summing Up

Cars may still be the cherished possessions of millions and fill the dreams of many more but it is no longer a foregone conclusion that they will inherit the earth. Eviction notices have been served on them in places as different as Yosemite National Park in California and the central streets of Cologne and Munich. A growing amount of public money has also begun to flow into the creation of alternatives.

In Britain the last great official trumpet call for what used to be known as democracy on four wheels was sounded in the plan for the new town of Milton Keynes in 1969. It stressed the need for '. . . the easy movement by private cars and their penetration to every point in the city. The individual car offers its users a freedom of choice and opportunity which more and more people will want—and be able—to take advantage of.' I know of no subsequent official document that is so unequivocal about the blessings of drive-in living.

The first important signpost to a different future was the 1972 report of the Urban Motorways Committee set up by the Secretary of State for the Environment. The Committee laboured long and hard before stating what was to most people already a glimpse of the obvious: that all sorts of innocent parties were harmed by new urban roads and left uncompensated. The Government duly made grants available towards sound-proofing and the effects of disturbance under the Land Compensation Act 1973. This Act makes a start at redressing the wrongs of traffic and it makes motorway madness more expensive in cities but it does nothing for people plagued in one way or another by traffic on existing roads.

A second signpost was put up in 1973 by the bi-partisan Expenditure Committee of the House of Commons which said : 'We feel it is right to recommend that national policy should be directed towards promoting public transport and discouraging the use of cars for the journey to work in city areas.'

The Government responded a few months later with a White Paper on urban transport planning which said : 'Local authorities will need to make wider use of bus priority measures even if this involves reduced road capacity for other vehicles.' This was the first occasion on which the Government had blessed the idea of squeezing cars off the roads.

The Expenditure Committee drew attention to one other vital issue. It looked at how policies for transport were determined by local authorities and found that they were drawn up largely by groups of engineers with the help of complex-seeming mathematical modelling techniques and computers. In other words, policy was decided by technocrats according to their priorities with little reference to non-transport considerations. The Committee therefore said : 'We recommend that transportation studies should be carried out within a clearly defined framework of general policy.'

Similar changes have been going on in other countries. In the United States the notorious ninety-per-cent grant procedure by which the states were blackmailed into building roads and offered scarcely a cent towards the improvement of public transport was finally killed in 1973. States and their cities may now say No to federal highway projects and demand that sums equivalent to their cost be made available for public transport.

Slowly but surely, the incredible expense of foisting on to the public the need to buy and run cars has begun to emerge. Brian Ketcham, a divisional head of the New York Department of Air Resources, estimates that the disbenefits of road transport in the United States in 1973 amounted to between $75,000,000,000 and $150,000,000,000 or between a sixteenth and an eighth of the 'wealth' created by Americans in that year.

No comparable calculations have been made for Britain but

the annual cost of road accidents in lost output, hospital care, police and law court time and destroyed property was estimated by the Transport and Road Research Laboratory to be running at about the same level as the country's investment in new highways in 1970. I am not one of those who think that economic growth is bad but I am convinced that this kind of economic growth is obsolete.

Let me give just one more illustration of the costs of assuming that it is the best of all possible worlds for everyone to have a car. In 1971 the Swedish Government set up a commission to examine public transport and the management of traffic in towns. The following year Bo Stenman, secretary of the commission said in an interim report :

> We know that people with low incomes often live a long way from their work and because of the inadequacy of public transport, are obliged to buy cars. But the cost of doing so leaves them with only the narrowest margin between solvency and financial disaster. As a result such families have to have recourse to social security payments in order to live.

Can anyone imagine anything crazier than a set of public policies that pushes people into buying cars and then humiliates them with handouts because they cannot make ends meet?

A child of ten could see that the solution to these problems is bound to lie, first of all, in better public transport. The events of the winter of 1973/4 and the subsequent steep rise in the price of fuel make it all the more self-evident. The trouble is that bus and urban railway services have in most places sunk to such a low ebb that they hardly seem a practicable alternative to going by car. Most people do not look with contempt upon public transport because it is beneath their dignity—though no doubt some do—but because the service is so poor. Wherever the service is being improved, whether it is by putting the trams in tunnels as in Brussels or by giving people a chance to park-and-ride as in Leicester or Oxford, extra passengers are being attracted. The steady growth in the use of taxis and hired cars, that forgotten branch of public transport, is further proof of the paramount importance of quality of service.

The message is perfectly clear. All the expertise and at least some of the funds that have hitherto been poured into building highways and trying to get quarts of traffic into pint pots of roads need to be devoted to giving buses and taxis priority over other traffic. Limits on parking and bus lanes will play a part in achieving this objective but 'planned congestion' will do much more. This is the idea of the 1970s. It involves nothing more than using traffic lights in a new way to hold private cars in queues where they obstruct only one another while allowing shared vehicles to bypass them. The technique can be seen on the approach ramps to freeways in Los Angeles and on ordinary roads in Southampton. It is being applied on a town-wide scale in Nottingham.

The absence of any traffic limiting concept of this kind made the ideas put forward by Sir Colin Buchanan in his *Traffic in Towns* report an expensive nonsense. The economists saw the fault at once and advanced the academic and inequitable idea of pay-as-you-drive road pricing. Now the practical men—the much abused traffic engineers—have come in on the act with their sheep-and-goats traffic management techniques. These new methods of regulating the entry of cars on to the roads, deployed in conjunction with parking controls and greatly improved passenger transport services, hold out the promise of mobility for all without profligate use of fuel and an ever deeper litter of parked cars.

What might these greatly improved passenger services be? The first step is to get more conventional buses into service and to pay their drivers better wages. About a sixth of all provincial and about one-third of all London buses have been axed during the past fifteen years. But fleets of smaller and quicker vehicles giving a door-to-door service are needed too. These may be mini-buses on fixed routes, taxis with destination signs that take three or four or five passengers for a flat fare, and dial-a-ride vehicles with radio telephones on board. Travellers would then have a much wider choice of kinds of public transport than today. The new services would also be much better suited than double deckers on fixed routes to carrying the growing numbers of people trying to make random movements within and between suburbs. Fixation with historic centres should not be allowed to distract attention from the steady spread of all cities and the need for public transport in the suburbs. The public transport of the future must serve the city of the future.

The first step is to clear away institutional antiques such as the 1930 Road Traffic Act and subsequent regulations that share its obsolete philosophy. This would permit bus and taxi operators to test new kinds of service without having to apply first for permission to some one in 'authority'. This may sound dangerously radical, but if traffic management is used to give public passenger services privileges on the Queen's Highway, as is already happening, it will be disastrous if only the vehicles of large, semi-monopolistic municipal transport undertakings are to be the beneficiaries. Any operator able to demonstrate that his drivers are fit, and his vehicles safe and marked distinctively as shared transport, should be allowed to offer services to the public. The danger is not that there will be too many operators cutting one another's economic throats but too few. There should therefore be no limit on the number of vehicles plying in one way or another for hire. It should be left to competition between taxi owners, dial-a-ride operators and busmen and the judgement of the travelling public to decide on the composition of the fleet of vehicles that is allowed to bypass points of planned congestion. This would necessitate revising the current practice of financing public transport. Instead of the blanket subsidies to operators now so widely canvassed and increasingly given, travel subsidies should be given to individuals in the form of vouchers usable on whatever form of transport is appropriate to their needs. Company tax law needs to be revised too. At present firms are encouraged to buy cars for their employees. The incidence of taxation should be changed so that they are encouraged to pay for travel instead.

Many firms already give their employees lunch vouchers. Why should they not give them travel vouchers too?

Car ownership will not be eliminated by any of these measures but the balance of advantage will be shifted in the direction of sharing rides and hiring cars rather than owning them and travelling singly. Freedom from being forced into the ownership of a car will be established as a right alongside the privilege of possessing one.

But mobility is not primarily a matter of transport. At the bottom it is a reflection of patterns of activity which are in turn governed by patterns of land uses. As towns turn into cities, and as their residents aspire to more space to live and work in, so a spreading process takes place. Journeys to the centre then become more lengthy. At the same time new factories, shopping centres, hotels and offices spring up in the suburbs. In the 1960s it was conventional to build undergrounds to help people to get to the city centre and networks of freeways to knit together the suburbs. Chicago and to a lesser extent Munich and Milan show the results—overdevelopment in the centre and sprawl every-where else. It is now clear that it would have been preferable to have served the centres with express buses and to have brought together homes and jobs in the suburbs. Linkages between these complete communities could then have been achieved by net-works of busways or tramways, sometimes running on exclusive ways and sometimes running on the roads, with priority over other traffic. Instead of commercial ghettoes in the centre and sprawl all round, the outcome would have been constellations of identifiable communities. Local opportunities would have been greater. More people would have been able to live and work in the same locality. Walking and cycling would have served more needs, but public transport would have existed to enable people to get to other parts of the city irrespective of the direction in which they lay. These are the objectives for the 1970s.

The forecasts of public expenditure published by the Treasury at the end of 1973 show spending on roads running at a rate about three times as high as that for bus services and British

Rail up until 1978. Some adjustments were made to these forecasts during the winter of 1973/4 but these leave expenditure on the construction and maintenance of roads running at over £1,000,000,000 a year until 1978. Furthermore, expenditure on the construction of new motorways and trunk roads, the majority of which are parts of the inter-urban system, is planned to rise to about £400,000,000 a year.

National transport policy is thus still geared to spurring on the use of cars for long-distance journeys and to providing an ever-more-extensive network of expressways for road juggernauts. It is not profoundly different from the policy pursued with such disastrous results in the United States throughout the 1950s and 1960s.

The prospects at local authority level are not much brighter. A marked turn-around may have taken place in Oxford and Nottingham and London but in many cities the thinking of the early 1960s is still all too evident. Cardiff is typical of these backwoods municipalities. As recently as November 1973 the chief officers presented the Council with a choice of three transport plans and recommended the one involving the greatest expenditure on highways and the grossest bulldozing of houses. And as in all such plans, no account was taken of the contribution of these roads to increased accidents, to air pollution, to the diminution of the city's over-stretched housing stock and to the enfeeblement of public transport. The Councils in Birmingham and Brighton, Bristol and Belfast, Glasgow and York are all hell-bent on creating similar disasters.

Only political action can rout the worn-out thinking of the 1960s. The technocrats have been given their turn and have produced only monuments to themselves. The fallacies they believed in have been exploded. We do not live now in countries in which everyone has a car and we never shall. Even if the most fervent prayers of the motor manufacturers were vouchsafed, there would be no more than twenty million cars for fifty million teenage and adult Britons in 1990. That would be too few for convenience but too many for comfort. It is time to create a different kind of city, one that meets the aspirations of women, children and the elderly and not just the ambitions of executives. It is time for transport systems that conserve energy instead of wasting it. These are the values of the 1970s. It is time to give them expression.

Postscript

The following report appeared in the *Guardian* on Monday, 17 April 1995. It is reprinted here with the permission of the editor, Mr Anthony Howard.

MOTORWAY PRESERVERS RALLY

Two Hundred Enjoy Sentimental But Smelly Journey

Two United Dairies diesel milk tankers, both in full orange livery, seven carefully-preserved British Leyland Minis and nearly thirty other petrol-driven vehicles took part yesterday in an inaugural rally organised by the London Motorway Preservation Society.

The Society was celebrating a decision by the Department of the Environment to rent it the now-defunct elevated motorway through North Kensington at a peppercorn rent. Elsewhere in the country other preservation societies are negotiating with the Department to rent other motorways including Mancunian Way in Manchester and the entire Glasgow Inner Ring. Before deciding to sign the Westway contract, the Secretary of State turned down a request from the Royal Borough of Kensington and Chelsea to use the viaduct as a platform for temporary houses for the Borough's 15,000 homeless families.

Leading the rally were Mr Stirling Moss, sixty-five-year-old ex-racing driver and Sir Alec Durie, seventy-nine-year-old former head of the Automobile Association. Sir Alec, who retired shortly after his heroic efforts to rescue victims of a 272-car pile up on the former M1 Motorway in 1978, was at the wheel of an electric bath chair.

At a press conference afterwards, Sir Alec said he had never for a moment regretted his years of driving. 'I still cannot understand why the Government ever thought it necessary to phase out motorways', he said.

Along the route several drivers had the pleasure of changing punctured tyres after they had traversed boards carefully prepared with upright nails. Their happy four-letter words could be heard ringing across the spacious swathe of concrete as they struggled with jacks and wheel-braces.

At Paddington Green other drivers were able to pull off the motorway into the forecourt of an antique petrol filling station which had been set up there for the rally. This important relic of the petrol transport era dates from 1966 and was rescued from demolition at Inveraray by Shell-Ecology Limited, formerly the Shell Oil Company.

Several pairs of original oil-stained white overalls, a partly-filled Redex gun (a special lubricant formerly added to the fuel of internal combustion engined vehicles) and a period plastic display rack, containing some packets of Smith's Crisps and Rowntree's fruit gums were on show at the filling station. The owners had hoped to exhibit the Gentlemen's and Ladies' lavatories in a state appropriate to the days of motorway motoring but were prevented from doing so by public health regulations.

Volunteers from the Motorway Preservation Society will be spending weekends throughout the summer putting down a new layer of asphalt on the elevated parts of the viaduct and rewiring and painting the forty-foot-high light masts. Their work will be made easier, though none the less grimy, by the chance discovery of an original, though encrusted, tar burner and spreader dating from the late 1950s. The name of the Trinidad Lake Asphalt Company can still just be made out through the encrustations.

Current smoke abatement laws will make it impossible for the enthusiasts to use the burner (it would send up a pall of acrid black fumes thirty feet high) though permission has been granted for one demonstration ignition during the Movement Show at Earl's Court in the autumn.

Among other conservation works contemplated by the Society

is the stripping away of ivy and virginia creeper planted by protesting residents around the stilts of the motorway shortly after it was built. These now enshroud the structure up to the parapet railings and since the road fell into disuse they have begun to crawl across the pavement itself like two advancing armies of green. The Society objects to this covering because it conceals from sight the powerful lines of the concrete structure.

Mr Paul Trott, Joint Director of Planning and Transportation at the Greater London Council before the second great wave of transport policy reversals of 1976, will be in charge of removing the creepers. Since his retirement from local government he has lived in North Kensington in a house backing on to the Westway viaduct which he still considers to be the most beautiful structure in London. When asked about the project yesterday he said: 'It has always puzzled me that the superb finish of the concrete was allowed by the authorities to be covered with creepers. I cannot imagine them allowing ivy to climb the buttresses of Westminster Abbey.'

Acknowledgements

Far more people than I can hope to thank individually have given me help with this book. I would therefore like to acknowledge their assistance collectively and to pick out only Neil Cooke and Paul Faldo for their excellent illustrations.

The car ownership forecasts facing p. 23 are taken from *Forecasts of Vehicles and Traffic in Great Britain: 1972 Revision* by A. H. Tulpule, Transport and Road Research Laboratory Report LR 543; the chart facing p. 33 is taken from 'The Moulton Bicycle' by Alex Moulton, Friday Evening Discourse, Royal Institution, London, February 1973; the chart facing p. 35 is taken from *The Motor Car and Natural Resources* by Gerald Leach, Organisation for Economic Co-operation and Development, Paris 1972; the chart facing p. 55 was prepared by the Commission to Promote Public Transport in the West of the Netherlands and is taken from *The Effect of Organisation of Transport Facilities* by H. J. Noortman, Council of European Ministers of Transport Fourth International Symposium, The Hague 1971; the map facing p. 74 is based on the 'Cambridge Transportation Plan: Final Report', R. Travers Morgan and Partners, 1972; the map facing p. 76 is taken from 'Cycleways in Greater Peterborough' by Roy Ashton, *Journal of the Royal Town Planning Institute*, March 1974; the drawings facing pp. 106 and 108 are from 'Zones and Collars: Suggested Traffic Control Measures for Peak Travel in Nottingham', Nottingham City Council, November 1973; the quotations on pp. 132, 135 and 139–40 are from *Demand-Responsive Transportation Systems*, Special Report 136, US Highway Research Board, Washington, D.C.; the map facing p. 175 is taken from 'Transport Policy Report 1970', Federal German Minister of Transport;

248

the plan and the drawing facing pp. 208 and 211 are from *Regional Transportation District Frontier*, vol. 2, no. 6, Denver, Colorado, USA (no date given). I am grateful to all those responsible for allowing me to reproduce their work.

Index